READING BOOKS

Reading Books

ESSAYS ON THE MATERIAL

TEXT AND LITERATURE

IN AMERICA

Edited by
Michele Moylan
and Lane Stiles

Foreword by Michael Winship

University of Massachusetts Press
Amherst

Copyright © 1996 by
The University of Massachusetts Press
Foreword © 1996 by Michael Winship
All rights reserved
Printed in the United States of America
LC 96-8322
ISBN 1-55849-062-0 (cloth); 063-9 (pbk.)
Designed by Melinda Nan OK Lee
Set in Adobe Caslon
Printed and bound by Braun-Brumfield, Inc.

Library of Congress Cataloging-in-Publication Data
Reading books : essays on the material text and literature in America / edited by
    Michele Moylan and Lane Stiles ; foreword by Michael Winship.
        p.   cm. — (Studies in print culture and the history of the book)
    Includes bibliographical references (p.   ) and index.
    ISBN 1-55849-062-0 (alk. paper). — ISBN 1-55849-063-9 (pbk. : alk. paper)
    1. American literature—Criticism, Textual. 2. Literature—Publishing—United
States—History. 3. Books—United States—Format—History—19th century.
4. Books—United States—Format—History—20th century. 5. Books and reading—
United States—History—19th century. 6. Books and reading—United States—
History—20th century. 7. Transmission of texts. 8. Literary form. I. Moylan, Michele,
1963– . II. Stiles, Lane, 1952– . III. Series.
PS25.R38 1996
810.9—dc20   96-8322
                                                                                           CIP

British Library Cataloguing in Publication data are available.
This book is published with the support and cooperation of the University of
Massachusetts Boston.

Contents

v

Foreword

One of the most exciting results of the development of the history of the book as a vital field of research has been the emergence of an energetic group of young scholars working in American literary and cultural history. Many of these scholars—including all but one of those whose work is represented here—have participated in the summer seminars sponsored by the American Antiquarian Society's Program in the History of the Book in American Culture, where they have worked together in developing and exploring their interests in book history. As a group, these scholars bring to their research, first, a recognition of the material nature of texts and of how this materiality is bound up with the ways that texts signify and perform cultural work and, second, a concern for the institutions and technologies that make the production, publication, dissemination, and reception of texts possible. The essays gathered here show, I believe, the promise of their work.

Book history has not been alone in shaping the way that we do literary and cultural history today, of course. In literary studies, reader reception theory, feminist criticism, deconstructionism, new historicism, and other "isms," have all contributed to our current interest in an expanded and expanding canon of literary texts; our current concern for the power relations inscribed in texts and how these are shaped by such issues as gender, class, and race; and our current focus on readers, on the various meanings that they construct out of texts, and on how these meanings shape and reflect their identities, beliefs, and actions. The result has surely been a livelier and richer historical understanding of American literature and culture.

If the history of the book has a special contribution to make in this effort, I believe that it does so because it is something more than a special form of cultural history. If literary culture can be seen to be "produced" in a metaphoric sense, literary texts as books are first produced in a material sense in printing shops and factories by living men and women. Can we overlook or ignore their part in literary culture? The literary marketplace may have emerged as an important cultural metaphor in the antebellum years, but let us not forget that simultaneously authors and publishers found themselves caught up in real marketplaces with their texts—ones where money, credit, and goods were exchanged.

The history of the book, as it has been practiced in the past and as it is now being practiced, involves not just cultural history but also material and economic history, bibliography and textual criticism, amateur antiquarianism, and archival compilation. If book history is to remain vital in the future, it must continue to incorporate and profit from this full range of scholarly activities. Most especially book historians must address the material book, as well as its cultural work, and explore the book trade as an economic and social, as well as a cultural, institution. The book, as physical artifact, acts finally as the touchstone with which we must test our abstract cultural insights and theories as we decide whether their gold is genuine or base.

Michael Winship
University of Texas, Austin

Acknowledgments

This book began as an idea tossed out over a couple of personal pan pizzas on an inauspiciously gloomy day in March 1992. (One has to have weathered a Minnesota winter to know just how gloomy a March day can be.) The idea seemed straightforward enough: to collect a volume of original essays examining the relationships between textual meaning and textual materiality. But even four years ago, institutional support for research in the history of the book in America was much less visible than it is today, and, though optimistic, we began the project with more than a little uncertainty.

We are very grateful, therefore, for the generous assistance we have received throughout the editing of this book. In particular, we wish to acknowledge the longstanding interest and support of Paul Wright of the University of Massachusetts Press. The increasing visibility of scholarship in the field of history of the book is due in no small part to publishing projects like the series which this collection helps to inaugurate and which Paul Wright has worked to develop. We are grateful, too, for the encouragement and advice of Michael Winship. Many of the contributors to this collection began their research during a summer seminar at the American Antiquarian Society led by Michael Winship as part of the Society's Program in the History of the Book in

American Culture. We are also indebted to the Department of English at the University of Minnesota and to the members of the Early American Literature Subfield, who read and commented on an early version of the introduction.

READING BOOKS

Introduction

MICHELE MOYLAN AND LANE STILES

> Claude Rivet had told them of the projected *édition de luxe* of one of
> the writers of our day—the rarest of novelists—who, long neglected by
> the multitudinous vulgar and dearly prized by the attentive . . . had had
> the happy fortune of seeing, later in life, the dawn and then the full
> light of a higher criticism—an estimate in which, on the part of the
> public, there was something really of expiation. The edition in
> question, planned by a publisher of taste, was practically an act of high
> reparation; the woodcuts with which it was to be enriched were the
> homage of English art to one of the most independent representatives
> of English letters.
>
> —Henry James, "The Real Thing"

℘ I. ℘

LET US IMAGINE FOR A MOMENT that we find ourselves brows-
ing for fiction on the shelves of our local bookstore. As we stroll past
hundreds of books we have never seen or even heard of, are we over-
come by a mass of chaotic information that we cannot interpret or
classify? Probably not. Rather, we are likely to distinguish categories of
texts—"literature" versus middlebrow novels versus pulpy paperbacks—
even in a pile of unshelved texts. If we are members of the literary
profession, we are likely to make even finer distinctions. Although, for
example, we may be searching for a collection of Hawthorne's short
stories, we may ignore the leather-bound, gilt-edged editions (unless
we find ourselves in a used bookstore and believe the edition is an old
one) in favor of a more pedestrian paperback with a dignified drawing
or portrait reproduction adorning the front cover.

What sorts of information do we use to make such literary distinctions at a glance? Certainly, in our example, the spatial placement of
books within the bookstore would play some part in our judgments.
Bookstore shoppers quickly internalize the conventions of the trade
and learn to look for Hawthorne and Melville in sections marked

"Literature." But location does not provide the entire answer. In a published lecture entitled "What's Past Is Prologue," British bibliographer D. F. McKenzie describes a classroom experiment in which he handed students a blank book and asked them to make decisions about what kind of text the book had been designed for.[1] He found their answers sophisticated and usually accurate. They could make fine distinctions about the type and margins the text would have, and they could predict the genre and the rough publication date of the text for which the book was designed—all from a book with no words. Similarly, even if our imaginary bookstore had no spatial logic, most of us would be able to make sophisticated decisions about the content of a book merely by looking at its packaging.

Clearly, when we read books, we really read *books*—that is, we read the physicality or materiality of the book as well as and in relation to the text itself. Literacy, then, may be said to include not only textual competence but material competence, an ability to read the semiotics of the concrete forms that embody, shape, and condition the meanings of texts.[2] Bindings, illustrations, paper, typeface, layout, advertisements, scholarly introductions, promotional blurbs—all function as parts of a semiotic system, parts of the total meaning of a text.

But while we may intuitively accept and even act on the notion that materiality is part of meaning, the nature of this relationship remains relatively unexplored. What is the relationship between materiality and meaning, between book and text? In the following essays, nine scholars explore this relationship in the context of individual authors, individual texts, or particular publishing projects. Each scholar demonstrates the complex particularity and variability of the relationship between materiality and meaning. Each demonstrates as well, however, that to ignore the semiotics of the book artificially wrenches texts from a complex system of cultural signification; to replace the text within the book, on the other hand, allows these scholars, each in his or her own way, to mine a rich vein of literary and cultural meaning that might otherwise have been inaccessible.

∽ 2. ∽

"Reading" the physical evidence in books is not a new scholarly practice, of course. Bibliographers have been doing it for years. But the broad exploration of materiality and meaning that we intend here reflects a relatively new approach to the study of books and texts. Fundamentally historical, this approach aims to situate the material text within those webs of production, dissemination, and consumption that constitute and determine meaning in any given place and time.[3] Sometimes referred to as "historical bibliography," such scholarship is generally classified under the more comprehensive interdisciplinary label "history of the book."[4] This label is somewhat misleading, though, since "the book" in this context can signify almost any sort of text: nonbook as well as book, script as well as print, nonverbal as well as verbal.[5]

In a 1982 essay "What Is the History of Books?" Robert Darnton, one of the earliest and most influential practitioners of history of the book in America, defined the field as "the social and cultural history of communication by print."[6] In the decade and a half since the essay was first published, the scope of history of the book has expanded to include preprint culture, but even in 1982 this definition barely seemed adequate to encompass a field so oblivious to methodological and theoretical boundaries and, as Darnton noted at the time, "so crowded with ancillary disciplines that one can no longer see its general contours."[7] In order to gain a perspective on such "interdisciplinarity run riot," Darnton proposed in the essay "a general model for analyzing the way books come into being and spread through society," which he described as "a communications circuit" flowing from the author to the publisher through the book trade to the reader and, in the sense that the writer is also a reader, full cycle back to the author.[8] "Book history," Darnton explained, "concerns each phase of this process and the process as a whole, in all its variations over space and time and in all its relations with other systems, economic, social, political, and cultural, in the surrounding environment."[9]

Darnton's model elaborated a relationship that had been posited many years before by perhaps the most seminal figure in the study of the history of the book in America, William Charvat. In an essay first published in 1949, Charvat, a literary scholar, argued that, rather than a line running from writer to reader, literary history could better be represented as a triangular relationship between writer, reader, and the book trade. "In this triangle," he wrote, "cultural forces or influence runs in both directions. The book trade is acted upon by both writer and reader, and in receiving their influence the book trade interprets it and therefore transmutes it. Correspondingly, writer and reader dictate to, and are dictated to by, the book trade."[10] Although Charvat may have lacked a theoretical vocabulary for justifying this model to other literary historians and even, ultimately, to himself, his work on nineteenth-century literary publishing, authorship, and book promotion remains a touchstone for contemporary historians of the book in America, including many of the contributors to this volume.

Charvat's scholarship largely predates the "new" book history, the birth of which is most often associated with the publication of Lucien Febvre and Henri-Jean Martin's *L'Apparition du livre* in France in 1958.[11] Febvre and Martin's work initiated the French school of *histoire du livre,* a provocative synthesis of intellectual, cultural, and social history largely concerned with the advent of print culture in France.[12] This school, along with the *"Annales* school" of French history, has, in turn, strongly influenced the development of the American version of history of the book, particularly through the writings of cultural historians such as Robert Darnton, Roger Chartier, and Elizabeth L. Eisenstein.[13] But "Frenchness," to echo Roger Chartier, has been only one of a number of influences on the history of the book in America; many people from many different disciplines have shaped the evolution of this diverse and wide-ranging field. One such person especially needs to be acknowledged here: Cathy N. Davidson, a literary scholar whose *Reading in America: Literature and Social History* (1989) is an important precursor to this collection. In this work and others, Davidson has brought a range of postmodernist literary theories and methods to bear on those of *histoire du livre* to produce an object-centered approach to literary history and criticism that is at once "material, aesthetic, and ideological."[14] Davidson offers a model for those scholars who want to connect—really, reconnect—the worlds inside texts with those outside; the gateways for these connections are books themselves, which in their varying morphologies and manifestations encode the histories of the texts they embody. We have attempted in this collection to build upon Davidson's work by testing its implications for textual interpretation and analysis and by exploring more specifically the relationships it implies between materiality and meaning.

Davidson points out in the introduction to *Reading in America* that "[a]ll good book history—including the most speculative and theoretical—begins with sound bibliography," and we would be remiss if we did not also acknowledge the influence of bibliographer G. Thomas Tanselle on the study of the history of the book in America.[15] Tanselle has long argued that bibliographical and textual scholarship is fundamentally intertwined with the history of the book.[16] We share with Tanselle the basic premise that the textual and material are inseparable—that texts are always material and that materiality is itself a kind of textuality.

There are, of course, many other scholars whose work, in one way or another, converses with the essays in this collection: David D. Hall, Richard D. Brown, William Gilmore-Lehne, Robert Gross, Joan Shelley Rubin, Carl F. Kaestle, Ronald J. Zboray, Michael Winship, Roger Stoddard, John B. Hench, Richard H. Brodhead, Lawrence Buell, Janice Radway, James L. W. West III, Michael Denning, Jonathan Rose, David Paul Nord, and Michael Warner are just a few. As the field of history of the book continues its steady process of institutionalization and formalization in various programs of academic study around the country, in research and publishing projects like that of the American Antiquarian Society's Program in the History of the Book in American Culture, in national and regional centers for the book, and in professional organizations like the Society for the History of Authorship, Reading and Publishing, this list will only continue to grow.

∾ 3. ∾

Although none of the essays included in this collection falls completely within one theoretical school, all are informed and linked by certain theoretical perspectives. Each argues, for example, that the book provides an index of the cultural work performed by the text and serves as a medium of cultural exchange, a conduit between the worlds inside and outside the text. Each argues as well for the significance of a text's movement through the "communications circuit"—from producer to consumer and back, in loops of reciprocal influence. And each argues for a relationship between materiality and readers' responses to texts, although this relationship is variously conceived and studied.

Because, on one hand, the concerns of these essays overlap in so many ways and, on the other hand, each essay proposes its own equation of interactions between book and text and between producer, distributor, and consumer, the essays refuse to be categorized into neat, self-contained groups. What we have done, therefore, is to organize the essays chronologically, according to the point of origin of the book or publishing project that constitutes the main subject of the essay. Admittedly, even this seemingly straightforward arrangement presents some problems. For one, arranging texts according to a point of origin may erroneously suggest that we want to privilege original or early editions of texts over later editions. In fact, we would argue that every edition of a text, every printing that adopts a different set of advertisements, every version with a different cover is a different literary object—a different configuration of the forces that shape meaning. No one edition has primacy, no one edition has final authority. Relationships certainly exist among the various forms of a text, but those relationships must be hypothesized and demonstrated by the scholar: they do not come in a given, hierarchized arrangement privileging a first edition or an "authentic" text.

Most texts are printed only once. Therefore, to argue against the primacy of a first edition is, by implication, to invoke a somewhat exceptional scholarly subject: that minority of texts with multiple material lives. As it happens, reprinted texts do present especially fruitful case studies for book historians since how and why texts have been repackaged can say much about the cultural and social uses of texts.[17] Not surprisingly, most of the essays in this collection are case studies of textual repackaging. The fundamentally diachronous nature of this sort of case study, however, further complicates chronology, as the first essay in the collection, Kathleen Verduin's "Dante in America: The First Hundred Years," exemplifies. In her essay, Verduin uses the material text as a tool to trace the influence of a developing and increasingly self-aware and powerful group of American literati on the production and dissemination of Dante's work in nineteenth-century America. Scarcely known in America before the nineteenth century, Dante was by the end of the century a ubiquitous and universally esteemed cultural commodity. Verduin claims that while there were many contributing cultural factors, "the American Dante was more specifically a product of the New England establishment . . . that comprised the most prestigious literary, academic, and publishing industries of the post–Civil War decades and enjoyed at least a generation of cultural dominance." Verduin argues that the New England establishment's fascination with and appropriation of Dante created a context of significance for his work that shaped the material form given the texts by American publishers. These writers and intellectuals, then, created an "American Dante"—one expressive of their own sense of American cultural and literary identity.

Where on our timeline does this essay belong? In the fourteenth century when the texts were originally produced? In the late eighteenth and early nineteenth centuries when the texts were reintroduced to English-speaking audiences in translation? Or in the latter half of the nineteenth century when the cultural machinery that had taken up

"Dante" was fully engaged? Since Verduin's narrative begins with the introduction of Dante to America, we have chosen the middle option; however, we have no interest in defending the choice except as matter of convenience and coherence for our readers. If anything, we would rather defend the untidiness of these essays, as evidence of their vitality and historicity.

There are, as we noted, many threads that connect and overlap the essays. One of these threads is the relationship between a text's material history and its reception history. In "The Material Melville: Shaping Readers' Horizons," Michael Kearns studies this relationship through the lens of German *Rezeptionsästhetik*. Just as Iser argues that the *text* works to create an ideal reader and a privileged interpretation, Kearns argues that the *book* helps shape a reader's "horizon of expectations" (a phrase he borrows from Jauss).[18] Kearns analyzes the endpapers, title pages, and running titles of the first editions of Melville's early novels, as well as magazine advertisements for the books, for evidence of how professional readers affiliated with Melville's publishers responded to his work and then marketed their responses to the general public. These same physical details also allow Kearns to speculate on how general readers may have been conditioned to receive the new author. Borrowing from Peter Rabinowitz's notion that literary conventions can position a "readerly standpoint" before the act of reading begins, Kearns argues that textual materiality is one of these systems of conventions shaping readerly predispositions.[19] In Melville's case, readers were materially predisposed to read the early novels as authentic travel narratives. Once this horizon of expectations was established, Kearns contends, Melville could never completely escape categorization as "Herman Melville, author of *Typee* and *Omoo*," no matter how much his texts violated the generic expectations of his audience.

Like Kearns, Jeffrey Groves "reads" the book semiotically, but where Kearns looks at aspects of the book that identify and individuate texts, Groves is more concerned with morphology that erases differences between texts. In "Judging Literary Books by Their Covers: House Styles, Ticknor and Fields, and Literary Promotion," Groves argues that the two house styles of binding developed by the Boston firm of Ticknor and Fields during the middle of the nineteenth century became both advertisements for the publishing house and a signifying system defining a new field of literature: American texts of high literary quality. The two uniform styles—the brown cover, which was developed in the late 1840s, and the blue and gold cover, introduced in 1856—

were both modeled on the editions of English literary houses, whose prestige Ticknor and Fields successfully borrowed and marketed on a mass scale. The Ticknor and Fields house styles commodified literary quality not only for consumers (who may have purchased the books as much to own as to read) but also for authors (who longed to have their works enshrined within such prestigious covers) and for other American publishers (who imitated the styles in their own editions).

In her essay, "Literature in Newsprint: Antebellum Family Newspapers and the Uses of Reading," Amy Thomas also explores the relationship between the physical appearance of a publication and readers' purposes for reading. However, "the book" that Thomas analyzes is a very different type of material and textual object from that with which the preceding essays were concerned. Thomas's subject is a popular newspaper—the Raleigh, North Carolina, newspaper *Spirit of the Age*—which began as a temperance paper but evolved under the direction of its publisher and editor, Alexander Gorman, into one of the South's most successful family newspapers during the 1850s. In her essay, Thomas describes how Gorman manipulated the form of the newspaper to create and sell a context of meaning for a variety of reading purposes. This form represented a delicate attempt to mediate between readers' expectations (that a newspaper would present only low-culture literature or that newspapers were primarily for "use") and the publisher's desire to promote new possibilities in the form and quality of literary journalism. Thomas demonstrates that the materiality of literature often includes a feedback mechanism through which the responses of readers ultimately shape the form of the text.

This feedback mechanism between reader and publisher is demonstrated even more concretely in Susan Williams's essay, "Manufacturing Intellectual Equipment: The Tauchnitz Edition of *The Marble Faun.*" Williams argues that the international success of Nathaniel Hawthorne's *The Marble Faun* owed much to its publication in 1860 by German publisher Bernard Tauchnitz. It was the Tauchnitz *Marble Faun* that, beginning around 1868, Italian booksellers encouraged American tourists to illustrate and bind as personalized guidebooks and souvenirs of their travels in Italy. Blank pages inserted in the book allowed tourists to decorate and inscribe each copy as they saw fit. Eventually, the Tauchnitz *Marble Faun* became such a conventional part of the American tourist's "intellectual equipment" that American publishers began to imitate it. Williams asks us to be open to different conceptions of reading; the uses American travelers made of the Tauchnitz *Marble*

Faun, she argues, pushed reading into a social realm in which readers could act out Hawthorne's narrative and, in essence, convert it into their own.

A feedback mechanism of a different sort is described in Nancy Cook's essay on the publication by subscription of Mark Twain's *The Innocents Abroad* (1869). In "Finding His Mark: Twain's *The Innocents Abroad* as a Subscription Book," Nancy Cook explains how Twain continually reshaped the form and content of his novel to meet the expectations and desires of his subscribers and, in the process, fashioned and reified the idea of "Mark Twain," successful author. Subscription publishing made explicit the implicit contract between writer and reader, and Twain's success in this mode of publication helped to establish audiences for a large body of popular (if low status) nationalist literature in addition to his own work. Reading closely this copiously illustrated subscription book, Cook speculates on how an original subscriber's experience of reading *The Innocents Abroad* must have differed significantly from readers' experiences of other editions.

Historian Scott Casper returns to an issue first raised by Verduin and then touched on by Groves: the influence of a New England cultural establishment on national culture and taste. Casper's essay, "Defining the National Pantheon: The Making of Houghton Mifflin's Biographical Series, 1880–1900," explores the ways in which a publishing house in the late nineteenth century attempted to use the material text to position and market two series of biographies, and, thereby, to participate in the delineation of a particular American identity. Houghton Mifflin designed the American Statesmen and American Men of Letters biographical series as American cultural canons, but, as Casper points out, "the publishing history of the series reveals not a coordinated program of cultural production but an uncertain and contested process, dependent on the schedules of writers and the desires of readers as well as on the aims of editors or publishers." The material uniformity of the series masked the untidy historical contingencies that complicated the publisher's effort to produce coherent and cohesive canons. These contingencies included the very mechanics of editing and publishing the series—defining what and who was a "statesman" or "man of letters," sequencing and scheduling volumes, selecting authors, and responding to readers' suggestions. Casper extends the arguments of Verduin and Groves by demonstrating that the intentions of a cultural establishment can be just as easily subverted as reinforced by the materiality of the literature it produces.

Using Helen Hunt Jackson's novel *Ramona* (1884) as a case study, Michele Moylan treats the material text as a dual repository of meaning: an expression of both reading and writing, interpretation and creation. The book, she argues, embodies an already-experienced interpretation of the text, an attempt to write that interpretation back into the text, and an attempt to take that meaning "on the road" to sell to future audiences or interpreters. In "Materiality as Performance: The Forming of Helen Hunt Jackson's *Ramona*," Moylan maintains that the myriad of editions of Jackson's "Indian novel" reflect the various meanings that readers have found in the text, beginning with Jackson's own meaning. As the meaning becomes expressed in the material form of the book, it then becomes part of subsequent readers' horizon of expectation, a sense of the text they must accommodate, whether they read with it or against it.

The final essay in the collection looks again at the ways in which the book mediates textual meaning in relation to the uses to which institutions and cultural formations put texts. In "Packaging Literature for the High Schools: From the Riverside Literature Series to *Literature and Life*," the institutional arena is the public schools. Lane Stiles's essay explores the transition from "separate classics" series to literature anthologies in American high schools after the First World War. Stiles centers his analysis on Scott Foresman's *Literature and Life* (1922–24), one of the first and most influential high school literature anthologies published in America. Stiles suggests that *Literature and Life* both positioned readers in relation to "classic" literature and embodied the cooperative venture of the American public school system and the textbook publishing industry. Thus, Stiles argues, the material form of the *Literature and Life* anthology demonstrates the effects of an educational and political agenda on the packaging and therefore the meaning and cultural work of literature in America.

These nine essays represent several different approaches to linking book and text, materiality and meaning, drawing from the theories and methodologies of history of the book, *Rezeptionsästhetik,* reader response, sociology of literature, new historicism, feminism, Marxism, and hermeneutics. Applying these techniques, each scholar argues that the book embodies and participates integrally in the meaning of a text as the point of mediation between culture and text, as a part of a system of conventions that shape and condition readings, or as a performance of meaning. To ignore the book, therefore, is to risk not having fully read the text. Furthermore, to ignore the book is potentially to miss many of the rich, complicated, various, and often unpredictable interactions between American literature and American culture.

∾ 4. ∾

One of our goals when we began this project was to develop a model of practical criticism and interpretation that incorporated material analysis into textual analysis. Fundamental to the essays in this collection, then, are challenges to traditional approaches to studying and teaching literature. Each essay, for example, probes the boundaries of the textual object, searching for the lines dividing the literary from the extraliterary. To what degree do we consider the advertisements included in a copy of Melville's *Typee* by a twentieth-century publishing house part of the meaning of the novel, the *literary* object? Are the ads irrelevant because they do not represent the author's intended meaning or because they are not an artifact of the book's original culture of production, or are the sheets centrally relevant because they form part of the context of meaning for any reader who engages the particular edition or form of that text?

Our assumptions about where literary meaning resides will dictate our answer to this and other related questions. Early book historians like William Charvat reacted against the limits of New Critical definitions of literature as an ideal object, but they also worried that a more sociological study of the book could not capture "literariness." The scholars represented in this collection conjoin literariness and materiality; they employ broad and sometimes amorphous definitions of the literary object, but they see and read a fundamental relationship between book and text. Illustrations, bindings, scholarly introductions— all function in their analyses as determinants of and participants in literary meaning. For none of these scholars is there a clear line between the "ideal" and the "material."

Even so seemingly simple an issue as the verb tense we use to write about literature comes under challenge when we collapse the boundaries between the literary and the extraliterary, between book and text. Each of the scholars represented here began writing their essays the way one usually writes within the professional literary community: using the present tense to refer to the literary text. No doubt most literary scholars have been taught some version of the explanation that since the literary text exists unchanging, able to be opened and read by anyone at any point in history, it is forever contemporary. Explicit in the methodologies represented in this collection, however, is the argument that literary meaning is not static: texts can change frequently and radically. The readers who encountered Mark Twain's *Innocents Abroad* in its original subscription book form encountered a different book than do readers of the contemporary Penguin edition. Literary books do not, in other words, transcend time and place but instead are very much products of historical forces.[20]

Finally, these scholarly methodologies of material analysis have pedagogical implications as well. Bringing the material text into the undergraduate classroom could open literary discussion and analysis in important ways, bridging the chasm that separates literature and history for many students. Analysis of the physical forms the book (or a book) has taken in America throughout history can bring sociocultural and literary forces into logical relation for these students by providing them with a methodological and theoretical link.

Furthermore, if, as the scholars in this text argue, the material book often represents interpretation—or meaning that others have previously found in the literary text—then an analysis of the various forms of a text in the classroom could decenter the teacher as final authority on meaning without opening the classroom to the chaos of absolute relativism. In other words, the instructor could demonstrate that, over time, many readers have found ways to make many meanings out of the literary text. Although those interpretations are often tied to the highly variable sociocultural needs and contexts of the readers, the meanings that survive, flourish, and sell are those that can persuade an audience to adopt their perspective. Students could be similarly challenged both to make their own meaning out of the text and to learn to shape that interpretation so they can "sell" it to others (tying interpretation to audience).

Too often scholars, particularly literary scholars, have tended to idealize books as "mere" texts—disembodied mental constructs transcending materiality, culture, and history. While the notion of a disembodied text may be a useful critical fiction, it is nevertheless an inherently distorting one, for there is no such thing after all as a text unmediated by its materiality. What we propose in this introduction, and what all the essays in this collection exemplify, is an approach to books aimed at restoring the materiality of texts in the fullest possible sense—an approach that specifically posits the material text as a nexus in the intersection of literature, culture, and history.

ᴥ NOTES ᴥ

1. D. F. McKenzie, "What's Past Is Prologue," The Bibliographic Society Centenary Lecture (14 July 1992) (N.p.: Hearthstone Publications, 1993).

For the purposes of this introduction, we shall use the terms "book" and "text" to distinguish between material form and textual content. When we wish to collapse this distinction (as we will wish to do often), we will refer to both book and text as the "material text."

2. For the historian, the study of material competence, like the study of literacy in general, presents a number of methodological challenges, particularly in terms of definition and evidence. (See Carl F. Kaestle, "Studying the History of Literacy" and "The History of Readers," in *Literacy in the United States: Readers and Reading since 1880,* ed. Carl F. Kaestle et al. [New Haven: Yale UP, 1991].) The essays in this collection attempt as much as possible to document the actual responses of actual readers to material texts. While we would argue that books themselves represent direct evidence of the actual responses of actual readers (the professional readers, editors, marketers, and designers associated with publishing houses), we recognize that it is problematic to use material texts to speculate on "intended" or "implied" readers and readings. Still, we believe that, at the very least, such speculation provides a useful and plausible starting point for further research.

3. As John B. Hench has pointed out, "[o]ne of the hallmarks of the 'new' history of the book, in contrast with the older fields of bibliography and printing history, is the emphasis that book history has placed on the distribution and consumption of printed materials in addition to their production" ("Toward a History of the Book in America," *Publishing Research Quarterly* [Fall 1994]: 14).

4. For brief overviews of the history of the book as practiced in America, see Michael Winship, afterword, *Literary Publishing in America 1790–1850,* by William Charvat (1959; rpt. Amherst: U of Massachusetts P, 1993); Cathy N. Davidson, "Toward a History of Books and Readers," *Reading in America: Literature and Social History* 1–26, ed. Cathy N. Davidson (Baltimore: Johns Hopkins UP, 1989); Robert Darnton, "What Is the History of Books?" in Davidson, *Reading in America* (orig. pub. *Daedalus* [Summer 1982]: 65–83; rpt. in Darnton, *The Kiss of Lamourette: Reflections in Cultural History* [New York: Norton, 1990] and in *Books and Society in History: Papers of the Association of College and Research Libraries, Rare Books and Manuscripts Preconference, 24–28 June 1980, Boston, Massachusetts,* ed. Kenneth E. Carpenter [New York: Bowker, 1983]).

5. Thomas R. Adams and Nicolas Barker define "the book" as any "bibliographical document" intended for public consumption, whether in manuscript or printed form ("A New Model for the Study of the Book," in *A Potencie of Life: Books in Society,* ed. Nicolas Barker [London: The British Library, 1993]). McKenzie proposes incorporating the new book history into

an expanded conception of bibliography as "the study of the sociology of texts" (*Bibliography and the Sociology of Texts* [London: The British Library, 1986]). McKenzie defines " 'texts' to include verbal, visual, oral and numeric data, in the form of maps, prints, and music, of archives of recorded sound, of films, videos, and any computer-store information, everything in fact from epigraphy to the latest forms of discography" (5).

6. Darnton in Davidson, *Reading in America* 27.

7. Darnton in Davidson, *Reading in America* 29.

8. Darnton in Davidson, *Reading in America* 29.

9. Darnton in Davidson, *Reading in America* 30. The model is still very useful, although, as several of the essays collected here demonstrate, there may be more reciprocity to the relationships in this circuit than Darnton's model implies. A variation on this model, focused more on the book trade, has been offered by Michael Winship ("Publishing in America: Needs and Opportunities for Research," *Needs and Opportunities in the History of the Book: America, 1630–1876*, ed. David D. Hall and John B. Hench [Worcester, Massachusetts: American Antiquarian Society, 1987]). Thomas R. Adams and Nicolas Barker have proposed a similar model, except that theirs uses books rather than people as its nodes.

10. William Charvat, "Literary Economics and Literary History," *The Profession of Authorship in America, 1800–1870*, ed. Matthew J. Bruccoli (1968; rpt. New York: Columbia UP, 1992) 284. Published posthumously, *The Profession of Authorship* contains unfinished as well as previously published work. Other important essays have been collected in Charvat, *Literary Publishing in America, 1790–1850*.

11. Lucien Febvre and Henri-Jean Martin, *The Coming of the Book: The Impact of Printing 1450–1800*, trans. David Gerard, ed. Geoffrey Nowell-Smith and David Wooten (1976; rpt. London: Verso, 1984).

12. The study of the history of the book has tended to coalesce around national publishing projects—*l'Histoire de l'édition française, Geschichte des Buchwesens, A History of the Book in Britain, A History of the Book in America*. For an overview of the American Antiquarian Society's Program in the History of the Book in American Culture, see John B. Hench, "Toward a History of the Book in America"; also, David D. Hall, "A History of the Book in American Culture," *Book Research Quarterly* (Summer 1990): 63–69.

13. Robert Darnton, *The Kiss of Lamourette, The Great Cat Massacre and Other Episodes in French Cultural History* (New York: Basic Books, 1984), and *The Business of Enlightenment: A Publishing History of the "Encyclopédie," 1775–1800* (Cambridge: Cambridge UP, 1979); Roger Chartier, *The Order of Books: Readers, Authors, and Libraries in Europe between the Fourteenth and Eighteenth Centuries*, trans. Lydia G. Cochrane (Palo Alto: Stanford UP, 1994), *The Cultural Uses of Print in Early Modern France*, trans. Lydia G. Cochrane (Princeton, N.J.: Princeton UP, 1987), and "Frenchness in the History of the

Book: From the History of Publishing to the History of Reading," *Proceedings of the American Antiquarian Society* 97 (1987): 299–329 (rpt. Worcester: American Antiquarian Society, 1988); Elizabeth L. Eisenstein, *Print Culture and Enlightenment Thought* (Chapel Hill, N.C.: Hanes Foundation, 1986) and *The Printing Revolution in Early Modern Europe* (Cambridge: Cambridge UP, 1983).

14. "A field of study that makes the book its focus constantly moves between material, aesthetic, and ideological planes, and assumes that a book, like meaning itself, is created within a specific historical context" (Davidson, *Reading in America* 2).

15. Davidson, *Reading in America* 7.

16. "A concern with the social repercussions of printing is ultimately a concern with texts—with what works, and what texts of those works, were disseminated through print at particular times. The study of variations in texts, and the reasons for them, is therefore basic to the broadest concerns of intellectual history; and analytical bibliography is thus fundamental not only to the history of printing but to 'book history' in its newest sense" (G. Thomas Tanselle, "Issues in Bibliographical Studies since 1942," *The Book Encompassed: Studies in Twentieth-Century Bibliography*, ed. Peter Davison [Cambridge: Cambridge UP, 1992], 31). See also G. Thomas Tanselle, "The Bibliography and Textual Study of American Books" in *Needs and Opportunities in the History of the Book*, and *The History of Books as a Field of Study* (Chapel Hill: Hanes Foundation and the University of North Carolina, 1981).

17. According to McKenzie, the presentation of a reprinted text "in different formats and typefaces, on different papers in different bindings, and its sale at different times, places, and prices, imply distinct conditions and uses and must vary the meanings its readers make from it. In that sense, the book (or script) as an *un*stable physical form in its descent through successive versions is the more valuable in offering ubiquitous evidence—in the physical signs embedded in the documents themselves—for 'history of the book' as a study of the changing *conditions* of meaning and hence of reading" (*Bibliography and the Sociology of Texts* 297).

18. Wolfgang Iser, *The Implied Reader: Patterns of Communication in Prose Fiction from Bunyan to Beckett* (Baltimore: Johns Hopkins UP, 1974) and *The Act of Reading: A Theory of Aesthetic Response* (Baltimore: Johns Hopkins UP, 1978). Hans Robert Jauss, *Toward an Aesthetic of Reception* (Minneapolis: U of Minnesota P, 1982).

19. Peter Rabinowitz, *Before Reading: Narrative Conventions and the Politics of Interpretation* (Ithaca, N.Y.: Cornell UP, 1987).

20. Even if we think of meaning as performative, every performance of a text occurs in time and is always already historical.

Dante in America: The First Hundred Years

KATHLEEN VERDUIN

A desire to know more of the earliest monuments of modern literature is at length manifesting itself among us; and before the expiration of ten years it is probable that the most important of these works will have emerged, so to speak, into the perpetual light of the press.

—Longfellow, *Outre-mer,* 1835

The cheap press and the universal reading, which have come in together, have caused a great many translations to be made from the Greek, the German, the Italian, and the French. . . . To me the command is loud to use the time by reading these books.

—Emerson, *Journals,* 1849

Literary works, it might be worth insisting, do not produce their own occasions. They are always produced within some cultural situation of the literary, within the particular set of relations in which literature's place is at any moment socially determined.

—Richard H. Brodhead, *Cultures of Letters,* 1993

In a memorable scene in Sinclair Lewis's 1922 novel, *Babbitt,* the title character's affable Rotarian friends and their wives attempt an impromptu séance. Asked which departed spirit should be summoned, Mrs. Orville Jones begs, "Oh, let's talk to Dante! We studied him in the Reading Circle. You know who he was, Orvy." Certainly Orvy knows—"the Wop poet. Where do you think I was raised?"—and Babbitt chimes in, "Sure—the fellow that took the Cook's Tour to Hell. I've never waded through his po'try, but we learned about him in the U." Later, secretly embarrassed by his friends' flippancy, Babbitt experiences "without explanation, the impression of a slaggy cliff and on it, in silhouette against menacing clouds, a lone and austere figure."[1]

The passage is fiction, but it offers a remarkably accurate synopsis of

Dante's various meanings in the culture of the period: widely if some-what imprecisely renowned ("the fellow that took the Cook's Tour to Hell"), a staple both of the academic canon ("we learned about him in the U.") and of improving organizations for women ("we studied him in the Reading Circle"), definitely highbrow and a marker of social status ("Where do you think I was raised?") but adaptable to lowbrow party games and even to the dubious rituals of spiritualism: in short, much more a ubiquitous and versatile construct than a literary text. Yet even on this level, one notices, Dante is inextricable from available forms of print culture, since Babbitt's mental picture recalls unmistak-ably the famous illustrations by Gustave Doré (Illustration 1).

Given that little more than a hundred years earlier Dante was scarcely known in the English-speaking countries at all, let alone a household word in small midwestern communities like Babbitt's Ze-nith, Lewis's vignette confirms the success of an amalgam of develop-ments that both promoted the *Divine Comedy* to a position of cul-tural authority and made it materially accessible to American readers. Whatever its virtues—and indeed those virtues are very great—Dante's work could hardly have circulated apart from the exigencies of the literary marketplace and the network of production, promotion, and reception that consolidated and perpetuated value. The general cul-tural factors cited in my epigraphs from Longfellow and Emerson—increased literacy, mass production of books, and a new enthusiasm for foreign literature—of course played a foundational role. But both as a literary and cultural commodity, the American Dante was more specif-ically a product of the New England establishment—a "culture of let-ters,"[2] in Richard Brodhead's phrase—that comprised the most pres-tigious literary, academic, and publishing industries of the post–Civil War decades and enjoyed at least a generation of cultural dominance.

∿ I. ∿

The American interest in Dante is traceable to an international revival of his works. To eighteenth-century taste the *Commedia* had epito-mized medieval barbarity and was in fact little known: Voltaire's flip-pant dismissal of Dante in the *Dictionnaire Philosophique* (1764)—"His reputation will always continue to be solid, because no one reads him"—complemented Goethe's observation that the *Inferno* was horrible, the *Purgatorio* ambiguous, and the *Paradiso* boring.[3] In England, Horace Walpole branded the poet in 1782 as "extravagant, absurd, disgusting, in

1. "A lone and austere figure." Illustration by Gustave Doré (1861) to *Dante's Inferno*, trans. Henry F. Cary (Cassell, 1901). Photo by Lou Schakel.

short a Methodist parson in Bedlam."[4] Yet Walpole's remark coincided exactly with the first English translations of Dante: three cantos by Blake's friend William Hayley in 1782, the *Inferno* the same year by Charles Rogers, and the *Commedia* in its entirety by Henry Boyd between 1785 and 1802. Within a few decades of these events, a wave of enthusiasm for Dante had swept across Europe.[5]

Crucial to this revival in the English-speaking countries was the blank-verse translation by the Reverend Henry Francis Cary, whose

biography, by his son, sheds some light on the process by which an antiquarian exercise became a bestseller. Cary published his *Inferno* in two
volumes between 1805 and 1806, but as the younger Cary reports, "The
success of the publication was not at all answerable to its merit. . . . and
the circulation was chiefly confined to a small number of personal
friends, and perhaps a few Italian scholars." When the persistent Cary
finished the *Purgatorio* and *Paradiso*, notes his son,

> Nearly eight years had elapsed since the publication of his version of the
> Inferno: but the work had attracted very little notice, by no means
> sufficient to induce a publisher to embark on the expense of printing the
> whole. My father, therefore, though his means could ill afford such an
> undertaking, resolved on publishing his translation at his own expense;
> but, from the same cause, was under the necessity of having it printed in
> a cheap form, one little calculated to attract the notice of critics or the
> public.

Cary's complete translation appeared early in 1814. "The book is a
cheap one," he wrote a friend, "if the quantity alone be considered. The
price is only twelve shillings for the three volumes in boards; and
though they are diminutive in size, yet they contain letter press in
abundance." "Pecuniary return for his labours," avows the pious son,
"was altogether out of the question."[6]

In 1818, however, Coleridge commended Cary's translation in a lecture, suddenly catapulting Cary's efforts into fame. "About a thousand copies of the first edition, that remained on hand, were immediately disposed of," according to the biography, and "in less than three
months a new edition was called for. The Edinburgh and Quarterly
Reviews re-echoed the praises that had been sounded by Coleridge,
and henceforth the claims of the translator of Dante to literary distinction were universally admitted." This dramatic reversal confirms a
principle as significant for future Dante publication as for any other
literary enterprise: the importance of authoritative endorsement. In
1825 Cary could savor the following incident:

> Henry [Cary's son] went yesterday to lay out part of his fee in a book-
> seller's shop in Piccadilly, and I must indulge a translator's vanity so far as
> to relate what there befel him. "I have some old College books that I
> should like to exchange," said Henry. "They would be of no use to me,"
> said the man, "but if you have any standard works I should like to see
> them." "What do you mean by standard works?" says H——, when the
> man beginning "Cary's Dante, Sir!" he burst into one of his laughs, at

which the man was so confused that H—— found it necessary to explain the cause of his mirth.[7]

Cary's elevation into a "standard work" attractive to publishers and booksellers reflects the vitality of the Dante revival in England: and as Theodore Koch acknowledged retrospectively to the Dante Society at Harvard in 1896, "From England we inherited many of our traditions and tastes; when Dante came to be widely read in England, we welcomed him here, read him, and began to study him for ourselves."[8] Since a genteel education for both sexes typically included training in the modern languages, preferably from a native speaker, privileged Americans were able to read Dante in the original language. The lessons of Mozart's exiled librettist, Lorenzo Da Ponte—to invoke the most famous example—incited enthusiasm for Dante among a generation of New Yorkers, and Pietro Bachi and others stirred similar interest in New England.[9] Copies of Dante in Italian were consequently in demand among the intelligentsia in the early Republic and were often procured as souvenirs or gifts during European travel. Margaret Fuller, for example, was delighted sometime during the 1830s with her uncle's gift, "the fine Athenaeum copy" printed in Rome in 1802.[10] Another important source was the bookseller Obadiah Rich, eventually the London agent for Harper's, who in his years as U.S. consul in Spain had amassed a large collection of books and manuscripts and supplied many American scholars and libraries with foreign volumes. The papers of historian W. H. Prescott show that Rich invoiced him for nearly a dozen titles by or relating to Dante.[11]

Still, as Angelina La Piana states in her informative study *Dante's American Pilgrimage,* it was Cary's translation that remained the primary medium of access, particularly as heralded in authoritative literary reviews.[12] The influential discussion of Cary in an 1818 issue of the *Edinburgh Review*—a magazine, as Charles Eliot Norton would recall, widely read in the Cambridge of his youth—reached the attention of Prescott, and fifteen-year-old Ralph Waldo Emerson copied excerpts from the piece for his brother Edward with the ingenuous note, "This is translation from the Italian I believe."[13] Cary's Dante is listed among the books Emerson withdrew from the Boston Athenaeum; it was also available to the young Longfellow at Bowdoin. In 1823 Prescott asked George Ticknor (who would later teach Dante at Harvard), "Do you know of a large edition of Cary's translation in town?"[14]

In his memoir of Margaret Fuller, therefore, Emerson correctly linked "the new vogue given to the genius of Dante" with the first American issue of Cary's translation, since which, in Emerson's account, "all studious youths and maidens [had] been reading the Inferno."[15] Emerson refers here to volumes 45 and 46 in the series The Works of the British Poets, published in Philadelphia in 1822.[16] This was the edition of Cary that Emerson himself purchased in 1825, and Longfellow also owned a copy.[17] I have located no information regarding the cost of these volumes: copies I have seen are leatherbound, but binding in leather was often executed by owners rather than publishers. Emerson's record—"all studious youths and maidens"—suggests however a fairly general readership, and the volumes, 5 1/2 by 3 1/2 inches, were conveniently pocket sized. What the volumes indicate incidentally is that in 1822 Dante's identity as an author had not yet solidified, at least on the visual level: the series title emphasizes not Dante but Cary, as a "British poet," and the charming frontispiece to volume 45, illustrating *Purgatorio* 9:28–30, depicts Dante not in the now familiar medieval scholar's garb but in eighteenth-century knee breeches (Illustration 2).

By midcentury, the American publishing industry had centered in New York, and publication of the increasingly famous Dante moved with it.[18] In 1845 Appleton and Company, founded two decades earlier, issued an edition of Cary's recently revised translation that they would reprint more than a dozen times before 1880. In line with newly sophisticated marketing strategies, the volume (6 3/4 by 4 inches) was available in gold-stamped leather binding as well as the more common cloth, which sold for $1.50; it carried the recently discovered and much celebrated Giotto portrait of Dante as a frontispiece, emphasizing the romantic genius-author, and reproduced twelve engravings by the eighteenth-century English artist John Flaxman (Illustration 3).[19] The Appleton edition closely resembled one published about the same time by the London firm of Henry Bohn (priced, according to a publisher's circular, at 7s. 6d.), worth mention because Bohn's Antiquarian Library series introduced many American as well as English readers to medieval works and also because it was the edition owned by Melville.[20] Poe commended the Appleton Dante in an 1845 review:

> This is one of the most beautiful volumes ever issued from the press of Appleton. It is a duodecimo of nearly 600 pages, exquisitely printed on *very* fine paper, embellished with a dozen carefully engraved plates from Flaxman's inimitable designs, and the whole tastefully and durably

DANTE.

And snatch'd me upward even to the fire

Canto 9

DRAWN BY T. UNDERWOOD.   ENGRAV'D BY G.S. LANG.

2. Frontispiece, volume 45 of The Works of the British Poets (1822). Widener Library, Harvard University.

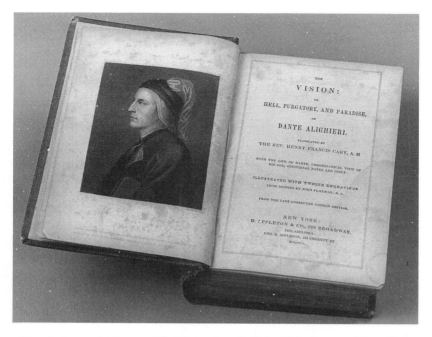

3. Frontispiece and title page, *The Divine Comedy* ("The Vision"), trans. Henry F. Cary (Appleton, 1845). Photo by Lou Schakel.

bound. The title fully conveys the contents of the book, with the exception of the frontispiece—which is a likeness of Dante, engraved by Phillibrown, from the "last portrait" by Giotto. This picture was discovered in the ancient castle of the Podesta, at Florence, in July 1840. When found, it was encrusted with whitewash.

The Messrs. Appleton in giving us this edition, have rendered a very important service to the literature of the country.[21]

Poe's remarks are clearly weighted in favor of the appearance of the book and its appropriation of the currently newsworthy portrait; like his allusion in one of his sketches to the Ugolino story, among the most habitually excerpted passages from the *Inferno* (canto 33), they suggest little more than a nodding acquaintance with the text.[22] But Margaret Fuller, who had read all of the *Commedia* in Italian, also took time to criticize the Appleton product on grounds of appearance in her review for the *New York Daily Tribune,* complaining, "'Tis pity that the designs of Flaxman are so poorly reproduced in this American book"; she disliked the Giotto frontispiece, preferring the putative death mask of Dante prefixed to contemporary British publications. Nevertheless,

4. Illustration by John Flaxman (1793) to *Inferno* 3 (the boat of Charon), included in "The Vision" (the *Divine Comedy*), trans. Henry F. Cary (Appleton, 1845). Photo by Lou Schakel.

Fuller agreed that "whoever wants Cary's version will rejoice at last to possess it in so fair and legible a guise, as we do."[23]

Fuller's attention to the Flaxman illustrations (Illustration 4), in her words "a really noble comment upon Dante," suggests the eagerness with which readers sought to visualize classic works.[24] Privately commissioned by the wealthy Thomas Hope in 1793, Flaxman's were the only English illustrations of Dante before those William Blake completed in 1827 (which as far as I know were never incorporated into publications of Dante before the twentieth century). Hope's private collection was quickly republished in pirated editions in France in 1802 and in England in 1807, and engravings after Flaxman thence appeared in editions of Dante across Europe (Fuller's "Athenaeum" copy also contained them).[25] Melville praised the Flaxman pictures effusively in his 1852 novel, *Pierre,* and Longfellow cited them as "a work which I would urge every reader of Dante to have by him as he reads."[26]

∾ **2.** ∾

One finds evidence that Dante was being read across the eastern seaboard in nineteenth-century America: men of letters like the New

Yorker R. H. Wilde, the Philadelphian George Henry Boker, and the
southerner William Gilmore Simms were all engaged with Dante to
some degree.[27] As my references already suggest, however, American
interest in Dante ran strongest in New England. Literacy rates were
higher in these states, but more importantly, literature had arguably
acquired a more complex social role. Puritan tradition had stressed
what Ronald Zboray calls "the nexus between reading and religion,"
laying groundwork for the blurring of religion and literature in later
generations; and the nineteenth-century Unitarian deemphasis of the-
ology in favor of a more generalized "self-culture" permitted easy accommodation of Dante, whose Catholicism might otherwise have
proved an ideological obstacle.[28] Extant records of reading remain in
largest number, not surprisingly, from the New England writers now
central or at least peripheral to the literary canon, but while these
figures cannot speak for all classes, even in their own region, they do
testify to a social institutionalization of Dante that radiated increasingly beyond them.

I have mentioned that New England historians like Prescott and
Ticknor were early readers of Dante; the first full-length article on
Dante in an American periodical was by John Chipman Gray in an 1819
issue of the Boston-based *North American Review,* and the young
Cambridge artist Washington Allston produced a portrait of Dante's
Beatrice the same year.[29] Traveling in Europe in the 1830s, future Massachusetts senator Charles Sumner gushed to his and Longfellow's
friend and fellow Italophile G. W. Greene, "You gave me the jewel I
have, for I should never have learned Italian without you. I think my
highest, maddest ambition—without the expectation of ever gratifying
that minimum—was to read the 'Inferno' of Dante!"[30]

The residual journals and correspondence of the New England
writers are especially detailed in documenting a cozy round of lending
and gift giving. Emerson lent his friend Samuel Gray Ward—so much
the Italophile that friends like Margaret Fuller called him "Raffaello"—
his copy of the *Vita Nuova,* itself a gift from George Bancroft; their
Concord friend Elizabeth Hoar was "emboldened," as she put it, to ask
Emerson for his copy of Cary in 1840, possibly the one he had received
from presumably grateful schoolboys in 1825.[31] Gifts of Dante's works
were supplemented by the exchange of related consumer items like the
engraving of Dante and Beatrice hanging in Fuller's house at Jamaica
Plain or the one Whittier received from his friend Lucy Larcom (probably both from the painting by Ary Scheffer that had recently been on

exhibit at the Boston Athenaeum).[32] The portrait of Dante discovered in 1840 and attributed to Giotto—featured, as I have mentioned, in the Appleton edition—was concurrently disseminated by the British Arundel Society; a copy still hangs in Longfellow's house in Cambridge, and Emerson received one from Charles Eliot Norton, responding cordially, "What a supernal figure! and how miraculously preserved, from the time when Dante was unknown, to the times of the Appreciation!"[33]

This network of transactions, at once personal and commercial, underlies also the integration of Dante reading into New England social patterns. Fuller, who started translating the *Vita Nuova* "as a piece of Sunday work," reported to Emerson in 1837 that she had spent an evening "reading bits of Dante" with William Ellery Channing; and Dante merged easily, the same year, with her temporary incorporation into the Emerson household: Emerson's baby son Waldo, she wrote a friend, "comes so natural after Dante and other poems."[34] Legend has it that at the Transcendentalists' experimental Brook Farm, Dante was read aloud in the barn during milking.[35] Dante was hardly the only author New Englanders were reading to each other, but the evidence suggests he was a particular favorite for parlor declamation, perhaps because the *Commedia* could so easily be broken up into manageable segments, as Longfellow later confirmed when he translated a canto a day while his morning kettle boiled.[36]

Perhaps predictably, then, the next American publication of Dante was instigated by the prime mover of the Transcendental circle. Having visited Thomas Carlyle during his European trip of 1847–48, Emerson brought home proof sheets of John Aitken Carlyle's prose translation of the *Inferno*, published in England by Chapman and Hall, and was transparently eager to please Thomas Carlyle by negotiating the American publication of his brother's work.[37] Though Emerson was already trying to prime the market with a review of the Carlyle version, the project proved more difficult than he anticipated, and it offers something of a case study in the frustrations of publishing in antebellum America.[38] Emerson turned first to Ticknor and Fields, a logical choice both for their proximity in Boston and because they had published the local poet-dentist Thomas W. Parsons's *The First Ten Cantos of the Inferno* in pamphlet form in 1843 (Ticknor and Fields would also issue J. C. Peabody's imitative "literal metrical version" of *Inferno* 1–10 in 1857), but Emerson was turned down "on account of the bad times."[39] Emerson's letter to his brother William (then living in New York) on 15 August 1848 indicates that he was not above the hard sell:

They advised me to try the Harpers. The Appletons, I believe, have printed *Cary*, & therefore would not be the right men. Wiley & P[utnam] have ceased to print.—I think tomorrow to send it to N.Y.—I shall perhaps send it to you, because of the difficulty of corresponding about a thing which can be spoke through in a few minutes. These are the facts. Here is a good book faithfully translated by Dr John Carlyle who has lived near seven years in Italy & probably knows more of Dante than anybody living. Dante is read every year, more & more, *in this country*, & in England. This is the book which students want, & which general readers want, & not *Cary*. Now will you print it, Gentlemen, & give the translator a commission on your sales, for his work?—If not; will you print it, & if it succeeds, give him something by & by? If not; will you print it well, & give him nothing?[40]

The fact that Cary's own revision was only a few years out and American booksellers eager to distribute it may have added to the Harpers' reluctance.[41] Fletcher Harper, the firm's chief editor, cautiously wrote William, "it is likely that we might reprint Dr. Carlyle's 'Dante' and get back our investment, provided we were not required to give anything more than a few presentation copies for the translation— And we would probably venture upon it, if informed that it would be agreeable to your Brother and the Doctor for us to do so."[42] Subsequent letters from Emerson to his brother trace his mounting frustration as the project dragged. Harper's apparently reneged in late September, but Emerson was able to tell John Carlyle in December 1848 that with the election of Zachary Taylor to the presidency "our people are in better spirits, and trade and, at last, booktrade will revive, it is believed"—though he confessed in the same letter, "I had no pleasure in my agency, since I found it had fallen on such evil times that a book so valuable was to be held so cheap. Did I tell you, you are to have nothing but American fame & ten copies?"[43]

Harper's then postponed the project again, inciting Emerson's wrath: "If you [William] should ever meet this 'Fletcher' again, I wish you would tell him that if he has never printed, & only destroyed my copy (which he was to take special care of), I will forgive [him] if he will only own it at once, & let me go with the book to somebody who prints with ink, instead of air. The book is really valuable, & ought on all accounts to appear at once."[44] When Harper's finally announced publication in May of 1849, Emerson demanded the only thing he could: "a good expiatory score of copies for the author."[45]

Was the Carlyle *Inferno* as "valuable" to American readers as Emerson insisted? With the loss of Harper's records by fire in 1853, sales

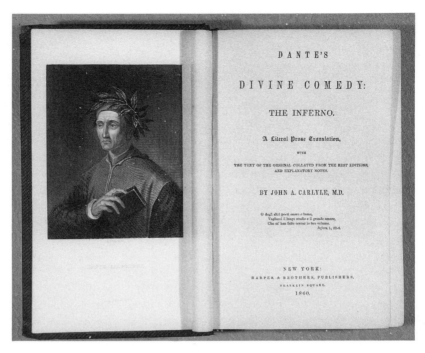

5. Frontispiece and title page, the Carlyle *Inferno* (Harper's, 1849). Department of Special Collections, University Libraries of Notre Dame.

cannot now be documented, but Emerson may have sensed an American preference for prose to poetry. Adorned with the now de rigeur portrait of Dante as a frontispiece (this one after the portrait by Raphael Morghen), the Harper edition (clothbound, 7½ by 4½ inches) offered the translation in paragraph form above the Italian text with the notes in very small type at the bottom of each page; the volume thus combined scholarly respectability with a text as readable as fiction (Illustration 5). Carlyle's was the version, interestingly enough, that was read by Walt Whitman. "As it happen'd," Whitman insisted, he had read his copy "mostly in an old wood." In his last years he was still calling Carlyle's translation "greatest among them—indisputably so."[46]

A remark by Elizabeth Hoar in a letter to Emerson in 1848—"I love the Carlyles Dr [John] Carlyle too, especially since he loves Dante"— indicates that Emerson had already spoken of Carlyle's work in the Concord circle, and he distributed seventeen presentation copies of the Harper edition once he had them in hand: "following in the distribution a mixed principle," as he wrote to John Carlyle, "for I gave them to some because they were good Scholars, and to some because they were

28

good talkers. They have gone for the most part to the best places, good
seed to good soil, and I look for the best fruit."[47] In fact his "principle"
was hardly mixed at all, since most of the recipients were Concord or
Boston neighbors (among them Thoreau, Alcott, Channing, Ward,
Theodore Parker, Sarah Ripley, and Sarah Freeman Clarke). The term
"good soil," however, would prove prophetic. Among the copies Emerson distributed was one to Longfellow, who responded, "Let me thank
you . . . for Carlyle's Dante; I have read it with great care. It is very
good; as good as a prose translation can be."[48] This rather qualified
praise—"as good as a prose translation can be"—anticipates Longfellow's own climactic contribution to the incipient Dante industry in
New England, the poetic translation he had already begun.

❧ 3. ❧

Like many of his New England contemporaries, Longfellow had been
a reader of Dante since his youth, when Dante "excited [him] more
than any other poet."[49] Though Ticknor had preceded him as a teacher
of Dante at Harvard, Longfellow certainly consolidated the formal
study of the poet in the American university setting and was eager to
disseminate the *Commedia* to an even wider audience: in 1853 he wrote
regretfully that he was "very sorry that very little has been done for
Dante in this country."[50] Having already experimented with translating
Dante in 1843, Longfellow resumed the project in the early 1860s, as is
well known, as consolation for the death of his wife. As he himself was
always ready to acknowledge, however, the private activity soon became a collaborative philological effort—encouraged, sustained, and
perfected in the Wednesday night "Dante Club" that began meeting
informally at his house to discuss his translation and then adjourn for
what Longfellow habitually deprecated as "a little supper." Dubbing
the group "the Dante Club" was in an important sense simply renam-
ing a social circle already in place—old friends such as one might find in
any community, now banded together in mutual support. In this case,
however, the list of members reads like a roster of literary, academic,
publishing, and even political luminaries. Included were James Russell
Lowell, who had replaced Longfellow as a teacher of Dante at Harvard
in 1855; Charles Eliot Norton, later to become professor of fine arts at
Harvard and the preeminent American Dantist of his time; G. W.
Greene, formerly U.S. consul to Italy; Longfellow's publisher James T.
Fields, also editor of the *Atlantic Monthly;* occasionally Massachusetts

senator Charles Sumner; later, author and *Atlantic* editor William
Dean Howells. The spontaneity and enthusiasm with which this group
assembled attests by itself to the cultural primacy of Dante among the
literati of New England.[51]

Whatever its original significance as grief therapy or social bonding,
therefore, Longfellow's translation was rapidly recast as a political
event, a gesture of pride and cultural parity precipitated by the immi-
nent international celebration of the sexcentennial of Dante's birth.
"Go to the Nortons' in the morning," Longfellow wrote in his journal
30 April 1863. "Find Charles there alone. He tells me that in 1865 the
six-hundredth birthday of Dante is to be celebrated in Florence; and
wants me to keep back my translation of the 'Divina Commedia' for
that occasion."[52] Norton, who had inherited a love of Dante from his
father, Harvard professor and "Unitarian pope" the Reverend Andrews
Norton, was preparing a study of the Dante portraits for the Italian
event; these were to accompany a third offering, seventeen cantos from
the laboriously progressing translation of Parsons. Longfellow finished
the first canticle in good time, much to the relief of his friends: "I could
not bear the thought," Greene told him (21 January 1865), "that the
great celebration should not have some record of American sympathy."[53] Entrusted to the care of Sumner, Longfellow's *Inferno*—printed
in a limited edition of only ten copies and handsomely bound in gold-
stamped scarlet leather with brilliantly marbled cover boards—was sent
to Italy by diplomatic pouch. Though he had joked about "descend-
[ing] among the Printers' Devils, the Malebranche [*Inferno* 21–22] of
the University Press," Longfellow took particular and pardonably
chauvinistic satisfaction in the appearance of his book. "I want you and
the [Italian] minister to look at the volume," he urged Sumner. "It is
beautiful, and worthy of the Italian press;—all written, printed, bound
in Cambridge, Middlesex County, Massachusetts."[54]

Issued for public consumption by Ticknor and Fields in 1867, the
Longfellow translation was thus mounted from the outset as an important literary and cultural event. Longfellow was the unofficial American laureate, and his name already carried immense weight: more than
a decade earlier Thomas Bulfinch had requested permission to dedicate
his *Age of Fable* to Longfellow "as a sort of guarantee to the public that
nothing worthless or mischievous is offered to them."[55] In La Piana's
words, "The fact that the most famous and most popular of all American poets of the time had turned his talents to making a translation of
the *Divine Comedy* was a potent factor in inducing American readers to

strike up an acquaintance with the great poem."[56] The format of this version accordingly locates the work on a continuum with Longfellow's poetic oeuvre. In place of the historical introduction preceding earlier versions, the three volumes are prefaced simply by double sonnets that Longfellow wrote for the occasion; Longfellow's notes do not intrude upon the poetic text (in unrhymed terza rima) but are relegated to the back of each volume. The notes, however, are copious and testify to Longfellow's scholarly as well as poetic investment in his work; following each canticle, in addition, are what he termed the "Illustrations," essentially small anthologies of Dante criticism compiled during his years of teaching and study. "There is no other comment on Dante to be compared to yours," Norton applauded, "for containing what,—and only what,—an intelligent reader desires to have before him, in order that he may appreciate better than he otherwise could do the essential qualities of the poem."[57]

Yet despite Longfellow's status as artist and scholar, it is with his translation that Dante materializes most unmistakably in American culture as a book in the literal sense, a possession as well as (and perhaps more than) a text to be mentally consumed. If tasteful design had factored into earlier editions, it was now a prominent consideration. Longfellow's correspondence indicates some negotiation on his own with John La Farge, probably the most sought after decorative artist in America at the time and later well known for his work on the interior of Trinity Church in Boston. Longfellow wrote James T. Fields in 1864, "I gave Mr. La Farge a note to you this morning. I hope you will think as well of him and of his drawings as I did. There are parts of Dante which I feel confident he would do well; for he evidently has a nature, which discerns things spiritual. But it will be a long, long labor. His idea of a vignette at the beginning and end of each Canto struck me very favorably."[58] La Farge was involved in a number of projects for book and magazine illustration in the 1860s, among them a series of wood engravings for a Ticknor and Fields edition of Tennyson's *Enoch Arden;* but many of them came to nothing because of prohibitive reproduction costs, and this was apparently the fate of the Dante project, of which so far as I can tell nothing remains.[59] Longfellow cautioned Fields that chances of getting high quality engravings were doubtful, and he added, "Is not the book handsome enough without?"[60]

Indeed, even without illustrations the Longfellow Dante marked a dramatic departure from earlier editions: Norton agreed that the "re-

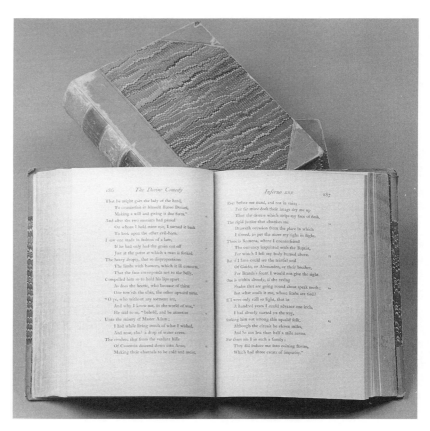

6. Longfellow's *Divine Comedy,* "royal octavo" edition (Ticknor and Fields, 1867). Photo by Lou Schakel.

markable beauty of the book is appropriate to the character of the translation, and the claim tacitly asserted by the elegance of the external appearance is justified and maintained by its intrinsic merit."[61] James R. Osgood, Fields's new partner, was notably concerned with improving the looks of the company's products, changing them from "muddy brown" cloth and uniform appearance to volumes designed to suit their contents. The recently established *Publisher's Weekly* praised Fields and Osgood's books in 1872, citing "the superb editions of Longfellow's *Dante,* Bryant's *Homer,* and Goethe's *Faust*" as "among the greatest triumphs of the publisher's art the world over."[62] The "royal octavo" version of Longfellow's translation resembled the original limited edition, with a spine of fawn-colored, gold-stamped leather and sides marbled in rich tones of red and blue (Illustration 6). As physical artifacts, these heavy volumes also dictated social function: their digni-

7. Longfellow's *Divine Comedy,* Houghton, Mifflin's one-volume edition (1870). Photo by Lou Schakel.

fied solidity prescribed a stationary and indoor location, and they joined other Dante paraphernalia—pictures, busts, even fragments of the Dante coffin (fortuitously if dubiously unearthed in time for the sexcentennial)—as objects befitting a genteel interior. Fields's socialite wife, Annie, in an inadvertent but telling juxtaposition, wrote in her diary that "the Ladies' Club, the Thursday Club, the Dante Club are now in full swing, also Mrs. Dorr's dinners."[63] Elsewhere, the painted head of Dante majestically crowned the domed ceiling of J. P. Morgan's New York palace (now the Morgan Library).

But the carriage trade could not by itself support the publishing industry, and Longfellow's publishers accordingly redirected their product at a wider range of customers. After charging five dollars for each of the "royal octavo" volumes, Fields and Osgood produced in 1870 both a cheaper three-volume edition and a one-volume edition (Illustration 7). The various forms in which the Longfellow *Divine Comedy* became available are summarized in a notice in the *Literary World* (26 February 1881) placed by the Boston company Houghton, Mifflin, who had by then absorbed the Ticknor and Fields stock:

TRANSLATION OF THE DIVINA COMMEDIA OF DANTE. With Notes and Literary Illustrations. 3 vols., royal octavo. I. Inferno. II. Purgatorio. III. Paradiso. Beveled boards, gilt top, $4.50 a volume, the set, $13.50; half-calf, $27.00; morocco, $35.00. THE SAME. 3 vols., 12 mo[duodecimo], $6.00; half calf, $12.00; morocco, $15.00. THE SAME. 1 vol., crown 8 vo[octavo], $3.00; half calf, $5.50; morocco, $7.00.[64]

In fact, as company records show, the "royal octavo" sold only moderately well: fewer than 100 copies between 1881 and 1891, and a mere 23 from then until 1907. The less expensive three-volume edition did far better: 930 copies sold before 1891, well over 5,000 in the next sixteen years. The single-volume edition, on the other hand, sold close to 10,000 copies in the same period, many of them probably destined for school libraries. Sales of the three-volume edition tapered to fewer than 50 copies per year after World War I, but sales of the one-volume edition were still fairly high in 1920. Houghton, Mifflin records list earnings for the single-volume edition at $1,760 between 1885 and 1891; they fluctuated between $300 and $400 per year until the end of the century.[65] Following his death in 1882, Longfellow's translation also became accessible in the collected "Riverside" edition of his works (1886).

Where Emerson had been forced to approach the Harpers cap in hand, Longfellow enjoyed a close friendship with his publisher, James T. Fields; Fields promoted the translation by placing advance cantos and Longfellow's Dante sonnets in the *Atlantic,* which he edited from 1859 to 1871 and built into an arbiter of high literary culture. A letter to Longfellow from Fields, Osgood, and Company (6 September 1869) regarding the forthcoming "cheaper edition of Dante" notes casually that "the form was left to be determined in consultation between you and Mr. Fields." A week later Osgood proposed separating text from notes in a two-volume edition, which might have permitted potentially more remunerative marketing of the text alone; but when Longfellow resisted, the firm politely deferred: "we doubt the commercial success of the three-volume edition but . . . we are desirous of meeting your views in the matter" (13 September). Meanwhile, the English company Routledge secured advance sheets of the *Inferno* at £150, a figure apparently set by Longfellow himself. The rush of new British translations might slow the market, the company warned, but they laid their hopes in "the additional value of your name" (10 May 1865, 31 March 1866).[66]

The undisputed value of Longfellow's name—exploited most visibly

in the Dante volumes of the "Riverside" edition, where his bust re-
places conventional portraits of Dante as frontispiece—might also
have obviated the need for favorable reviews. In his 1899 memoir, *Old
Cambridge,* Thomas Wentworth Higginson credits the Cambridge
authors of Longfellow's generation with an admirable distaste for self-
promotion: "they did not copy the tricks of politicians, pulling their
own wires, lauding their own achievements, asking puffs from others,
and exhibiting themselves in attitudes."[67] In truth, however, Longfellow's cultural position was aggressively augmented for him by faithful friends like Norton, who supported Longfellow's achievement in
the channels he himself commanded. Attempting to prepare the way
for Longfellow's work, Norton published a learned disquisition on
translations of Dante for the *North American Review* in April of 1866;
this was followed by reviews championing his friend in *The Nation*
(4 May 1867), which he had founded, and again in the *North American*
(July 1867), where he retained strong influence. Greene supplied a
review for the *Atlantic* (August 1867), and Howells, an eager newcomer
to the Cambridge establishment, reviewed Longfellow in the *Round
Table* (19 May 1866).[68]

Howells's biographer points out that in the *Round Table* review
Howells "virtually challenged his audience to read the poem or admit a
lack of taste for the exquisite things in poetry."[69] Not all reviewers
matched the adulation of Longfellow's personal friends: as La Piana
notes, Longfellow's work was criticized by some for "his crude literal-
ness, his method of line-by-line translation, his use of Latin-English
rather than Anglo-Saxon words, his inversions, and his rhythmical
irregularities."[70] Such storms, however, could confidently be endured.
"Our Dante stock is rising in the market daily," Fields assured Longfellow, "the gibes of 'the Press' not at all affecting our operations"
(30 July 1867).[71]

∾ 4. ∾

Longfellow's achievement, as I have noted, was almost from the outset
a collective local activity, banked, sponsored, promoted, and financed
by a literary nucleus that, consciously or innocently, affirmed its authority by taking possession of a world-class poet. The members of
Longfellow's circle basked in his success as though it had been their
own—as in an important sense it was. "Parsons, yourself, Lowell, and
I," Norton told Longfellow with some satisfaction in 1865, "are, I be-

lieve, the only American writers who have done anything worth mention or preservation in Dantesque literature."[72] The momentum generated by publication of Longfellow's translation provoked a palpable
flurry of "Dantesque" activity among his friends, all directed at the
agency of Fields. Greene was soon proposing his own translation of
Dante's epistles for publication in the *Atlantic,* a project Longfellow
loyally did his best to commend: "Now here is our good Fields, fright-
ened at the length of the Dante Letters, but at the last Dante Club,
Lowell and Norton, as well as myself, were so positive that they ought
to go into the Magazine, that he seemed to take heart."[73] This fragment
offers a glimpse of the way the Cambridge circle operated. Norton had
already published his translation of Dante's *Vita Nuova* serially in the
Atlantic in 1859; this was revived by Ticknor and Fields in 1867 to
accompany the Longfellow *Commedia.* Gratified by Longfellow's approval of his essay on translation in the *North American,* Norton quickly
offered Fields "a little volume . . . to contain all the English versions of
the 5th Canto of the Inferno" with an illustrative essay by Norton.[74]

Though this project was dropped, Norton's own translation of the
Commedia, published by Houghton, Mifflin between 1891 and 1892,
marks the next important landmark in American Dante publication.
The first complete prose translation in English (John Carlyle had
offered the *Inferno* only), Norton's presented the text in paragraph form
and included minimal editorial apparatus. The Norton volumes were
thus easily accessible to readers inexperienced in both poetry and scholarship, and indeed this was Norton's expressed intent: he noted in the
preface that he meant his version "first, for those who, unable to read
the *Divine Comedy* in the original, desire to obtain knowledge of its
contents."[75] Issued in three medium-sized (8 by 5) clothbound volumes
at $1.25 each (half-calf binding was also available), the Norton version
was also less formidable economically than Longfellow's (Illustration
8). Decorative touches were confined to gilt-top pages and binding in
either deep red or dark green (for the initiated, of course, the colors
worn by Beatrice in *Purgatorio* 30).

The Houghton, Mifflin catalog description is almost defensive
regarding this simplicity of design: "These volumes are 12mo[duo-
decimo] form, printed on good paper, with clear, handsome type, and
although severely plain are admirable library editions."[76] Norton's correspondence with the firm indicates nevertheless that he was highly
sensitive to the appearance of books and almost dictatorial about the
appearance of his own: in the summer of 1891, for instance, he fussed

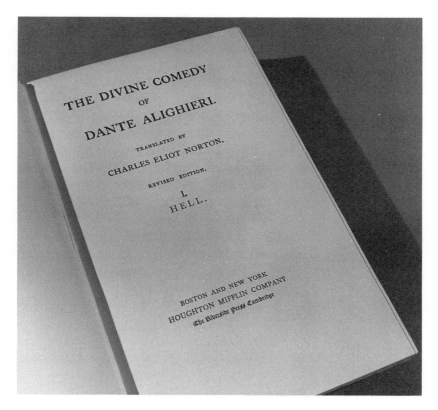

8. Title page, the Norton *Divine Comedy* (Houghton, Mifflin, 1891–92). Photo by Lou Schakel.

about details of the title page, with Houghton, Mifflin bowing readily to his preference. As publication of the *Purgatorio* and *Paradiso* approached, Norton proposed a revision of his *Vita Nuova*, envisaging the project in precise material terms:

> The new edition . . . ought, of course, to correspond with the Divine Comedy. But should you be willing to print, also, (*not* to electrotype), a small, exquisite edition of the original text and the translation without any body of notes, as a book for lovers? I should want it done through-out, and in every respect to suit the most fastidious and exacting taste,— with nothing of the common Christmas gift book about it. I think an edition of 500 copies would be likely to sell,—if really well got up.[77]

Nothing seems to have come of this "exquisite edition," but Norton's revised "New Life" earned Houghton, Mifflin close to $1,800 before his death in 1908 and sold more than 600 copies between 1905 and 1923. A special "large paper" edition of his *Divine Comedy* with the *Vita*

Nuova as a fourth volume sold out its 250 copies in two years, earning Houghton, Mifflin $830 in profits. The three-volume *Commedia* also sold well—beyond, as Norton admitted to the company (May 1903), his own expectations: 4,000 copies in the first seven years, 1891–98, earning nearly $5,000, and 4,533 more between 1905 and 1923.[78]

While Longfellow's translation was made desirable by his stature as a poet, Houghton, Mifflin attempted to capitalize on Norton's reputation as a scholar, advertising his volumes as "of more than ordinary importance, as Professor Norton is recognized in America and in Europe as not only one of the best Dante scholars, but as one of the few masters of English prose."[79] Norton, however, firmly resisted his transformation into a marketing device, refusing to supply a photograph of himself—"I have no inclination to have my likeness presented to the public" (14 March 1897)—and reacting with unconcealed irritation (14 March 1907) to the company's spring bulletin:

> You say that you hope I shall like the appearance of the page containing the announcement of my little sketch of Longfellow's life, and the description of the book given there. I am sorry to say that nothing is ever less pleasing to me than a flattering advertisement of my own work, whatever it may be. While recognizing the kindly intention, I submit to such advertisements only as supposing them to be in the interests of the publishers. I am not likely to get over my dislike of having my work treated as though it were in the class of patent medicines or Pears' soap. I wish that my feelings in this matter were more common among my literary confreres.[80]

Though the instance may be trivial in itself, Norton's distaste here reflects in a nutshell the embattled campaign against vulgarity with which his name was by then synonymous. In the brief biography of Longfellow mentioned above, he noted that in the older man's time "the perils of prosperity, of unlimited democracy, of unchecked immigration, were not foreseen; they were gradually to manifest themselves. The generation which grew up before 1830 had neither experience nor dread of them."[81] Norton himself was keenly aware of these "perils," however, and set about to combat them with the weapons at hand. In his 1853 treatise *Considerations upon Some Recent Social Theories*, Norton had eloquently stressed the educational responsibility of the privileged:

> Taking no low standard of duty, satisfied with no partial performance, no incomplete statement, dazzled by no show of outward success, deluded by no selfish plans, turned aside by no popular enthusiasms, yielding to

no fatigue or indifference,—it is for each one of us to do his best, feeling that not only his happiness, but that of the fortunes of his country, depends upon his deeds. The trust committed to the hands of the intelligent and prosperous classes here is the future of their country. It is for them to provide against the evils which threaten it, by spreading and improving education, by laboring to throw open freely every opportunity for advantages that may be shared by all.[82]

Deeply disturbed by the growing commercialism around him, Norton quixotically projected Dante as a deterrent and corrective. Affectionate memoirs by some of his students (Norton began teaching Dante at Harvard in 1877) indicate some degree of success: Rollo Walter Brown maintained that Norton "read Dante with such affectionate reverence that undisciplined youths who customarily spent lecture periods carving initials on classroom furniture slipped away at the end of the hour and bought all of Dante's works"—presumably, one infers, in Norton's tastefully understated volumes.[83] While this reminiscence may be a little hard to credit, it is clear that Norton also did his best to propagate Dante beyond academia: Longfellow informed Lowell in 1878, "Charles Norton is reading Dante to a class of ladies at the new Hawthorne Rooms in Park Street," and Norton's own letters record him rushing off to lecture on Dante in Baltimore.[84] As the acknowledged dean of American Dante studies by the turn of the century, Norton edited, supervised, or granted his imprimatur to a number of related Houghton, Mifflin publications: the Dante epistles translated by Charles Sterrett Latham and edited by Norton's friend G. R. Carpenter, in 1891; the Parsons translation, finally completed in 1892; a compilation of Ruskin's comments on Dante in 1903; and *Aids to the Study of Dante* by the Boston clergyman Charles Dinsmore the same year. Norton also counseled and encouraged the translation of Dante by Melville Best Anderson, ultimately published in 1922.[85]

✑ 5. ✑

So pronounced was the identification between Dante and New England by the beginning of the twentieth century that commentators like the southerner Thomas Nelson Page were manifestly aware of territorial trespassing: "We know that [Dante] is said by the Brahmin class of Intellectuals, or would-be Intellectuals, to be a great poet, and we accept this theory as we accept their theory of the Laws of Gravitation and would equally accept that of Relativity if generally held, without knowing or caring very much about it," he allowed in 1922.[86] The deprecatory assessments of mid-twentieth-century literary historians intimate the extent to which Dante had come to suggest Boston snobbery. "The cult of Dante had woven itself into the fabric of Boston life," Van Wyck Brooks asserted in 1940, a fabric he judged to be "higher and dryer than ever"; another scholar observed the same year that "Boston once excelled in cultural achievement by the simple device of defining culture in terms of those things in which Boston excelled."[87] "In New England they decided the culture needed an epic and elected Dante," Hugh Kenner pronounced in the same vein some decades later.[88]

In fact, however, interest in Dante was steadily moving westward, and had been for some time; Longfellow's immigrant friend Emmanuel Scherb, for example, was lecturing on Dante in Buffalo and Cincinnati as far back as the 1850s. Norton's personal influence in this transmission is again obvious: in 1878 he wrote Longfellow commending "a law student from the West [who] is reading Dante with me," and in 1907 we find him asking Houghton, Mifflin to send copies of his translation to "the the Public Library, Eldon, Iowa, as a gift from the author."[89] By the last decades of his life, to his gratification, Dante reading groups were sprouting up well beyond New England. Norton noted in the 1890s, appropriately in one of his public lectures, "Such clubs for reading his great poem as that which has existed here during the past winter have been found in many places from the Pacific to the Atlantic shore. I found one last week in Newton, Massachusetts, I heard of one within a few weeks in Colorado."[90] Karen Blair cites Dante along with Shakespeare and Browning as a standard topic for women's literary societies (perhaps like that of Mrs. Orville Jones in *Babbitt*) from the 1870s on.[91]

Recent historians like Jackson Lears and James Turner have pointed to the decline in religious faith in the late nineteenth century as the basis for contemporary fascination with Dante, and Lawrence Levine has similarly emphasized the "sacralization of culture" pervasive in the period.[92] Certainly the New England Dante enthusiasm reflected this trend: reading Dante with Norton, a former student recalled, "was almost an act of worship."[93] Levine outlines also, however, a concurrent bifurcation between "high" and "low" culture exemplified by Shakespeare's assumption into the academic province, and one senses something of the same bifurcation of Dante, a dramatic and rather sudden branching into elite and popular and perhaps even vulgar forms. The meticulously researched translations of Dante by Longfellow and Norton gave way in the popular market to the very commercialization and sensationalism that Norton had so strenuously opposed. Given the absence of international copyright before 1891, opportunistic newer publishers fell back on the putatively obsolete translation of Cary, reprinting it from English editions throughout the last quarter of the nineteenth century: Scribner's, Hurst, Worthington, John Alden, Estes and Lauriat, Lippincott, and A. L. Burt all issued copies before 1900, as did Thomas Crowell and J. W. Lovell of New York.

Especially subversive to the Longfellow and Norton versions was the spate of Cary reprints adorned to one degree or another with the engravings of Doré, originally published in Paris in 1861. As noted above, Longfellow had happily eschewed the expense and delay of illustrations by La Farge, though Houghton, Mifflin did revive the Flaxman illustrations for a special limited edition of Longfellow in 1906; a similar plan to embellish Norton's work with illustrations of Botticelli was abandoned about the same time.[94] Both Longfellow and Norton took an interest in visual interpretations of Dante by Flaxman, as we have seen, but also by Scheffer and Rossetti.[95] Doré was introduced to the American public in 1863 in portfolio form by Frederick Leypoldt, the German immigrant who later founded *Publisher's Weekly;* Norton quickly acquired a copy of the French edition and showed it to the clearly mesmerized Longfellow, who found Doré "a prodigality of horrors."[96] Unlike those of Flaxman, which recalled the statues of classical antiquity that were his inspiration, the pictures of Doré are consummately Gothic: "What chiefly excited the public," one art historian charges, "was the Grand Guignol horrors of Dante's infernal freak show, and these Doré exhibited with characteristic flamboyance, adding a few erotic *frissons* of his own."[97]

From the 1880s, cheap editions of Cary with a limited number of shamelessly reduced cuts from Doré inserted into the text block were issued by a number of American firms, including Jordan, Marsh (Boston), Pollard and Moss (New York), Altemus (Philadelphia), and Belford and Clarke (Chicago). Most competitive, however, were the massive editions of Cary lavishly adorned with full-page reproductions of Doré published by the Cassell company, a British house that had established an American office shortly after the Civil War (Illustration 9). Cassell, who started his company with the intention of "improving the social condition of the working classes," made a specialty of illustrated works, beginning with Doré; Tebbel describes his firm as one of the largest in the world at the time.[98] In what was perhaps an unintentional

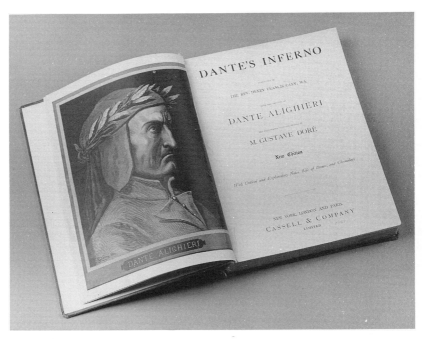

9. Frontispiece and title page for the Cassell *Inferno* (1901), trans. Henry F. Cary, illustration by Gustave Doré (1861). Photo by Lou Schakel.

capitulation to a dubious popular taste for the gruesome, Cassell issued the *Inferno* as a separate volume, extending the already disproportionate cultural emphasis on Dante's first canticle and promoting Doré's reputation, even in our own time, as a purveyor of horror. Along with indifferent perpetuation of Cary, the foregrounding of illustration in Cassell's widely distributed volumes served almost conclusively, one gathers, to displace serious emphasis on Dante's text: as one historian of publishing observes, "Anyone who has seen Gustave Doré's *Inferno* will have a hard time if he tries . . . to remember Dante without it."[99] Doré's popularity converted Dante into a lurid picture book. The Boston medium "Margery" fascinated Houdini around the same time with messages from Dante; in 1924 Dante's *Inferno* was transmogrified into a horror film.[100]

Levine's theory of cultural bifurcation is borne out as well by other forms of Dante publication in America in the early decades of the twentieth century. The rise of the textbook trade initiated editions of Dante's Italian text in specialized academic packaging: D. C. Heath's *Commedia,* edited and annotated by Norton's successor, Charles Grandgent, appeared in 1909 in their Modern Language series; Putnam's released

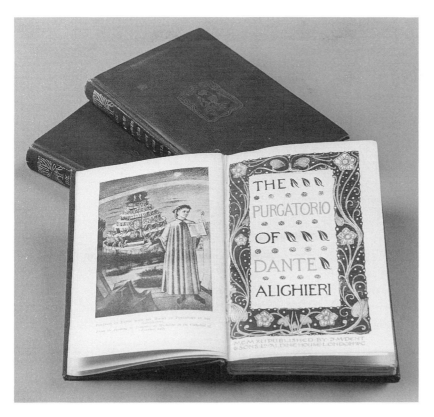

10. Frontispiece and title page, the Temple Classics *Purgatorio*, trans. Thomas Okey (J. M. Dent, 1899). Photo by Lou Schakel.

an Italian text edited by the British Dantist Paget Toynbee in 1900, and Crowell's 1897 edition of Cary, though hardly a new text, bore an introduction and notes by the Dantist Oscar Kuhns. For the literary generation represented by Eliot and Pound, on the other hand, the Dante of choice was the Carlyle-Okey-Wicksteed bilingual edition in the British company J. M. Dent's Temple Classics series, priced at one shilling in England and widely available through the firm's American connection, E. P. Dutton (Illustration 10).[101] Along with its low price and attractive, vaguely *Jugendstil* title-page design, an important feature of the Temple Dante was its portability: unlike the ponderous Doré versions or even the Longfellow and Norton editions, which seem stuffy by comparison, the Temple Dante (at 6 by 4 close in size to the 1822 edition of Cary) had once again become a vade mecum, read by enthusiastic young disciples like Eliot "lying in bed or on a railway journey."[102]

In other quarters, however, where a new breed of middle-class Americans were, in the view of Norton, "seeking material comfort in a brutal way," Dante continued to solidify into a fixture, a tangible item of conspicuous consumption.[103] In 1924 the popular novelist Edna Ferber capped her description of a typically pretentious interior with a reference to "Dante's saturnine features sneering down upon you from a correct cabinet," and Tebbel's history includes a provocative fragment: the Chicago company of Baird and Dillon, described as "a landmark house in the subscription trade" who distributed their wares to fifteen different installment houses across the nation, counted among their "bread-and-butter bestsellers" family Bibles, imported photograph albums, *Hill's Manual of Social and Business Forms,* and editions of Milton and Dante as illustrated by Doré.[104] Taken together, these titles seem to sum up the dimensions of an America far removed from the genteel New England whose cultural properties it had so eagerly commandeered: the very democratization of Dante's work facilitated by Longfellow and principally by Norton had brought about, ironically, an increasingly carnivalesque appropriation of the poet by an emergent diversity of social groups. Even the "lone and austere figure" of Lewis is a blend: invoked in judgment of Babbitt's mediocrity but derived paradoxically from popular illustration.

Yet it is ultimately not the popular reinvention, I would propose, that accounts for the vitality of Dante interest in subsequent decades of the century. Instead, one may credit the endorsement by Pound and Eliot— both of them, it should be noted, highly academic poets (and indeed related by blood respectively to Longfellow and Norton)—and more probably the formal, even aggressive repossession of medieval studies, and with them of Dante, by the American academy (though admittedly in the context of an increasingly democratized conception of higher education). Dante may still be encountered in popular fiction like Pournelle and Niven's *Inferno,* and the Doré illustrations remain available in an inexpensive reprint.[105] But it is more likely that readers come to the *Commedia* now in the pages of a college anthology—and in the classrooms of Dantists trained in an academic *stemma* leading back to the Harvard of Longfellow and Norton. Once again Dante has become the property, it might be said, of a definable culture of letters, and one with a recoverable line of descent: and in our own time it must be within this culture, apparently, that the continuing *libro* of human memory may be reinscribed once more with Dante's image.[106]

∾ NOTES ∾

1. Sinclair Lewis, *Babbitt* (New York: Harcourt, Brace and World, 1922) 126, 128.

2. Richard H. Brodhead, *Cultures of Letters: Scenes of Reading and Writing in Nineteenth-Century America* (Chicago: U of Chicago P, 1993).

3. Voltaire's remarks are excerpted in *Discussions of Dante,* ed. Irma Brandeis, Discussions of Literature (Boston: D. C. Heath, 1961) 12–14; for Goethe, see Johann Wolfgang von Goethe, *Italian Journey,* trans. Robert R. Heitner, ed. Thomas P. Saine and Jeffrey L. Sammons, Goethe Edition 6 (New York: Suhrkamp, 1989) 303.

4. Horace Walpole, *Selected Letters,* ed. W. L. Lewis (New Haven: Yale UP, 1973) 251.

5. For surveys of the nineteenth-century Dante revival, see Werner P. Friedrich, *Dante's Fame Abroad 1350–1850: The Influence of Dante Alighieri on the Poets and Scholars of Spain, France, England, Germany, Switzerland, and the United States,* University of North Carolina Studies in Comparative Literature 2 (Chapel Hill: U of North Carolina P, 1950); Paget Toynbee, *Britain's Tribute to Dante in Literature and Art: A Chronological Record of 540 Years* (London: Oxford UP, 1921); Steve Ellis, *Dante and English Poetry: Shelley to T. S. Eliot* (Cambridge: Cambridge UP, 1983); David Wallace, "Dante in English," *The Cambridge Companion to Dante,* ed. Rachel Jacoff (Cambridge: Cambridge UP, 1993) 237–58; and most recently Ralph Pite, *The Circle of Our Vision: Dante's Presence in English Romantic Poetry* (Oxford: Clarendon P, 1994). A useful bibliography is Thomas Werge, "Dante and Modern Literature: A Review of Scholarship 1960–1981," *Studies in Medievalism* 2.3 (Summer 1983): 115–58.

6. Henry Cary, *Memoir of the Rev. Henry Francis Cary, M.A., Translator of Dante, with His Literary Journal and Letters,* 2 vols. (London: Moxon, 1847) 1:227, 276–77, 299.

7. Cary 2:28, 123.

8. Theodore W. Koch, *Dante in America: A Historical and Bibliographical Study* (Boston: Ginn, 1896) 9 (reprinted from the *Fifteenth Annual Report of the Dante Society,* 1896).

9. Sheila Hodges, *The Life and Times of Lorenzo Da Ponte, Mozart's Librettist* (New York: Universe, 1985) 196–97, 204–5; Angelina La Piana, *Dante's American Pilgrimage: A Historical Survey of Dante Studies in the United States 1800–1944* (New Haven: Yale UP, 1948) 26–28, 34–38.

10. Margaret Fuller, *The Letters of Margaret Fuller,* ed. Robert N. Hudspeth, 5 vols. (Ithaca: Cornell UP, 1983–90) 1:279.

11. A[dolph] Growoll, *Book Trade Bibliography in the United States in the XIXth Century* (New York: Dibdin Club, 1898) xlv–xlvi; Eugene Exman, *The*

Brothers Harper: A Unique Publishing Partnership and Its Impact upon the Cultural Life of America from 1817 to 1853 (New York: Harper and Row, 1965) 159; William Hickling Prescott, *The Papers of William Hickling Prescott,* ed. C. Harvey Gardiner (Urbana: U of Illinois P, 1964) 69, 70–74, 82, 94.

12. La Piana 24.

13. Charles Eliot Norton, *Reminiscences of Old Cambridge* (Cambridge, Mass.: Cambridge Historical Society Proceedings, 1905–6) 18; William Hickling Prescott, *The Literary Memoranda of William Hickling Prescott,* ed. C. Harvey Gardiner, 2 vols. (Norman: U of Oklahoma P, 1961) 235; Ralph Waldo Emerson, *The Letters of Ralph Waldo Emerson,* ed. Ralph L. Rusk, 6 vols. (New York: Columbia UP, 1939) 1:71. The review, by the celebrated Italian exile Ugo Foscolo and James Mackintosh, appeared in the February 1818 issue of the *Edinburgh Review* (453–74).

14. Kenneth Walter Cameron, *Ralph Waldo Emerson's Reading* (Raleigh, N.C.: Thistle Press, 1941) 67; J. Chesley Mathews, "H. W. Longfellow's Interest in Dante," *Papers Presented at the Longfellow Commemorative Conference April 1–3, 1982* (National Park Service, Longfellow National Historical Park) 47; Prescott, *Papers* 43. As my notes testify, Professor Mathews must be credited with substantial work on the American reception of Dante.

15. *Memoirs of Margaret Fuller Ossoli,* ed. Ralph Waldo Emerson, William Henry Channing, and James Freeman Clarke, 2 vols. (Boston, 1852) 1:240.

16. The series was The Works of the British Poets, 50 vols. (Philadelphia, 1819–23); the editors were Ezekiel Sanford and Robert Walsh. Though two similar series had previously appeared in Britain, this was an American undertaking. McCarty and Davis of Philadelphia are credited as publishers of the Dante volumes in Koch's bibliography: the title pages, however, list Samuel F. Bradford and John Laval of Philadelphia as publishers for volume 45 (a later copy adds American poet James Eastburn of New York) and Charles Ewer and Timothy Bedlington of Boston for volume 46. Volume 45 names William Brown as printer; according to information kindly supplied to me by Rosalind Remer, McCarty and Davis were simply job printers for the second volume. See Remer's *Printers and Men of Capital: Philadelphia Book Publishing in the New Republic,* forthcoming from the U of Pennsylvania P.

17. *The Journals and Miscellaneous Notebooks of Ralph Waldo Emerson,* ed. William Gillman et al., 16 vols. (Cambridge: Harvard UP, 1960–82) 3:347; J. Chesley Mathews, "Longfellow's Dante Collection," *ESQ* 68 (1971): 14.

18. On the movement of American publishing from Philadelphia to New York, see John Tebbel, *A History of Book Publishing in the United States,* 4 vols. (New York: Bowker, 1975) 1:203.

19. On marketing practices, see Ronald Zboray, *A Fictive People: Antebellum Economic Developments and the American Reading Public* (New York: Oxford UP, 1992) 11. Price of the Appleton edition is given in Grant Overton, *Portrait*

of a Publisher and the First Hundred Years of the House of Appleton 1825–1925 (New York: Appleton, 1925) 34, and in Gerald R. Wolfe, *The House of Appleton* (Metuchen, N.J.: Scarecrow, 1981) 27. On the impact of the Giotto portrait, see Ellis 104.

20. Merton R. Sealts, Jr., *Melville's Reading,* rev. ed. (Columbia: U of South Carolina P, 1988) 171.

21. Edgar Allan Poe, *Writings in the Broadway Journal: Nonfictional Prose. Part I: The Text,* ed. Burton R. Pollin (New York: Gordon, 1986) 290–91.

22. Edgar Allan Poe, *Tales and Sketches,* vols. 1–2 of *Collected Works of Edgar Allan Poe,* ed. Thomas Olive Mabbott (Cambridge: Belknap P of Harvard UP, 1978) 1128.

23. Margaret Fuller, *The Writings of Margaret Fuller,* ed. Mason Wade (New York: Viking, 1941) 356–57.

24. Fuller, *Writings* 356.

25. David Irwin, *John Flaxman 1755–1826: Sculptor Illustrator Designer* (New York: Rizzoli, 1979) 94.

26. Herman Melville, *Pierre, or, the Ambiguities,* The Writings of Herman Melville 7 (Evanston: Northwestern UP and the Newberry Library, 1971) 42; Henry Wadsworth Longfellow, "Lecture on 'Divina Commedia,'" Longfellow Papers, Houghton Library, *54M.8/MsAm 1340 (06). All manuscript material is cited by permission of the Houghton Library, Harvard University.

27. See J. Chesley Mathews, "The Interest in Dante Shown by Nineteenth-Century American Men of Letters," *Dante Alighieri: Three Lectures* (Washington, D.C.: Library of Congress, 1965) 1–22.

28. Zboray 89; see also Lawrence Buell, *New England Literary Culture: From Revolution to Renaissance* (Cambridge: Cambridge UP, 1989) 166–90.

29. John Chipman Gray, rev. of *La Divina Commedia* of Dante Alighieri, *North American Review* 8 (1819): 322–47, rpt. in *Dante in America: The First Two Centuries,* ed. A. Bartlett Giamatti (Binghamton: Medieval and Renaissance Texts and Studies, 1983) 3–26; William H. Gerdts and Theodore Stebbins, Jr., *"A Man of Genius": The Art of Washington Allston* (Boston: Museum of Fine Arts; Charlottesville: U of Virginia P, 1979) 134.

30. *Memoirs and Letters of Charles Sumner,* ed. Edward L. Pierce, 2 vols. (Boston, 1877) 2:118–19.

31. Emerson, *Letters* 3:183, 5:78 (see also 4:534); Elizabeth Maxfield-Miller, "Elizabeth of Concord: Selected Letters of Elizabeth Sherman Hoar," *Studies in the American Renaissance* (1986): 116 (see also Emerson, *Journals* 3:347); Emerson, *Letters* 1:160.

32. *Memoirs of Margaret Fuller Ossoli* 2:31–32; *Letters of John Greenleaf Whittier,* ed. John B. Pickard, 3 vols. (Cambridge: Belknap P of Harvard UP, 1975) 2:295–96.

33. Emerson, *Letters* 5:230.

34. Fuller, *Letters* 3:102, 1:269, 272.

35. Madeline B. Stern, *The Life of Margaret Fuller,* rev. ed. (New York: Greenwood, 1991) 252.

36. *The Letters of Henry Wadsworth Longfellow,* ed. Andrew Hilen, 6 vols. (Cambridge: Belknap P of Harvard UP, 1966–82) 4:316.

37. Emerson, *Journals* 10:336.

38. Emerson's review was placed in the *Massachusetts Quarterly Review* in Sept. 1848 (see Emerson, *Letters* 4:103).

39. *Cost Books of Ticknor and Fields and Their Predecessors 1832–1858,* ed. Warren S. Tryon and William Charvat, Bibliographical Society of America Monograph Series 2 (New York: Bibliographical Society of America, 1949) 451, 462; Emerson, *Letters* 4:105.

40. Emerson, *Letters* 4:105–6.

41. Cary 2:341.

42. Quoted in Exman 150.

43. Emerson, *Letters* 4:124–25.

44. Emerson, *Letters* 4:134.

45. Emerson, *Letters* 4:149. For additional details of this transaction, see Exman 250–53.

46. *Walt Whitman: Complete Poetry and Prose,* ed. Justin Kaplan (New York: Library of America, 1982) 665; Horace Traubel, *With Walt Whitman in Camden,* 6 vols. (New York: Rowman and Littlefield, 1961–) 5:74.

47. Maxfield-Miller 155; Emerson, *Journals* 11:134–35; *The Correspondence of Emerson and Carlyle,* ed. Joseph Slater (New York: Columbia UP, 1964) 457 (see also 471).

48. Longfellow, *Letters* 3:215.

49. Longfellow, *Letters* 2:50–51.

50. Longfellow, *Letters* 3:389.

51. For a memoir of the Dante Club, see William Dean Howells, *Literary Friends and Acquaintance: A Personal Retrospect of American Authorship,* ed. David F. Hiatt and Edwin H. Cady, A Selected Edition of William Dean Howells 32 (Bloomington: Indiana UP, 1968) 154–64.

52. Longfellow journals, Houghton *54 M./bMsAm 1340.

53. Greene to Longfellow, Houghton bMsAm 1340.2 (2379).

54. Longfellow, *Letters* 4:400, 464 (see also 408, 463, 489). Bookseller Charles Goodspeed noted in his autobiography that this limited edition was one of the first American first editions to bring more than a thousand dollars in the rare book trade. See his *Yankee Bookseller* (Boston: Houghton, Mifflin, 1937) 197.

55. Bulfinch to Longfellow (29 Aug. 1855), Houghton bMsAm 1340.2 (838).

56. La Piana 109–10.

57. Norton to Longfellow (11 Oct. 1866), Houghton bMSAm 1340.2 (4150).

58. Longfellow, *Letters* 4:386.

59. On La Farge, see Barbara Weinberg, *The Decorative Work of John La Farge* (New York: Garland, 1977), and James L. Yarnell, *John La Farge: Water-colors and Drawings* (Yonkers: Hudson River Museum of Westchester, 1990).

60. Longfellow, *Letters* 4:473. Apparently Longfellow and Fields later planned a book to be titled *Landscape Illustrations of Dante* (see Longfellow, *Letters* 5:266). Andrew Hilen speculates in his note to Longfellow's letter to Fields on 19 October 1866 (*Letters* 5:87) that the plan was thwarted by announced republication of the Cary translation with all of the Flaxman illustrations by the London firm of Bell and Daldy (this book appeared in 1867), though Fields and Longfellow's intention seems have run more along the lines of geographical vignettes. In fact, Sarah Freeman Clarke, sister of the Reverend James Freeman Clarke, realized something of this notion in a two-part article illustrated with her own sketches ("Notes on the Exile of Dante," *Century* 17 March 1884: 734–52, 27 April 1884: 833–49), a project Longfellow warmly encouraged (see *Letters* 5:332, 6:558, 564).

61. Charles Eliot Norton, "Mr. Longfellow's Translation of the Divine Comedy," *The Nation*, 4 May 1867: 369.

62. Quoted in Carl J. Weber, *The Rise and Fall of James Ripley Osgood: A Biography* (Waterville, Me.: Colby College, 1959) 112.

63. Quoted in Judith A. Roman, *Annie Adams Fields: The Spirit of Charles Street* (Bloomington: Indiana UP, 1990) 29.

64. Houghton, Mifflin company scrapbook, Houghton MsAm 2030 (247), n.p.

65. Houghton, Mifflin Records of Sales, Houghton MsAm 2030 (31–37).

66. Fields, Osgood, and Co. to Longfellow, Houghton bMsAm 1340.2 (1972); Routledge to Longfellow Houghton bMs 1340.2 (4813). Longfellow's translation was simultaneously published in Germany by Tauchnitz.

67. Thomas Wentworth Higginson, *Old Cambridge*, National Studies in American Letters (New York: Macmillan, 1899) 34.

68. Charles Eliot Norton, "Dante, and His Latest English Translators," *North American Review* April 1866: 509–29; Norton, "Mr. Longfellow's Translation of the Divine Comedy," 369–70; [G. W. Greene], "Longfellow's Translation of Dante's *Divine Comedy*," *Atlantic Monthly* Aug. 1867: 188–98; William Dean Howells, "The Coming Translation of Dante," *The Round Table* 19 May 1866: 305–6.

69. James Woodress, *Howells and Italy* (Durham, N.C.: Duke UP, 1952) 109.

70. La Piana 111.

71. Fields to Longfellow, Houghton bMsAm. 1340.2 (1972).

72. Norton to Longfellow, Houghton bMs.Am 1340.2 (4150).

73. Longfellow, *Letters* 5:28.

74. Norton to Longfellow, Houghton bMsAm 1340.2 (4150).

75. Charles Eliot Norton, Preface, *The Divine Comedy*, trans. Norton, 3 vols. (Boston: Houghton, Mifflin, 1891–92) 1:v.

76. Houghton, Mifflin company scrapbook Houghton MsAm 2030 (247).

77. Norton to Houghton, Mifflin (12 Jan. 1892), Houghton bMsAm 1925 (1322).

78. Houghton, Mifflin Records of Sales, Houghton MsAm 2030 (31–37); Norton to Houghton, Mifflin, Houghton bMsAm 1925 (1322).

79. Clipping, Houghton, Mifflin company scrapbook.

80. Norton to Houghton, Mifflin, Houghton bMsAm 1925 (1322).

81. Charles Eliot Norton, *Henry Wadsworth Longfellow: A Sketch of His Life* (Boston: Houghton, Mifflin, 1907) 3.

82. Charles Eliot Norton, *Considerations upon Some Recent Social Theories* (Boston, 1853) 157–58.

83. Rollo Walter Brown, *Harvard Yard in the Golden Age* (New York: Current Books, 1948) 153.

84. Longfellow, *Letters* 6:346; Charles Eliot Norton, *The Letters of Charles Eliot Norton*, ed. Sara Norton and M. A. De Wolfe Howe, 2 vols. (Boston: Houghton, Mifflin, 1913) 2:219.

85. Charles Eliot Norton, Preface to *Dante's Eleven Letters*, trans. Charles Sterrett Latham, ed. G. R. Carpenter (Boston: Houghton, Mifflin, 1891); *Comments of John Ruskin on the Divina Commedia*, ed. Charles Eliot Norton (Boston: Houghton, Mifflin, 1903); Charles Allen Dinsmore, *Aids to the Study of Dante* (Boston: Houghton, Mifflin, 1891); Melville Best Anderson, trans., *The Divine Comedy of Dante Alighieri* (Yonkers-on-Hudson, N.Y.: World, 1922).

86. Thomas Nelson Page, *Dante and His Influence* (New York: Scribner's, 1922) 7.

87. Van Wyck Brooks, *New England: Indian Summer 1865–1915* (New York: Dutton, 1940) 435, 442; Richard Shryock, quoted in William Charvat, *Literary Publishing in America 1790–1850* (1959; rpt. Amherst: U of Massachusetts P, 1993) 20–21.

88. Hugh Kenner, *The Pound Era* (Berkeley: U of California P, 1971) 320.

89. Norton to Longfellow (26 Nov. 1878), Houghton bMsAm 1340.2 (4150); Norton to Houghton, Mifflin (24 Jan. 1907), Houghton bMsAm 1925 (1322).

90. Norton, Dante Lectures I (c. 1890), Houghton bMsAm 1088.5 (Box 13).

91. Karen Blair, *The Clubwoman as Feminist: True Womanhood Redefined 1868–1914* (New York: Holmes and Meier, 1980) 57.

92. T. J. Jackson Lears, *No Place of Grace: Antimodernism and the Transformation of American Culture 1880–1920* (New York: Pantheon, 1981) 155–59; James Turner, *Without God, without Creed: The Origins of Unbelief in America* (Baltimore: John Hopkins UP, 1985) 252; Lawrence W. Levine, *Highbrow Lowbrow: The Emergence of Cultural Hierarchy in America* (Cambridge: Harvard UP, 1988).

93. William Roscoe Thayer, "Professor Charles Eliot Norton," *Twenty-Eighth Annual Report of the Dante Society* (1909) 5.

94. Ellen Ballou, *The Building of the House: Houghton Mifflin's Formative Years* (Boston: Houghton, Mifflin, 1970) 537.

95. Longfellow journal 13 Jan. 1855, 18 April 1860.

96. On Leypoldt, see Tebbel 2:309–10; Growoll lxvii–lxix; and Jay H. Beswick, *The Work of Frederick Leypoldt, Bibliographer and Publisher* (New York: Bowker, 1942) 10, 76, 80. Longfellow remarks on Doré in his journal for 8 Feb. 1862.

97. Milton Klonsky, *Blake's Dante: The Complete Illustrations to the Divine Comedy* (New York: Harmony Books, 1980) 18.

98. Tebbel 2:353–54; the copy I have seen is *Dante's Inferno,* trans. H. F. Cary (New York and London: Cassell, Petter, & Galpin, 1866). Regrettably, Cassell's records were destroyed during World War II by the London Blitz.

99. Roger Burlingame, *Of Making Many Books: A Hundred Years of Reading, Writing, and Publishing* (New York: Scribner's, 1946) 227.

100. Peter Haining, *Ghosts: The Illustrated History* (Secaucus, N.J.: Chartwell 1987) 88–89; Carlos Clarens, *An Illustrated History of the Horror Film* (New York: Capricorn, 1967) 185. "Dante's Inferno" was also the title of a 1935 film starring Spencer Tracy.

101. *The Works of Dante Alighieri,* 6 vols., Temple Classics (London: J. M. Dent, 1899–1906); see Tebbel 2:244, Kenner 76.

102. T. S. Eliot, "What Dante Means to Me," *To Criticize the Critic* (New York: Farrar, Straus and Giroux, 1965) 125.

103. Norton, *Letters* 2:220.

104. Edna Ferber, *So Big* (New York: Doubleday, 1924) 310; Tebbel 2:428.

105. Larry Niven and Jerry Pournelle, *Inferno* (New York: Pocket Books, 1976); *The Doré Illustrations for Dante's Divine Comedy* (New York: Dover, 1976).

106. The phrase *libro della memoria* occurs in the opening line of Dante's *Vita Nuova.*

The Material Melville: Shaping Readers' Horizons

MICHAEL KEARNS

I AM CONCERNED HERE ONLY tangentially with two well-known Melvilles: the actual person who wrote *Moby-Dick* and other prose pieces and the personified aesthetic intention that can be inferred from the works themselves. Instead, I am going to consider some of the tangible facts external to those works, facts that helped shape the "horizon of expectations" (a term coined by Jauss)[1] with which Melville's first readers approached his early novels, especially *Typee* and *Omoo*: endpapers, title pages, running titles, and magazine advertisements. In her work on early American novels, Davidson notes that such "seemingly nonliterary considerations still suggest the scope and nature of a particular work's use and appeal."[2] These physical details reflect how professional readers affiliated with Melville's publishing houses responded to the words he wrote when he was unknown or just becoming recognized as an author. They probably also influenced the purchaser's actual reading experience of this writer who was totally unknown until 1846, who subsequently had several notable successes and three times as many notable failures, and who in spite of his efforts never escaped being known as a "man who lived among cannibals"[3] and "Typee"— Evert Duyckinck's characterization of him in 1857.[4] "Herman Melville, author of *Typee* and *Omoo*" is my primary subject—constituted in these artifacts and localized in the literary culture of his time.

Rabinowitz provides another way of thinking about the horizon of expectations. "Readers need to stand somewhere before they pick up a book," he writes; basic to this readerly standpoint are the "conventions of reading," which influence "what happens *before* the act of reading even starts."[5] "Conventions of reading" and "horizon of expectations" highlight different aspects of the same process: the horizon can be thought of as reading conventions that exist in potential, ready to be evoked by a specific reading experience. In concentrating on the tangible details surrounding Melville's early works I am concerned more with the potential than with the activated conventions, with the expectations Melville's early readers took to the reading experience more than with the experience itself.

Nor will I be dealing with what Levenston calls "the stuff of literature": spelling, punctuation, layout, and other aspects the author controlled in order to signal the presence of "literary meaning."[6] It is certainly important in reading Melville to study how an audience's perception of authorial intention can be influenced by the author's perceived adherence to and deviations from the conventions of print; most of Levenston's examples from *Tristram Shandy* could be replaced or supplemented by examples from *Moby-Dick*. But my focus here is on the "stuff" extraneous to the words in which Melville embodied his intentions; this extraneous material both reflects what professional readers thought of Melville's words in manuscript form and influences the "horizon of expectations" within which those words were read once they were published, once the author "Herman Melville" became a commodity. The writer Herman Melville generated a handwritten manuscript that had to be received, contextualized, and transmitted by what we often carelessly refer to as "the publisher"—actually a collection of individuals whose tasks included reviewing that manuscript, editing, designing, and marketing it, and so forth.[7] Each of these had a definite idea of the buying public's different horizons and a pecuniary motive for situating a given work within one or several of those horizons. Their decisions helped create the author "Herman Melville" by providing readers with expectations about the value, significance, and genre of this author's early productions.

Exploring how these knowledgeable readers decided to design and market an actual book helps set straight the historical record we might call "the reception of Herman Melville, author of *Typee, Omoo,* etc." The problem with this record, as William Charvat noted years ago, is that there is so little "reliable evidence" of how readers actually responded to Melville's works.[8] Sales figures and payment records, as detailed by Tanselle, reflect how badly this author's works fared in the literary marketplace (except for *Typee, Omoo,* and the magazine stories) but not how the ordinary readers who *did* buy or borrow them responded.[9] Contemporary reviews are problematic as evidence of response, according to Charvat, because they were so closely tied to marketing. Disagreeing with Charvat, Baym writes that novel reviewing "was directed toward readers, was conducted in a constant awareness of what people were reading, and was always trying to understand the reasons for public preferences. The reviews offer guidance and correction in a way that enables us to see what they thought they were guiding and correcting."[10] Not every historian will agree with Baym. I find it difficult reliably to infer anything about what the reviewers thought or what they were trying to understand; until the rhetoric of historically distant reviews has been more closely studied in the context of the literary marketplace, cautious use of this evidence is advisable. Two other types of evidence, comments about Melville's productions in personal letters other than those related to his own biographical record, and readers' marks in copies that were actually read, could be enormously useful. Unfortunately, no hardy sub-sub librarian of a scholar has yet gathered this material, although Davidson's study of the readers of early American novels shows how the work should be done and the rich results it can yield.[11]

Because there is so little evidence, and because literary scholars have only recently become centrally concerned with issues of the reception of literary works, for most of this century Melville has been taken at his own word: he was an author-hero misunderstood and misprised in his time. There is truth in Melville's lament and in the Melville myth created from the 1920s through the 1960s. However, the evidence we do have shows that the whole picture is considerably more complicated. From the beginning of his career this author was placed in literary company that was presented to the public as both respectable and valuable. Such placement could have led to the kind of reception Melville came to desire for his writings, if he had been able to recognize and accommodate himself somewhat to the horizon of expectations implied by Wiley and Putnam's Library of American Books, which published *Typee: A Peep at Polynesian Life* in 1846.[12]

That publishing series and its companion grouping the Library of Choice Reading, which included foreign works, featured "Books that are books," according to Wiley and Putnam's advertising. Although some of the works published in each series have come to be held in slight regard, that evaluation has at least as much to do with the institution of literary study in the twentieth century as with intrinsic value. The fact that Wiley and Putnam offered both Hawthorne's *Mosses* and James Hall's *The Wilderness and the War-Path* in the Library of American Books actually increases the list's usefulness as a window into American literary culture of the 1840s. According to Ezra Greenspan, the Library of American Books was the "most important series of original works of American literature ever published to that date or since"; this series actually "marked the coming of age of American literature."[13] In presenting these lists to the public and in touting them as "Books that are books," Wiley and Putnam appealed to several desires common among the American book-buying public of the first half of the nineteenth century: the desire to own a tangible piece of culture, the wish to display possessions that represented economic achievement as well as cultural sophistication, and the inclination to support endeavors that were both practical and American. In fact, the Library of American Books was unusual in its commitment to "issue only American works, many of which were original and all of which were paid for on a royalties or lump sum basis."[14]

Baym has written that readers in the nineteenth century wanted to read and own novels but did not expect them to stimulate thoughtful inquiry about the culture or the processes by which they were written and read.[15] This generalization needs to be somewhat qualified, at least in the case of the fictional works within Wiley and Putnam's Libraries, because readers were authorized by the advertising slogans to respond with some depth to the works of imagination listed in them. On the other hand, as I will explain later, readers did discriminate both among and within genres on the basis of the value of the content: true accounts (histories, biographies, travel narratives for example) were valued more than imaginary creations.

Wiley and Putnam's advertising reveals that the factors of "use and appeal" identified by Davidson at the end of the eighteenth century were still important in the 1840s. In the words of one ad, the works in the Library of American Books had all been written by "sundry citizens of this good land prompted by a certain something in their nature." Another description, from the endpapers of William Gilmore Simms's *The Wigwam*, as printed in 1845, situates the Library project more precisely:

The Publishers of the Library of Choice Reading beg leave to call attention to the following classification of the books published in the series,
by which it will appear that novelty, variety and standard merit have
always been preserved, and the promise of the original prospectus faithfully kept. It was proposed [in that prospectus] to publish "the best
books of Travels, Biographies, works of Classic Fiction—where the
moral is superior to the mere story, without any sacrifice of the interest—
occasional choice volumes of Poetry, Essays, Criticism, contributions to
History, and generally such single volumes, written by men of genius, as
will equally delight the scholar and the general reader."

Key phrases in the announcement—"standard merit," "moral," and
"equally delight the scholar and the general reader"—suggest that
Wiley and Putnam intended these works to be recognized as informative, entertaining, and respectable. The phrases invited readers *not* to
behave like the "superficial skimmer of pages" Melville scorned in his
1850 review of *Mosses from an Old Manse*.[16] Instead, the reader who
picked up *Typee* in a bookstall and encountered on the first page the
imprint "Wiley & Putnam's Library of American Books" would immediately be invited to think of this physical object as both *choice* and
American—lasting, valuable, and of the American spirit and experience.
(Illustration 1 is a reproduction of that page.) Items in this series were
not escape literature, not ephemera, not to be confused with sensationalism or romance.

That invitation would have been supported when readers turned
another page and encountered—still before beginning to read the text
itself—a list of travel books published by Wiley and Putnam. This list
does not identify *Typee* as a travel narrative but certainly implies a
kinship; "the reading audience of that era would have found far less difference between Melville's *Typee* and Taylor's *Views A-Foot* or Head-
ley's *Letters from Italy* than would readers today."[17] Even those individuals who tended to read against the grain of advertisements would have
had that kinship in mind and would have been more likely to read it
within that horizon rather than another. By association with other
travel books, readers could have expected *Typee* to be factual, hence
lasting and valuable. (The playful subtitle, "A Peep at Polynesian Life,"
would have added an interesting fillip but would not have contradicted
the work's potential value.) The prefatory map and the running title
"Residence in the Marquesas" further emphasized the work's ground-
ing in the real world and supported the promise extended by Wiley and

WILEY & PUTNAM'S

LIBRARY OF

AMERICAN BOOKS.

TYPEE:

A PEEP AT POLYNESIAN LIFE.

PART I.

1. First page of Melville's *Typee* (Wiley and Putnam, 1846). Courtesy, American Antiquarian Society.

Putnam that their series volumes would "equally delight the scholar and the general reader"—they would inform and entertain.

The ads preceding part 2, shown in Illustration 2, reaffirm these messages.[18] The boldness of the "library" line reminds readers of the importance claimed for this publishing project, while the titles reiterate

2. Ad for Wiley and Putnam's Library of American Books series, inserted in *Typee* between parts 1 and 2 of the text. Courtesy, American Antiquarian Society.

the generic link with works of travel. Likewise in the endpapers: of the six items advertised, three are travel: *Journal of an African Cruiser, Wanderings of a Pilgrim,* and *Western Clearings.* These intermediate and final ads could have confirmed what a reader had already experienced in passing through the pages. They also could have shaped that experience because many readers, if engaged in recreational rather than academic reading, do not proceed linearly through the pages of a book but instead begin by getting a feel for the object in their hands—flipping through the pages and looking over the cover. Those who bought *Typee* in paper wrappers could have encountered all of these ads while cutting the pages, that is, before reading a single page of text.

The overall effect of the tangible details of these advertisements, especially when included with the actual work—literally framing it, in the case of the endpapers—is to suggest a relative seriousness of purpose and a generic kinship with travel narratives. Familiar with the series' goals, readers could organize their encounter with the book's various elements, giving somewhat less weight to its adventure and mild sensationalism, somewhat more to the parts reporting on Typee customs and values. They could feel justified in looking for a moral or for a somewhat popularized scholarly interest. They could trust that the work was mostly true although certainly embellished, designed to "delight" as well as to instruct.

Typee by and large met readers' expectations, judging by the generally favorable reviews,[19] although it might not have fared nearly as well without the context suggested by the Library of American Books. Gerald Graff has commented on how today's untrained readers will rely on the "unofficial interpretive culture" embodied in book-jacket designs, advertising, and so forth.[20] Wiley and Putnam's advertising strategy contributed to the "unofficial interpretive culture" surrounding *Typee;* by associating the book with other autobiographical travel narratives, the publisher may be considered to have made the reading possible. The potential problem with *Typee* is that its generic identity as a travel narrative is frequently strained. Like the rest of Melville's works, *Typee* honors the genre contract more in the breach than in the observance, from one paragraph to the next becoming a cultural critique, an adventure, a romantic love story, or even (although less so than *Moby-Dick* or *Pierre*) a metaphysical treatise. The plot, built on the conflict between Tommo's desire to leave the valley of the Typees and their mysterious desire to keep him there, the strong narrative line, and the polished quality of the writing caused some reviewers and probably other readers to doubt the work's veracity; either the actual author was not the "I" of the narrative, or the whole work was a product of the imagination. This problem of generic identity does not seem to have crippled the reception or sales of *Typee* because the tangible details of advertisements and so forth provided readers with an interpretive map that helped them identify certain sections as digressions and others as belonging to the main narrative. In addition, readers who were disposed to seek out and celebrate the special "American" characteristics of literary works might have felt authorized to regard the digressions themselves as such a characteristic.

One other potentially problematic aspect of the horizon within which *Typee* was read was the relationship between authorial identity and truthfulness. Baym has determined that in the nineteenth century the author's identity was second only to "subgenre classification" as a means of signaling to readers what to expect in a book's contents: "Granting that every novel was a unique instance of a literary form, reviewers also assumed that all works by one person had real resemblances and could be properly thought of as forming one class."[21] But the author of *Typee* was an unknown quantity; for all most readers knew, "Herman Melville" could have been a pseudonym. Hence the question of truthfulness could have been extremely important to reviewers and general readers alike.[22] It was an issue, of course, but less so than it might have been. One explanation for the relatively minor tempest is that Wiley and Putnam was a respected house; if their Library imprint represented *Typee* as valuable, it could not be an outright fabrication. When Melville was actually able to present his publishers with documentary evidence that he had been in the Marquesas Islands, and when his companion on that adventure surfaced and provided additional written testimony that Melville incorporated into the second edition of *Typee,* this issue was effectively put to rest. Yet that resolution of the problem surely also solidified the public's perception of "Herman Melville, author of *Typee*" as a writer of factual rather than fictional works. This perception, in turn, became part of the horizon that Melville's third work, *Mardi,* so thoroughly violated.

The reader of *Typee* who encountered *Omoo* the following year would probably have been struck by the more impressive quality of the physical object. Compared to the binding of *Typee,* that of *Omoo* conveys a sense of greater value: on the spine a gold-stamped floral pattern and on the front cover a blind-stamped scene of two ships. A reader buying the book in wrappers would get a similar impression: the title in maroon standing alone on the title page and every second line on the imprint page done in the same rich maroon, in contrast to *Typee*'s plain black. In a reciprocal relationship, these tangible objects helped situate the author as a known literary figure, as someone whose star was climbing and who could now be identified with a body of work: "Herman Melville, author of *Typee* and *Omoo.* "

As with *Typee,* the incorporated ads suggest that serious readers should be interested in *Omoo,* an important detail because Melville had jumped the Wiley and Putnam ship and had signed on with Harper and Brothers. His second publisher accepted and built on the context established by the first, a consistency that probably contributed to those labels Melville so disliked, associate of cannibals and "sea-dog" philosopher. The knowledgeable readers affiliated with the house of Harper—editors, advertisers, and so forth—regarded *Typee,* and by extension "Herman Melville," as a commodity whose appeal to the buying public had been accurately assessed and developed by Wiley and Putnam. Local history may also have played a role in this regard. The house of Harper had reviewed a draft of *Typee* and had declined to publish it on the grounds that it could not be "true" and, hence, was of no "value."[23] But by 1847 that value had been established, and the work was accepted as largely autobiographical. Similarly, as a work of fact, *Omoo* would appeal to a range of buyers including those interested not just in reading for entertainment but in acquiring items of substance. In line with this appeal, *Omoo* in paper covers touts, on the back cover, "Works of Sterling Value Published by Harper and Brothers, New York"—the word "sterling" perhaps intended to make potential purchasers think of fine silver or English currency. These works included William H. Prescott's *History of the Conquest of Peru* and a forty-part edition of *The Pictorial History of England* projected to result in "Four splendid octavo Volumes"—splendid, presumably, as both a bookshelf display and a compilation of knowledge.

However, the running titles of *Typee* and *Omoo* suggest that the staffs of the two publishing houses would not have agreed about the generic identity of these books. The full American title, *Typee: A Peep at Polynesian Life,* conformed to the ads framing this edition, which emphasized the slightly prurient activity of *peeping.* The running title, however, conveys the impression of a travel book: "Residence in the Marquesas." By contrast, the running title of *Omoo* is "Adventures in the South Seas." One possible explanation for Harper and Brothers' choice of "Adventures" is that they desired to narrow and focus the appeal of Melville. The running title of *Omoo* could have steered readers to an impression somewhat at odds with that conveyed by *Typee;* readers might have regarded a book of adventures as somewhat less valuable, as of less lasting significance, than one emphasizing residence. At the very least, encountering "Adventures in the South Seas" at the top of every other page could have caused readers to pay more

attention to the narrative portions and less to those with a more sociological, anthropological, or ethical slant. This effect could have been
pronounced for someone who had purchased either book in wrappers
and had to cut the pages before beginning to read. The prereading
experience of encountering the running title as many as several hundred times could have helped establish an expectation as to genre and
content.

The magazine ads for the early novels flesh out the portrait of the
professional readers who contributed to the creation of "Herman Melville, author of *Typee*" and help us understand more clearly his place
within the literary culture of his time—that is, the place the literary
persona "Herman Melville" actually occupied in contrast to the place
the historical Melville hoped to occupy. The ads in the *Literary World*
are especially instructive in this respect. This literary periodical, which
first appeared on 6 February 1847, described itself as "a paper in which
all persons interested in literature may be certain of seeing the FIRST
announcement of every new literary undertaking." The promise was
fulfilled in several ways, including the one most pertinent to consideration of the tangible Melville, the final section, called the "Publishers'
Circular." Here Harper and Brothers was prominent as the sole adver-
tiser on the highly visible last page of almost every number during the
major phase of Melville's career, through 1852.

The first *Literary World* advertisement for Melville appeared on the
last page of number 11 (17 April 1847) as part of a descriptive list of
recent Harper publications, including *Omoo*. This ad, reproduced as
Illustration 3, sends an interestingly mixed message. On the one hand,
the bold first line does not just state but virtually shouts out that these
works are new and important; *Omoo* not only leads the list but garners
nearly half of the full-page ad. Its "importance" is especially easy to
understand in relation to the other titles listed, which are factual, historical, and in the case of *The Writings of George Washington* prominently American. The ad's selections from reviews of *Typee* convey a
similar impression, emphasizing that work's charm, freshness, and elegance. Just as important, these selections do not refer to adventure or
"peeping." The stated comparisons with *Robinson Crusoe* and Irving's
biography of Columbus and the implied comparison with Johnson's
Rasselas, among other works, indicate that Harper and Brothers were
claiming for *Typee* the status of an American classic, a status that
presumably would add value to the "NEW WORK BY THE AUTHOR OF
'TYPEE.'" On the other hand, the "Extract from the Preface" of that

IMPORTANT NEW LITERARY PRODUCTIONS.

PREPARING FOR SPEEDY PUBLICATION BY

MESSRS. HARPER & BROTHERS, NEW YORK.

I.

NEW WORK BY THE AUTHOR OF "TYPEE."

IN A FEW DAYS WILL BE PUBLISHED, BY

MESSRS. HARPER AND BROTHERS, NEW YORK,

SIMULTANEOUSLY WITH ITS PUBLICATION IN LONDON, BY MR. MURRAY,

OMOO: A NARRATIVE OF ADVENTURES IN THE SOUTH SEAS.

BY HERMAN MELVILLE, ESQ.,

AUTHOR OF "TYPEE."

This work forms the true sequel and counterpart of the author's popular production—"TYPEE." The adventures in the present volume embrace both sea and land. The Nautical incidents of the book are extremely interesting, and the Rambles and Excursions on the Islands of Tahiti and Omoo, most romantic and extraordinary. With respect to "Typee." "Omoo" is the reverse of the medal; as the former work presents the only account ever given of the state of nature in which the Polynesians are originally found, so the latter production will exhibit them as affected by a prolonged intercourse with foreigners.

"Nowhere, perhaps, are the proverbial characteristics of sailors shown under wilder aspects, than in the South Seas. For the most part, the vessels navigating those remote waters, are engaged in the Sperm Whale Fishery; a business which is not only peculiarly fitted to attract the most reckless seamen of all nations, but, in various ways, is calculated to foster in them a spirit of the utmost license. These voyages, also, are unusually long and perilous; the only harbors accessible are among the barbarous or semi-civilized islands of Polynesia, or along the lawless western coast of South America. Hence, scenes the most novel, and not directly connected with the business of whaling, frequently occur among the crews of ships in the Pacific.

"Without pretending to give any account of the whale-fishery (for the scope of the narrative does not embrace the subject), it is, partly, the object of this work to convey some idea of the kind of life 'to which allusion is made, by means of a circumstantial history of adventures befalling the author."—Extract from the Preface.

Criticisms on the Author's Previous Work.

"TYPEE is a work of even greater interest than De Foe's *Robinson Crusoe*, or Miss Porter's *Sir Edward Seaward Narrative*."—*Albany Evening Journal.*

"We can honestly say of this work, that it is curiously charming, and charmingly instructive."—*Standard*

"Mr. Murray's *Library* does not furnish us with a more interesting work than this: it is full of the captivating matter, upon which the general reader fastens, and is endued with freshness and originality to an extent that cannot fail to exhilarate."—*London Times.*

"A charming book, full of talent—composed with singular elegance, and as musical as Washington Irving's Columbus. 'Typee' is a new Eutopian of Savagedom, and continually reminds us of Bishop Berkeley's gorgeous invention—Gaudentio Lucca's City of the Sun. A more fascinating picture of Life was never equalled."—*Western Continent.*

"It is a very entertaining and pleasing narrative, and the Happy Valley of the gentle cannibals compares very well with the best contrivances of the learned Dr. Johnson to produce similar impressions."—*Tribune.*

"Chateaubriand's *Atala* is of no softer or romantic tone: *Anacharsis* scarce presents us with images more classically exquisite."—*Mirror.*

"One of the most captivating books we ever read."—*Douglas Jerrold's Magazine.*

"A book full of fresh and richly colored matter: Mr. Melville's manner is *New World* all over."—*London Athenæum.*

II.

IN TWO VOLUMES OCTAVO, EMBELLISHED WITH PORTRAITS FROM ORIGINAL PAINTINGS, EXECUTED IN THE FINEST STYLE OF ART, WITH MAPS, ETC.

THE HISTORY OF THE CONQUEST OF PERU;

WITH A PRELIMINARY VIEW OF THE CIVILIZATION OF THE INCAS.

BY WILLIAM H. PRESCOTT, ESQ.

AUTHOR OF "HISTORY OF THE CONQUEST IN MEXICO," "HISTORY OF FERDINAND AND ISABELLA," "BIOGRAPHICAL AND CRITICAL MISCELLANIES," ETC.

This work is arranged on the same general plan with that of the "Conquest of Mexico," to which it naturally forms a counterpart. It is devoted to an account of the celebrated Inca race; their empire, social and military policy, progress in the mechanic arts, &c., and presents a complete picture, in short, of the sanguinary revolution which established the Spanish rule over the ancient empire of the Incas.

III.

IN 12 MONTHLY VOLUMES OCTAVO, WITH ENGRAVINGS ON STEEL, BEAUTIFULLY PRINTED, BOUND, AND GILT. PRICE $1 50 EACH.

THE WRITINGS OF GEORGE WASHINGTON:

BEING HIS CORRESPONDENCE, ADDRESSES, MESSAGES, AND OTHER PAPERS, OFFICIAL AND PRIVATE, SELECTED AND PUBLISHED FROM THE ORIGINAL MANUSCRIPTS, WITH A LIFE OF THE AUTHOR, AND NOTES AND ILLUSTRATIONS.

BY JARED SPARKS.

The great reduction in the price of this beautiful re-issue—being *less than half the original cost*—will, for the first time, render this splendid national publication accessible to every person who venerates the name of Washington. Such a work may be said to be indispensable, as well as an honor, to every private library.

IV.

IN MONTHLY NUMBERS, COPIOUSLY EMBELLISHED BY ORIGINAL DESIGNS, ENGRAVED IN THE BEST STYLE.

THE WORKS OF FLAVIUS JOSEPHUS.

A NEW TRANSLATION.

BY REV. ROBERT TRAIL, D.D.

WITH NOTES, EXPLANATORY ESSAYS, AND NUMEROUS PICTORIAL ILLUSTRATIONS.

This splendid edition of the Writings of the Jewish Historian, comprising all the works of the author known to be extant, will possess many important advantages over all its predecessors, in the novelty, beauty, and extent of its graphic embellishments—derived in most instances from ancient monumental relics, bas-reliefs, medallions, coins, architectural remains, &c.; also in the greater accuracy of its translation, and the further elucidation of the text by the aid of notes and expositions—the fruit of much laborious research in archæological lore—by the editor and translator.

V.

IN MONTHLY PARTS, IN LEGIBLE TYPE, ILLUSTRATED BY NUMEROUS ENGRAVINGS ON WOOD, EXECUTED IN THE BEST STYLE.

THE NATIONAL CYCLOPÆDIA OF USEFUL KNOWLEDGE.

The design of the above work is to comprise all the elements of human science, including all the recent improvements and discoveries in its several departments. All that is valuable in previous productions of its class will be combined in the present work.

"If the steamboat and the railway have abridged space and time, and made a large addition to the available length of human existence, why may not our intellectual journey be also accelerated—our knowledge more cheaply and quickly acquired,—its records rendered *more accessible and portable*,—its cultivators increased in numbers,—and its blessings more rapidly and widely diffused ?"—*Quarterly Review*, No. 139.

3. Harper and Brothers' prominently placed advertisement in *Literary World* for 17 April 1847. Courtesy, American Antiquarian Society.

new work, reproduced in the ad, contains language that evokes the "adventures" of the subtitle and the running title: "wilder aspects," "reckless," "spirit of the utmost license," for example.

Together, these suggestions of value and adventure define that commodity effectively owned by Harper and Brothers, "THE AUTHOR OF 'TYPEE'" and *Omoo*—a commodity as important as the other tangible products named in the ad's third-largest type (used for *The History of the Conquest of Peru* and other works). The design of this ad shows that

4. Harper and Brothers' ad featuring *Mardi* in *Literary World*, 7 April 1849. Courtesy, American Antiquarian Society.

within the literary culture of his time, "Herman Melville" had been quickly identified as the voice behind these books. The ad also suggested that the book-buying public could expect this voice to combine narratives of adventure with cultural criticism: the paragraph introducing this extract accurately describes *Omoo* as "the reverse of the medal" (the other side being *Typee*), depicting the once-natural Polynesians

64

after their "prolonged intercourse with foreigners." In sum, it was another classic like its predecessor, deserving comparison with *Crusoe*.

Two weeks later, *Omoo* was still at the top of the Harper and Brothers page, although all but the first paragraph of the 17 April ad had been replaced by other titles. The work continued to be listed as late as 24 July among the house's "Valuable Literary Novelties Recently Published." In fact, the Harper and Brothers ads from 1847 through 1851 suggest that the house was doing its best to keep Melville's name before the public eye. Illustration 4, from the *Literary World* of 7 April 1849, is a good example. Featuring Melville's third work, *Mardi*, this ad used even heavier display type than did those for *Omoo*. The ads for this work follow the same pattern as the earlier ones: the top third of the ad of 7 April 1849 devoted to *Mardi*, the top two-thirds of the following week's ad, the top quarter the week after that. All three of these ads give additional prominence to this new work by dividing the remainder of the page, under the *Mardi* material, into columns. The tangible effect is to "headline" *Mardi* among the new productions from Harper and Brothers. Because the twentieth-century Melville myth gives such prominence to reviewers' hostile reception of *Mardi*, it is important to keep in mind that whatever might have been the private opinions of the various Harpers' staff members who participated in producing and advertising this work, the house's public stance remained supportive.[24]

Each novel through *Moby-Dick* received similar treatment. The ad on the last page of Number 250 (15 November 1851) announced in heavy type that "Harper and Brothers have just published: Moby-Dick; or, the Whale. By Herman Melville, Author of 'Typee,' 'Omoo,' 'Whitejacket,' 'Redburn,' 'Mardi.'" But this was the house's last strenuous effort. Melville's next novel, *Pierre*, was not touted so vigorously, and in fact the publishers seem finally to have accepted that "Herman Melville, Author of 'Mardi'" was an albatross. Announcing *Pierre* on 27 November 1852, they noted only that it was by the "Author of 'Typee' and 'Omoo.'"

The magazine and endpaper ads, the title pages, and the running titles of the first two works by "Herman Melville" surely contributed to the albatross effect. They helped to establish a horizon of expectations for the voice "Herman Melville" that did not include the genre toward which the actual writer was moving with *Mardi* and that he reached with *Moby-Dick*. This genre can be best characterized as "anatomy" presented through a "philosophical dialogue" (this apt phrase is Wenke's)[25] with an implied readership that is both interested in and relatively well informed about the topic and is also willing to accept, even enjoy, a prominently displayed and playful imagination. For American readers around 1850, "Herman Melville, author of *Typee* and *Omoo*" simply did not write this sort of thing. I would not go as far as Charvat and assert that the "general reader" displays a "latent, deep-rooted hatred of the seriously experimental,"[26] but the fact is that readers' impressions of the commodity "Herman Melville" were converging on the author of (and barely disguised hero of) *Typee* at the same time the actual human being was broadening both his goals for those readers and his sense of himself as a writer.[27]

For all but the few hardy specialists, *Mardi* remains readable if at all only as a measure of how far Melville's intellectual reach outgrew his rhetorical grasp during the first several years of his career. This "romance" might have failed even had the general reader not expected from "Herman Melville" more of what he had already produced; nevertheless, it is worth pondering whether the literary culture of mid-nineteenth-century America might have found a more prominent place for this proto-Voltaire or adolescent Rabelais had *Mardi* sprung from as unknown a pen as did *Typee*. Another possibility—suppose *Mardi* had been prefaced by a map, as were *Omoo* and *Typee*. Might such a tangible representation, even of a wholly fictive realm, have made it more accessible to readers? More interesting? More valuable?

We might think of two stories here that overlap very little: the story of the actual writer's growth and that of the expanding, then shrinking, of the "Herman Melville" constituted by the physical objects. The first is germinal even in *Typee*, with its interplay between the rhetorics of experience and romance and its progressive discovery of the power of the latter.[28] The story's rising action begins with the writing and publication of *Mardi*. This romance was Melville's first violation of "Herman Melville" the publicly recognized author.[29] In keeping with this attempt to establish an identity different from the one created by the reception of his first two works, he even requested that the title page not mention his authorship of *Typee* and *Omoo*.[30] Although his wish was honored by Harper and Brothers, their advertising campaign guaranteed that only those readers who had been entirely absent from the contemporary literary scene would be able to take *Mardi* as the "romance" Melville intended; any regular reader of the *Literary World* would expect another *Typee*-like production by "Herman Melville." This story climaxes in 1857 with the publication of *The Confidence-Man* and has as its denouement the long silence thereafter. This silence of course was only relative; he was no longer publishing fiction but was engaged in a serious apprenticeship in the craft of poetry as well as in drafting *Billy Budd*.[31]

The second story climaxes with the page-long ads for the first three novels that were inserted at the end of *Redburn*, with the title page of *White-Jacket* ("By Herman Melville, author of 'Typee,' 'Omoo,' 'Mardi,' and 'Redburn'"), and with the ads for these four novels inserted at the end of *White-Jacket*. What these ads said to someone who bought either *Redburn* or *White-Jacket* was that "Herman Melville" existed as a set and, by implication, was worthy of being owned in this way. Further supporting this suggestion is the prominence of the author's name in the ad—in contrast, for example, to the handling of Lyell's *Second Visit to the United States*, advertised in the same collection of pages. (Illustrations 5 and 6 show this contrast.) Obviously, in 1849 and 1850 Harper and Brothers still hoped, perhaps even believed, that "By Herman Melville" had significant appeal and commercial value in the eyes of the reading public.

And the denouement of this story? We might see it foreshadowed in the final word of both *Moby-Dick* and *Pierre*, "Finis" rather than the customary "The End." The title page of *Moby-Dick* lists "Herman Melville" as the "author of 'Typee,' 'Omoo,' 'Redburn,' 'Mardi,' 'White-Jacket.'" Harper and Brothers still seemed to be hoping that Melville would justify their investment in him. He was still a known author; they owned the plates for all of these works; they hoped that the reading public might yet be persuaded to acquire a set. But the jeering, antagonistic reception of *Pierre* shattered this hope, and Melville's next publishers applied the triage principle. The title pages of *The Piazza Tales* and *The Confidence-Man*, published by Dix and Edwards, list Herman Melville as "author of 'Typee,' 'Omoo,' etc., etc., etc." *Israel Potter*, that almost unknown work published by Putnam between these two, cuts even more deeply: "author of 'Typee,' 'Omoo,' etc." It is in the nature of Melvillean stories to be incomplete, of course—Melville's magazine fiction sold well, he seems to have pleased that public as well as meeting his own needs as a writer, and there is no good explanation either for the poor sales of *The Piazza Tales* or for his decision not to return to fiction after *The Confidence-Man*.[32]

The significance of these two stories—we might also say, with Stubb, of these several renderings of one text—lies in what Mailloux calls "rhetorical hermeneutics," which focuses on "the rhetorical dynamics among interpreters within specific cultural settings. . . . rhetorical her-

BY HERMAN MELVILLE.

O M O O.

One Volume, 12mo, Muslin, $1 25 ; Paper, $1 00.

After the pungent and admirably written narrative of that accomplished, able sea-man, Herman Melville, few books of the same class but must appear flat and unprofitable. Omoo would have found readers at any time ; and that although twenty publishers had combined with fifty authors to deluge the public with the Pacific Ocean during the five previous years.—*Blackwood's notice of Coulter's Cruise.*

Let Mr. Melville write as much as he will, provided always he writes as well as now, and he shall find us greedy devourers of his productions. He has a rare pen for the delineation of character ; an eye for the humorous and grotesque which is worth a Jew's ; for the description of natural scenery he is not to be beaten, either on this side of the Atlantic or the other. His pencil is most distinct, the coloring beautiful and rich. As for invention, he will bear comparison with the most cunning of the modern French school. * * * At the last page of his second work, Mr. Melville is as fresh and vigorous as at the first line of the book which preceded it. Lkie his reader, he leaves off with an appetite.—*London Times.*

Unlike most sequels, Omoo is equal to its predecessor. The character of the composition is clear, fresh, vivacious, and full of matter.—*London Spectator.*

The adventures are depicted with force and humor.—*London Athenæum.*

Some of the scenes are like cabinet pictures.—*London Critic.*

Written in a style worthy of Philip Quarles or Robinson Crusoe.—*Lon. Lit. Gaz.*

It would be difficult to imagine a man better fitted to describe the impressions such a life and such scenes are calculated to call forth, than the auther of Omoo. Every variety of character, and scene, and incident, he studies and describes with equal gusto.—*London People's Journal.*

A stirring narrative of very pleasant reading. It possesses much of the charm that has made Robinson Crusoe immortal—life-like description. It commands attention, as if old interest were created by the narratives—

> "Of Raleigh, Frobisher, and Drake—
> Adventurous hearts, who bartered bold
> Their English steel for Spanish gold."

The history is one of comparatively new lands and new people. His account of the natives corresponds with that of Kotzebue and others.—*Douglas Jerrold's Paper.*

Mr. Melville has more than sustained his widely-spread reputation in these volumes. Omoo and Typee are actually delightful romances of real life, embellished with powers of description, and a graphic skill of hitting off characters, little inferior to the highest order of novel and romance writers.—*Albion.*

A curious and fascinating narrative.—*Anglo American.*

These volumes contain a vast amount of exceedingly entertaining and interesting matter.—*Philadelphia Courier.*

Omoo is characterized by all the animation, picturesqueness, and felicity of style which commended the author's first writings to a second reading, even after curiosity is satisfied by tracing out the singularity of the story.—*Literary World.*

Harper & Brothers, Publishers, New York.

5. Bound-in advertisement in *Redburn* (1849), a full-page advertisement for Harper and Brothes' previous success, *Omoo*. Courtesy, American Antiquarian Society.

6. Another bound-in advertisement in *Redburn*. The reduced prominence of the author's name in this ad, compared with the emphasis given to Melville in the Harper ad for *Omoo* (Illustration 5), is striking. Courtesy, American Antiquarian Society.

meneutics describes the ebb and flow of the cultural conversation" and preserves "the rhetorical context of history."[33] Melville the writer was trying to move into the realm of the imagination and away from the realm of experience, trying to develop a romantic rhetoric to replace a rhetoric emphasizing control and experience.[34] The generic identification of *Typee* as travel narrative and its commodity aspect within the Library of American Books series worked against the favorable reception of that move by his public. Had Melville realized before offering *Mardi* to the public that "Herman Melville" was already solidly associated with *Typee* and *Omoo*, he might have considered some sort of disguise—a pseudonym, for instance. Or else he might have attempted to recast *Mardi* so that its early chapters were easily recognizable as romance, thus making a relatively unambiguous claim on the public's thoughtful side as did the works of Hawthorne. Literary history has tended to regard the *Mardi* affair as both a serious literary mistake and a serious public-relations mistake. It certainly was the latter but was not necessarily the former, and it might not have been either had Melville understood that he had a certain amount of control over how "Herman Melville" was perceived and his works were received, but also that his readers would expect him to remain true to that authorial identity.

It is possible that Melville did come to this understanding, although not soon enough to avoid dealing his fragile reputation that near-fatal blow with *Mardi*. His 16 March 1850 review of Cooper's *The Red Rover*, titled "A Thought on Book-Binding," has almost nothing to say about the novel itself, praising instead the cover for its "felicitous touch of the sea superstitions of pirates."[35] The praise could have been ironic; Melville surely saw that, like Cooper, he too was being forced into a mold. Or it could have been intended honestly. The clear irony in these two stories is that the contemporary reception of this writer who always began with the tangible facts of his personal history (however far into the ethereal realms he may have carried them) was influenced by the material realities of book publishing. His words, hunted down in the far Pacific of his mind, were presented to the reading public as suitable for the utilitarian illumination of a dining table or a desk.

In the spirit of Melville's endings, which always add one more twist or a little deeper layer, it is fitting to end this account with some questions arising from the words of one anonymous reader of *Israel Potter: His Fifty Years of Exile*, neatly penciled into the endpapers, possibly around 1855 (the date of publication): "50 years in exile well written book." What might this reader have meant by "well written"? Why is there no comment about the author? Had Melville finally succeeded, too late to make any difference to his literary career, in bringing about the reception of his books as "foundlings" rather than authored by "Herman Melville, author of *Typee* and *Omoo*"? (He expresses this wish in "Hawthorne and His Mosses.") These questions illustrate how much more can still be learned about the transmission and reception of literary works as material artifacts.

∾ NOTES ∾

Thanks to the American Antiquarian Society and to the University of Texas of the Permian Basin for financial support that allowed me to attend the 1990 Seminar in the History of the Book in America, organized by the Society. The research base for this paper was put in place during that seminar. Thanks also to the staff of the Society for their assistance in locating and photocopying materials, and especially to Babette Gehnrich, Chief Book and Paper Conservator, for details on book production.

1. Hans Robert Jauss, *Toward an Aesthetic of Reception* (Minneapolis: U of Minnesota P, 1982).

2. Cathy N. Davidson, *Revolution and the Word: The Rise of the Novel in America* (New York and Oxford: Oxford UP, 1986) 3.

3. *The Letters of Herman Melville,* ed. Merrell R. Davis and William H. Gilman (New Haven: Yale UP, 1960) 138.

4. Jay Leyda, *The Melville Log* (1951; rpt. New York: Gordian Press, 1969) 563.

5. Peter J. Rabinowitz, *Before Reading: Narrative Conventions and the Politics of Interpretation* (Ithaca and London: Cornell UP, 1987) 2.

6. E. A. Levenston, *The Stuff of Literature: Physical Aspects of Texts and Their Relation to Literary Meaning* (Albany: State U of New York P, 1992).

7. John Murray, Melville's English publisher, insisted on more details about the Typee natives. Melville included these details, which then became part of the proof-sheet version in which G. P. Putnam first encountered *Typee* and on which he based his offer to publish the American edition. (See Leon Howard, "Historical Note," in Harrison Hayford, Hershel Parker, and G. Thomas Tanselle, eds., *Typee* [Evanston and Chicago: Northwestern UP and the Newberry Library, 1968] 280–81.) Although not significant for the public reception of *Typee,* this stands as an interesting example of the complicated relationship among writer, publishers, and text.

8. William Charvat, *The Profession of Authorship in America, 1800–1870: The Papers of William Charvat,* ed. Matthew J. Bruccoli (Columbus: Ohio State UP, 1968) 285.

9. G. Thomas Tanselle, "The Sales of Melville's Books," *Harvard Library Bulletin* 18 (April 1969): 195–215.

10. Nina Baym, *Novels, Readers, and Reviewers: Responses to Fiction in Antebellum America* (Ithaca and London: Cornell UP, 1984) 19.

11. My quick search through the Melville editions at the American Antiquarian Society turned up only one such mark, which I discuss in my conclusion.

12. The first English edition of *Typee* was titled *Narrative of a Four Months' Residence among the Natives of a Valley of the Marquesas Islands; or, A Peep at Polynesian Life*, which immediately gives a slightly different impression, emphasizing the narrative aspect, than does the full American title. Melville probably had nothing to do with these differences, preferring the title *Typee* (see Howard 284).

13. Ezra Greenspan, "Evert Duyckinck and the History of Wiley and Putnam's Library of American Books," *American Literature* 64 (1992): 678.

14. Greenspan 682–83.

15. Baym, *Novels* 63.

16. Herman Melville, "Hawthorne and His Mosses," Harrison Hayford, Alma A. MacDougall, G. Thomas Tanselle, and others, *The Piazza Tales and Other Prose Pieces, 1839–1860* (Evanston and Chicago: Northwestern UP and the Newberry Library, 1987) 251.

17. Greenspan 689–90.

18. In these ads, did the publishers feel a twinge of cognitive dissonance when they placed pieces by "Mrs. C. M. Kirkland" (*Western Clearings*) or by "S. Margaret Fuller" (*Papers on Literature and Art*) among those "written by men of genius"? I suspect that the phrase "men of genius" was intended to evoke a general sense of value rather than any notion as specific as "brilliant human of the male gender."

19. Howard 286–300.

20. Gerald Graff, "Narrative and the Unofficial Interpretive Culture," James Phelan, ed., *Reading Narrative: Form, Ethics, Ideology* (Columbus: Ohio State UP, 1989) 3–11.

21. Baym, *Novels* 250.

22. Rabinowitz suggests that most readers are concerned to identify an authorial intent (30); I would broaden this suggestion to say that readers—general as well as academic—begin by making assumptions about the author's identity and about the genre. Such broadening is supported by Baym's study of novel reviewing, by Arac's discussion of Melville's probably conscious consideration of the role of action in a novel (a consideration his audience might have shared), by Lodge's claim that readers need to assume the existence of a "creative mind" behind the text, and by many other historians and theorists of literature. My point is that the "intentional fallacy" is only a problem from a New Critical perspective. No reception study can proceed without assumptions about how readers approach books, and it seems clear that readers want to attach any sort of text to a human purpose. We still need to know how important this aspect of the reading experience is relative to readers' assumptions about genre, to their knowledge about the actual author, and to other components of the experience. In fact I would suggest that neither the "rhetorical hermeneutics" described by Mailloux nor any other variety of historical/rhetorical study can get very far without a theory of reading, which still

remains to be developed. See Rabinowitz, *Before Reading;* Baym, *Novels;* Jonathan Arac, "'A Romantic Book': *Moby-Dick* and Novel Agency," *boundary 2* 17 (1990): 40–59; David Lodge, "After Bakhtin," *The Linguistics of Writing: Arguments between Language and Literature,* ed. Nigel Fabb, Derek Attridge, Alan Durant, Colin McCabe (New York: Methuen, 1987) 89–102; Steven Mailloux, *Rhetorical Power* (Ithaca: Cornell UP, 1989).

23. Howard 278. What the staff readers at Harpers' meant by "true" and "of value" Howard doesn't say, but the readers were probably having a problem similar to the one Murray had with the book, that it was too well written to be the actual autobiography of a sailor. If it was not true in that sense, then it could not be valuable; it would be mere fiction.

24. The historian who enjoys running the clock backwards may speculate on whether this ad's quotation from the preface of *Mardi* stands as advance notice of *Moby-Dick*.

25. John Wenke, "Ontological Heroics: Melville's Philosophical Art," *A Companion to Melville Studies,* ed. John Bryant (New York, Westport, London: Greenwood P, 1986) 567–601.

26. Charvat 233.

27. This broadening is described and interpreted by, among others, Nina Baym, "Melville's Quarrel with Fiction," *PMLA* 94 (1979): 921; Charvat; Michael Kearns, "How to Read *The Confidence-Man,*" *ESQ* 36 (1990): 209–37; Stephen Railton, *Authorship and Audience: Literary Performance in the American Renaissance* (Princeton: Princeton UP, 1991).

28. Bryan Short, *Cast By Means of Figures: Herman Melville's Rhetorical Development* (Amherst: U of Massachusetts P, 1992) 41.

29. Instead of seeing *Mardi* as breaking the implied contract, Kenneth Dauber asserts that "Melville keeps faith with his readers, come what may. He takes, as authorizing his work, the assent of his audience to his right of authorship despite his differences with it" (*The Idea of Authorship in America: Democratic Poetics from Franklin to Melville* [Madison: U of Wisconsin P, 1990] 210). It is a fascinating question, what nineteenth-century American writers, or indeed writers of any era, take as authorizing their work, their right to come before the public and ask not only for an ear but an income. To answer this question requires more than looking at reviews, the life, and the statements in the books; Dauber seriously oversimplifies the authorizing of Melville by applying uncautiously the paradigm of "democratic poetics."

30. Charvat 233.

31. *Billy Budd* stands as a fascinating coda to Melville's life as a writer of prose fiction, but it lies outside the scope of this study of how the tangible details surrounding the publication of Melville's works influenced the reception of these works.

32. For details on these sales see Merton M. Sealts, Jr., "Historical Note," Harrison Hayford, Alma A. MacDougall, G. Thomas Tanselle, and others,

eds., *The Piazza Tales and Other Prose Pieces, 1839–1860* (Evanston and Chicago: Northwestern UP and the Newberry Library, 1987) 498–514.

33. Mailloux 144–45.

34. Short passim.

35. "A Thought on Book-Binding," Harrison Hayford, Alma A. MacDougall, G. Thomas Tanselle, and others, eds., *The Piazza Tales and Other Prose Pieces, 1839–1860* (Evanston and Chicago: Northwestern UP and the Newberry Library, 1987) 237.

Judging Literary Books by Their Covers: House Styles, Ticknor and Fields, and Literary Promotion

JEFFREY D. GROVES

WRITING FOR THE New York *Literary World* in 1850, Herman Melville complained that there was a "sad lack of invention in most of our bookbinders." While publishers' bindings occasionally displayed some "clever device" to catch the eye of the reader, generally they tended to bear little or no relationship in terms of color, material, or design to the literature they contained. Rather than being cased in generic "sober hued muslin," Melville playfully averred, "books should be appropriately apparelled. Their bindings should indicate and distinguish their various characters."[1]

Melville's prescription—that a book's cover should function as a sign of distinction—paralleled the growing realization on the part of mid-nineteenth-century publishers that they could achieve such a qualitative statement through the appearance of their books. The perfection of case binding in the 1820s and 1830s had given publishers the chance to design uniform exteriors for their books, an opportunity rarely available before the nineteenth century when books were typically sold without permanent covers to be bound later to the tastes of retailers or purchasers.[2] As Ruari McLean points out, "the profession of publishing was beginning to take its modern shape: men were emerging who commissioned books to meet commercial needs . . . and who, having created the contents, gave thought also to their appearance."[3] Having previously been able to identify themselves only on the title pages of their books, publishers could now utilize cardboard, cloth, and decorative stamping to create edition bindings, uniform exteriors that characterized many of their publications visually and potentially distinguished them from the products of a rival publisher.[4]

In fact, while Melville was calling for increased attention to the external design of books, publishers were already utilizing recently developed binding techniques to create what are often called "house styles," uniform bindings that, rather than being associated only with particular titles or editions, were used for many of the books published by a single house.[5] Such bindings became signs—even advertisements—for the publisher: the repeated design alerted consumers, almost as surely as the publisher's name on the spine or the title page, about who had produced a particular book. Given sufficient publisher reputation and prestige, a house style also communicated a message of literary quality: if some of the books brought out by a publisher achieved canonical status, and the external design of most of the publisher's books looked identical, then the intended message from producer to consumer seems to have been that, like their appearance, the quality of the publisher's books was consistent. Moreover, the development of house styles as texts for communicating such value judgments was historically concurrent with publishers' increasing sophistication in literary promotion, and the synthesis of book design and promotion encouraged consumers to read bindings as guarantors that literary quality awaited within.

Unfortunately, the signatory, communicative aspects of nineteenth-century book bindings have too often been missed by literary historians and scholars. Despite two decades of celebrating textuality, contemporary critics usually fail to acknowledge that a binding is itself a textual element, not just the container for a text. As G. Thomas Tanselle laments, "Most readers, if they pay any attention at all to the physical features of the books they read, do not connect those details to their attempt at associating meaning with the verbal texts they find in books."[6] While recent scholarship and an *MLA Newsletter* survey[7] suggest that at least some readers are coming to understand material and verbal texts as interdependent constructs, critics and historians in general need reminding that books are "texts which have been given a particular physical form."[8]

Charting the relationship of form to meaning is necessarily a historicist project that entails interpreting how books in their total structure—binding as well as printed text—were devised and interpreted by their original producers and consumers.[9] Analyzing mass-produced binding designs for literary texts urges generalizations both about how books were understood in a given time and culture and about how "literature" as an embodiment of cultural power was fashioned and maintained. A book bound for the customer might reveal a great deal about a bookbinder, a book buyer, or the prevailing tastes of a given period, but a binding commissioned and perhaps designed by a nineteenth-century publisher lays open an attempt to feel the pulse of hundreds or thousands of buyers at once, both to perceive and to shape their notion of what "literature" meant and looked like. The decision to produce house styles discloses assumptions about growing national and international markets, about the creation and transmission of literary value, and sometimes about how literary canons were formed. As D. F. McKenzie argues, "In the pursuit of historical meanings, we move from the most minute feature of the material form of the book to questions of authorial, literary and social context."[10]

One of the firms that made a significant use of house styles was Ticknor and Fields of Boston, the most prestigious literary house in the United States during the mid-nineteenth century. Ticknor and Fields published Browning, De Quincey, Dickens, Emerson, Holmes, Longfellow, Lowell, Tennyson, Thoreau, Stowe, and Whittier, as well as many other once-prominent authors.[11] Their two famous house styles, the brown cover and the blue and gold, sold well and were often commented on during the 1850s; when tied to the development of literary promotion during that decade, these two styles demonstrate how literary books could in fact be judged by their covers.[12]

∾ TICKNOR AND FIELDS'S ∾
BROWN COVERS

In 1850, the same year that Melville published his thoughts on book binding, Ticknor and Fields issued the first American edition of Tennyson's *In Memoriam*.[13] In their advertisements for this volume, they noted that it was "uniform" with their 1848 edition of Tennyson's *The Princess*.[14] The "uniform" designation referred to the way the books were bound and suggests that, at least to the publisher's way of thinking, how those books looked on a shelf was a serious issue. In fact, the visual appeal and consistency of Ticknor and Fields publications seemed so important to the firm's owners that the same binding that covered Tennyson's poetry had by 1850 become the standard binding for a majority of the house's books.[15] The firm, it should be noted, used many other binding designs for its books during this period, and like other major publishers it offered specialty bindings to its customers. Indeed, as its catalogues indicate, Ticknor and Fields books could be purchased in several "extra" formats: with gilt edges, gilt stamping on the sides, or colors other than their regular brown. Buyers, of course, paid extra for these luxuries. However, as John Pye notes, "The majority of the books in any collection of Ticknor and Fields imprints will be in their classic style of binding. . . . Then as now, it was a symbol of the quality contained therein."[16] Such a profusion on the market of visually similar books meant that buyers of literary texts could identify a Ticknor and Fields book at a glance, which was certainly a factor contributing to the firm's celebrity.[17]

The brown cover design consisted of several components. Most important, the cloth used was dark brown with fine vertical ribs. Although there were slight variations in size, the bindings of the brown covers typically measured 5 by 7 inches. The spine was divided into panels by blind-stamped double rules, with the title and author's name gold-stamped in the second panel from the top and the publisher's imprint gold-stamped at the foot (see Illustration 1). The sides were blind-stamped with a rule frame, floral cornerpieces, and a central, ornately stylized floral pattern (see Illustration 2). Not as elaborate or flashy as some contemporary bindings, the brown cover came to suggest gravity, elegance, and good taste. However, though it was not ostentatious, the binding remained eminently identifiable on a retailer's shelf.

The brown cover bindings were very popular with readers and reviewers, and the firm utilized the design for many years. Warren S. Tryon suggests "It was in the binding of books that Ticknor & Company's volumes were most distinctive,"[18] and the nineteenth-century book-buying public bears out that generalization. William Dean Howells "loved the plain brown cloth" of Ticknor and Fields books.[19] A writer for the Boston *Republican,* reviewing James Russell Lowell's *Complete Poetical Works,* enunciated a common opinion when he stated, "These volumes are got up in the neat and elegant style that eminently distinguishes the publications of this House."[20]

James T. Fields, the junior partner of the firm, almost certainly helped to design the brown covers. His younger brother George worked for Benjamin Bradley and Company, the firm that bound most of

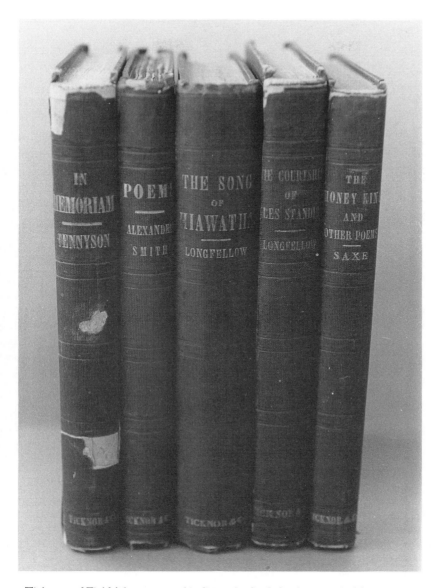

1. Ticknor and Fields's brown cover bindings, the firm's first house style. Tennyson's *In Memoriam* (far left) dates from 1850, Saxe's *The Money King* (far right) from 1860. Although they span a decade, the bindings for all these books share an identical design.

Ticknor and Fields's books in the 1840s and early 1850s,[21] and so Fields had a close personal as well as professional relationship with the bindery. Moreover, the brown cover style reflects Fields's anglophilic tastes, for he "relied heavily on the volumes of the London publishers, especially Edward Moxon, as his models."[22] Many English publishers, like

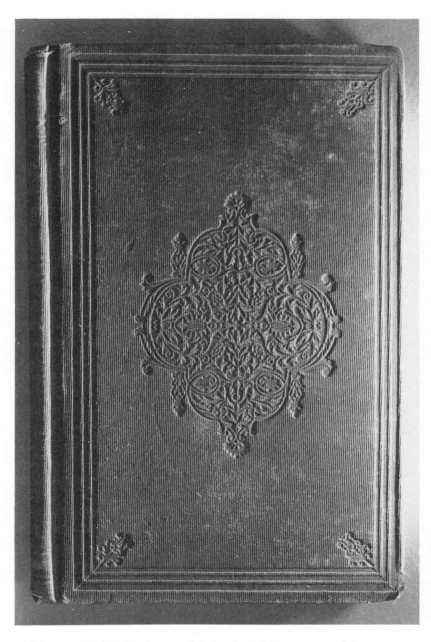

2. Ticknor and Fields's blind-stamped design for their brown cover editions.

Moxon, Murray, and Pickering, brought out books in the 1840s that were similar in volume size and spine design to the standard Ticknor and Fields binding; any number of their publications could have served as models for Fields as he worked to create a visual link between books published in Boston and the celebrated literary works published by prestigious English houses.

Another appeal to the visual prestige of English editions is made by the blind-stamped design so closely associated with the brown cover books (see Illustration 2). This design is based on Macaulay's *Lays of Ancient Rome*, published in London by Longman, Brown, Green, and Longmans in 1842.[23] The Macaulay book, which like a Ticknor and Fields volume is bound in a brown, fine-ribbed cloth, has a centered cover ornament inside a decorative frame. The frame is noticeably different from the one on Ticknor and Fields's books covers, but the ornament in the center looks almost exactly like that manufactured for the Boston firm several years later. In fact, except for a slight difference in size, there are no significant variations between the original design and the American copy. As this borrowing suggests, the similar appearance of an English and an American book could forge an iconic connection between an established national literary tradition and a fledgling one.

When it was first conceived, the English design of the brown cover editions was meant to impart a certain status to Ticknor and Fields books, but the design quickly became so identified with the firm and the popular authors it published that the house style acquired a prestige of its own.[24] The brown cover design thus succeeded in conveying a distinctive image of the firm and was retained for some editions long after the style itself was out of fashion, and long after the firm itself had begun binding most of its books in very different looking covers.[25] For instance, Ticknor and Fields's celebrated edition of Thomas De Quincey's writings began publication in 1850 and was bound in brown cover style (see Illustration 3).[26] In 1874, the De Quincey series was still being bound in brown cloth even though Ticknor had died in 1864 and Fields had sold out to his junior partner, James R. Osgood, in 1871.

Twenty-four years is a protracted life for a binding design, but there are at least three reasons why Osgood continued what his predecessor had initiated a quarter of a century before. First, the De Quincey edition was a very well-known series, being the first complete collection of the author's writings published on either side of the Atlantic. The buying public knew this work, and they knew what it should look like.

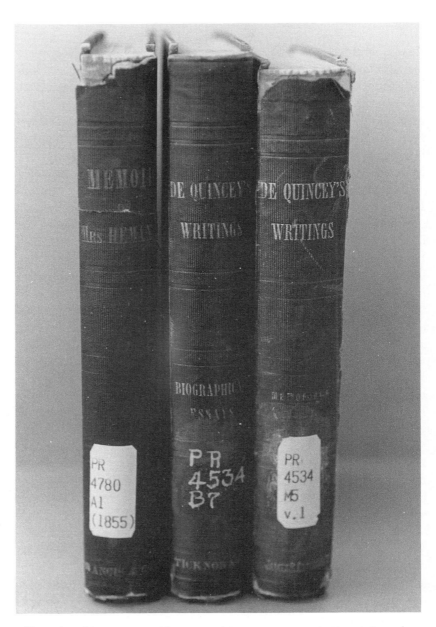

3. Examples of the prestige and longevity of the brown cover style. From left to right: an imitation brown cover, *Memoir of the Life and Writings of Felicia Hemans* (published by C. S. Francis, 1855); an authentic brown cover, Thomas De Quincey's *Biographical Essays* (Ticknor and Fields, 1861); and a brown cover used by a successor firm to Ticknor and Fields for De Quincey's *Memorials and Other Papers* (James R. Osgood, 1874).

Second, in the 1860s and 1870s some owners of a partial De Quincey set might have wanted to purchase missing volumes in the uniform binding, and this desire for visual consistency might have prompted the publisher to continue binding volumes of the edition in the brown cover. Third, utilizing the brown cover linked Osgood visually and promotionally to the success of the firm whose book list he had inherited; again, the brown cover functioned as an advertisement for literary quality.[27]

The prestige of the brown covers became so affixed to Ticknor and Fields that their own bindings, begun as imitations, themselves became models for other American publishers, some of whom imitated the binding very closely. For instance, a book published in 1855 by C. S. Francis, *Memoir of the Life and Writings of Felicia Hemans* (see Illustration 3), copies certain elements of the brown cover style exactly: the spine, including panel and rule design, is the same; the fine-ribbed brown cloth is a match; and the frame surrounding the front and back blind-stamped design is identical to the brown covers, although the central design itself is different. Such imitations were not meant merely to fool consumers into buying books; rather, the primary exchange was one of cultural capital. In a sense, this imitation, like Fields's imitations of English bindings, is a gesture toward literary greatness: if the Hemans volume were visually linked with Ticknor and Fields's stable of prestigious authors, then it gained status through the association.[28]

Nathaniel Parker Willis's relationship with Ticknor and Fields further attests to the prestige of the brown cover. Willis is now best known through *Ruth Hall*, his sister Fanny Fern's novel in which he is satirized as the character Hyacinth Ellet, but in the mid-nineteenth century he was one of the leading poets and journalists in the United States. Not bashful when seeking either monetary gain or literary distinction, Willis in 1849 wrote to Fields requesting that Ticknor and Fields bring out a collection of his plays: "Now, your press is the announcing-room of the country's Court of Poetry, and King People looks there for expected comers. . . . I should, of course, like the Edition, of your handsome fashion."[29] Fields declined the request, but Willis did not give up easily. In 1853 he again wrote to Fields, this time about the possible publication of several books:

> Now Scribner would take . . . my "Out-doors at Idlewild" on terms fair enough—but, to confess an undemocratic feeling,—the "society" is better at your corner. I would rather come out under your imprint, from the Company I should keep. . . .

> I feel that I am entering on a rising & new round of my ladder, & want
> to be well god-father'd—& your house is now the pleasantest to an
> author's pride.[30]

Sadly for him, Willis was never able to convince Ticknor and Fields to
publish his works. His letters suggest, however, a connection between
"the society" at Ticknor and Fields and the "handsome editions" of
their publications. The latter is the physical sign of "an author's pride,"
an advertisement ensuring that a book belongs to "the country's Court
of Poetry."[31] Willis's desire to have his work appear within a Ticknor and Fields brown cover demonstrates that the outside of a cloth-
covered book had become an effective space—made available by nineteenth-century developments in bookbinding—for literary promotion.

∾ THE BLUE AND GOLD EDITIONS ∾

In 1856, Ticknor and Fields introduced a second house style, the blue
and gold cover. Like the brown cover, this design was modeled on
English books.[32] The blue and gold books were characterized by their
deep blue cloth and their gold page edges and gold-stamped spine (see
Illustration 4). In place of the fine ribs that dignified the brown covers,
the cloth chosen for the blue and golds featured a flashy, diagonal wave
pattern. The books were conceived as pocket editions, and the covers
measured approximately $3^3/4$ by $5^3/4$ inches. Their spines were gold-
stamped for more than half their length with an intricate floral ornament that framed the title and author's name (see Illustration 5).
The "Ticknor & Co." imprint, in gold, stood at the foot of the spine.
Like the brown covers, the blue and golds bore an identifiable blind-
stamped design on the front and back covers (see Illustration 6).

The first book issued in the blue and gold format was Tennyson's
Poems in 1856.[33] In its first year of release, over eleven thousand copies
of the book were printed,[34] a figure that justifies labeling the new house
style a success. The press was as enthusiastic about the new design as
the buying public. A reviewer for the New York *Daily Tribune* opined:

> Every admirer of Tennyson will rejoice in this beautiful pocket edition
> of his favorite poet. Within the compass of a brief volume, which can be
> taken without inconvenience on a journey or on a walk, are comprised all
> the poems which have placed Tennyson on such a lofty eminence among
> the contemporary bards of England. Immortality in miniature was never
> more excellently presented.[35]

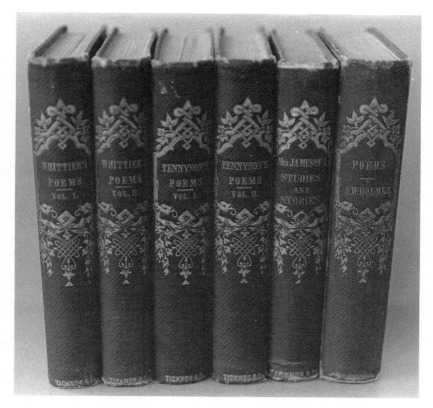

4. Ticknor and Fields's blue and gold bindings, the firm's second house style, introduced in 1856.

A reviewer for *Putnam's Monthly* called the edition "convenient" and "beautifully printed and bound," and went on to add that "the poems of one of the truest poets that ever illustrated our language, may [now] be had for the price of the last worthless novel."[36] The format of the blue and gold books caused the editor of *The Knickerbocker* to gush, "how exquisite they are, in the 'first appeal, which is to the eye,'"[37] and a writer for *Ballou's Pictorial* christened the volumes "gem-books."[38]

While a few of Ticknor and Fields's immediate associates—most notably Henry O. Houghton[39]—may have thought the binding was garish, most figures associated with the house felt the blue and golds were striking. In a letter to Fields, Sophia Hawthorne exclaimed of the new house style, "you have surpassed yourself in the beauty of its execution."[40] John Greenleaf Whittier wrote that he liked the new edition "exceedingly," and he let his publisher know that he hoped "some means could be devised to get my verses into somewhat similar

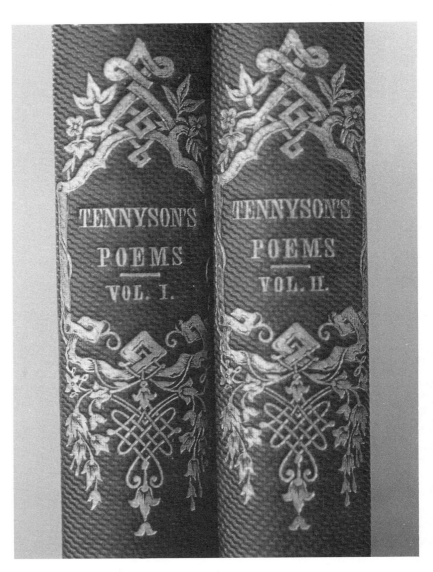

5. Detail of the blue and gold spine design.

shape." Fields obliged, and a blue and gold edition of Whittier's poetry appeared in 1857.[41] Several house authors wrote poems that either alluded to or directly addressed the blue and gold format. Oliver Wendell Holmes used the binding as a symbol for worldly beauty in a prefatory poem to his collection: "How long before your blue and gold / Shall fade and whiten in the dust?"[42] In another prefatory poem, Bayard Taylor asked of the blue and gold design, "Shall this an emblem be of

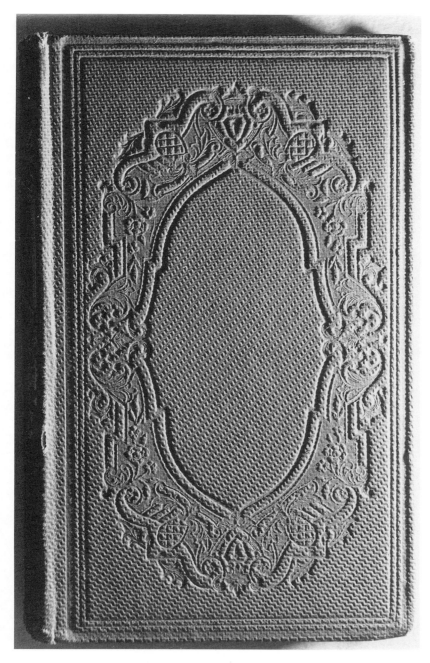

6. Ticknor and Fields's blind-stamped design for their blue and gold editions.

that blue sky / Wherein are set the golden stars of song?"[43] The most elaborate celebration of the new house style, a thirty-two-line poem by George S. Hillard addressed to James T. Fields, was quickly added to the front of the second printing of Tennyson:[44]

> When your new Tennyson I hold, dear friend,
> Where blue and gold, like sky and sunbeam, blend,—
> A fairy tome—of not too large a grasp
> For queen Titania's dainty hand to clasp,—
> I feel fresh truth in the old saying wise,
> That greatest worth in smallest parcel lies.
>
> . . . .
>
> And thanks to you, who put this precious wine,
> Red from the poet's heart, in flasks so fine,
> The hand may clasp it, and the pocket hold;—
> A casket small, but filled with perfect gold.

Despite the new binding's popularity with consumers, the press, and with authors, the most telling index of its success resides in the many imitations of the blue and gold by other publishers who wanted a share of Ticknor and Fields's cachet. Other important houses in Boston, Philadelphia, and New York—Little, Brown, Appleton, Miller, Francis, Scribner—began to issue books in blue and gold almost immediately after Ticknor and Fields's release of Tennyson.[45] In fact, the imitations appeared in such quantity that the phrase "blue and gold" became almost dissociated from the firm that originated the design, evolving instead into a generic term for a pocket edition bound in this style by any publisher.[46]

Ticknor and Fields fought this tendency by claiming that their blue and golds were the best of the genre. For instance, when they published a blue and gold edition of Gerald Massey's *Poems,* they included a letter from the poet to Fields that applauded both the format and the publishing house: "[O]f all pocket editions I think yours the choicest and am proud to find myself in its good company. The Blue and Gold are true colors also to sail under in crossing the Atlantic, and I desire to thank your firm for their fair and generous dealing with myself, and for their manner of getting up a bonny little book."[47] In printing this encomium at the front of Massey's book, Ticknor and Fields coyly advertised the virtues of their own firm under the auspices of a house author's pen.

Little, Brown's "Pocket Edition of the Poets, in Blue and Gold" was the most extensive imitation of the Ticknor and Fields format (see

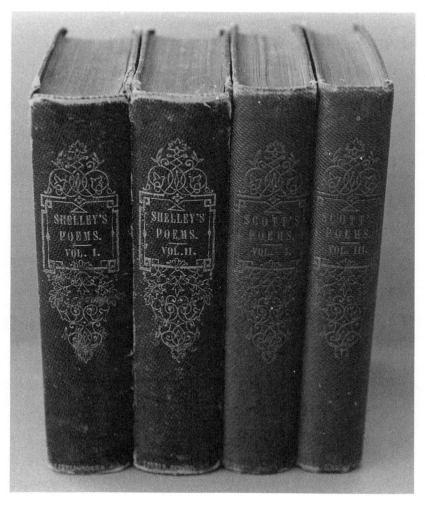

7. Little, Brown's blue and gold books, imitations of the Ticknor and Fields house style. Both the Shelley and the Byron editions appeared in 1857.

Illustration 7). By 1857, the works of Campbell, Hood, Scott, and Shelley were in print, and those of Coleridge, Keats, Milton, and Pope were advertised as in press.[48] The Little, Brown binding almost exactly copied Ticknor and Fields's original blue and gold, the 1856 Tennyson, which had a different spine design than subsequent issues of the same text. (For the design Ticknor and Fields used from 1857 on, see Illustration 4.) The same blind-stamped design was used on the front and back covers. The only significant difference between the blue and gold books produced by these two Boston houses was the imprint at the foot of the spine. Other publishers also appropriated the prestige of the Ticknor

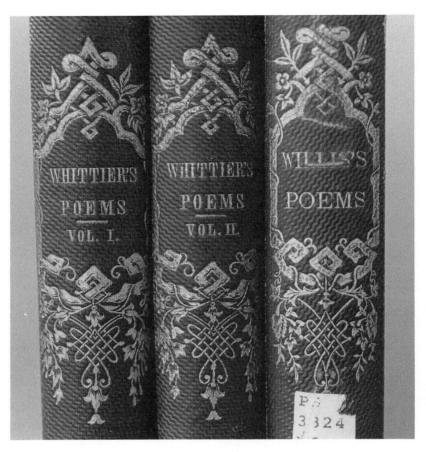

8. Next to two Ticknor and Fields blue and golds, another imitation, N. P. Willis's *Poems* (Clark, Austin, Maynard, 1861).

and Fields binding by almost precisely imitating it. Nathaniel Parker Willis, for instance, who had once begged Fields to publish him in the firm's "handsome fashion," finally saw his name associated with a Ticknor and Fields house style, only the book in question, Willis's *Poems*, was published by Clark, Austin, Maynard (see Illustration 8).

The prestige of the blue and gold editions was so great that in at least one case Ticknor and Fields attempted to transfer it to a book of a different size. When Tennyson's *Enoch Arden* was published in 1865, Ticknor and Fields released it in both blue and gold and a new binding style. The latter was the same size as the old brown cover but utilized a very different design and cloth (see Illustration 9). However, even though the two books were different in size, and even though they were printed from different plates, they shared the decorative title frame

9. Repeated spine design on two different formats of Tennyson's *Enoch Arden*, both published by Ticknor and Fields in 1865.

featured on the spines of blue and gold editions. The eyes of con-sumers, trained to recognize the blue and gold design, could now asso-ciate it and the status it carried with a new binding.

❧ HOUSE STYLES ❧
AND LITERARY PROMOTION

In the decade following 1850, Ticknor and Fields became a leader in publisher promotion of literary wares. William Charvat points out that in the second quarter of the nineteenth century, publishers began to shed their local sensibilities and seek wider distribution and readership for their products.[49] To accomplish such a task, new and improved methods of publicity were needed to develop national markets. Pub-lishers began to systematize their network of newspaper and journal contacts so that their books would be reviewed; they founded or ac-quired house journals in which they could publicize their own titles; they sent out catalogues of their complete book lists to retailers; and they printed "shew bills"—posters for new books that were distributed to booksellers for display in their stores. In short, they took advantage of any possible avenue for increasing the visibility and prestige (and hence the saleability) of their books and their firm. Ticknor and Fields was in the forefront of these efforts, and James T. Fields was the acknowledged master; while he "may have been neither the first nor the only publisher to recognize the value of promotional ideas for the successful dissemination of books . . . he was their outstanding exemplar."[50]

Given this development, it is not then surprising that book covers came to be seen as a kind of advertising space.[51] While a binding format might not communicate in a direct, denotative way like a shew bill, a newspaper advertisement, an inserted booklist, or a printed cata-logue, it could nonetheless powerfully imply certain notions about quality and value. In such a context, it is impossible not to read the Ticknor and Fields house styles as visual signs crafted and repeated to encourage consumers to associate good literature with specific binding designs.

In his biography of Fields, *Parnassus Corner*, Tryon comes close to making this point: "An aspect of publishing which was . . . pleasant to Fields was his role in making up the format of the books the house published. Undeniably this problem was related to promoting books, for there was a prestige value in books of distinction, but at the same time Fields possessed a true feeling for good formats which bore no relation to his promotional activities."[52] Tryon clearly understands the linkage between literary promotion and book design, and yet his opposition of "promotional activities" and "good formats" is troubling for it suggests that the two are easily separable. Yet the communicability of Ticknor and Fields's house styles belies such a strongly stated contrast. For major publishers with wide-ranging markets, by 1850 binding was becoming a promotional tool; by 1860 binding and literary promotion were dynamically linked.

Of course, bindings did not communicate only with readers looking for quality literary texts; then as now, a consumer might buy a book for reasons other than literary appreciation. In considering the profusion of "extra" bindings offered by nineteenth-century publishers, Ronald Zboray asks:

> How many people bought books and never intended that they or anyone else would read them? . . . A number of books in ornately gilded morocco upon the mantelpiece or in a sideboard bookcase testified to the owner's expensive taste in selecting fine commodities. . . . The conspicuous consumption of books during the era meant that some readers preferred owing books over reading them.[53]

A similar point might be made for Ticknor and Fields's house styles: they presented a prestigious spine to the world and so could function as status statements on a bookshelf. But whether bindings were treated as containers for textuality or as furniture, they remained textual themselves. As sign systems, house styles were constructed to communicate specific information; in the case of Ticknor and Fields, they served to condition the ways in which consumers thought about literature, about how it looked as a total structure, not just how it appeared on the individual page.

Bindings were an important component of textual production and consumption in the nineteenth century. Their design mattered to publishers, to authors, and to readers, and it is therefore incumbent on modern audiences to remember that technological developments changed the face of nineteenth-century publishing, that this change brought about new relationships between the producers and consumers of literary texts, and that these relationships, played out on a mass-marketing scale, encouraged the consolidation and extension of a national literary culture. If we are to understand literature in its historical context—if we are to comprehend what the category "literature" meant in the nineteenth century—then we must take pains to read the material text.

∾ NOTES ∾

I would like to thank Michael Winship for his comments on this essay and his assistance in describing the physical details of Ticknor and Fields's house styles. Some of the research for this essay was carried out in the Pye Collection of Ticknor and Fields Imprints, Wilson Library, University of North Carolina at Chapel Hill; I am indebted to the librarians at Wilson Library for their assistance and to the National Endowment for the Humanities for a travel grant that partially funded my visit.

1. Herman Melville, "A Thought on Book-Binding," *The Piazza Tales and Other Prose Pieces, 1839–1860,* ed. Harrison Hayford, Alma A. MacDougall, and G. Thomas Tanselle (Evanston and Chicago: Northwestern UP and the Newberry Library, 1987) 237–38. Melville's lighthearted response to the uninspired cover of a new edition of Cooper's *The Red Rover* was not aimed at those artisans who bound books to order for private customers. As his mention of "Mr. Putnam" in the first sentence of his essay makes clear, Melville's critique is directed toward mass-produced bindings manufactured for large publishing firms.

2. Sue Allen notes, "The use of cloth in the late 1820s and the perfection of the stamping press in the early 1830s opened the way to instant design and to the issuing by publishers of uniform editions, all bound in the same format" (*Victorian Bookbindings: A Pictorial Survey,* rev. ed. [Chicago: U of Chicago P, 1976] 1–2). Mass utilization of edition binding proceeded from several developments in cloth manufacturing, binding technology, and publisher finances. Concerning these developments, see Allen; Jacob Blanck, *Bibliography of American Literature,* vol. 1 (New Haven: Yale UP, 1955) xxviii–xxxv; John Carter, *The Origins of Publishers' Cloth Binding* (N.p.: Rasmussen Press, 1972) and *Publisher's Cloth: An Outline History of Publisher's Binding in England, 1820–1900* (New York: Bowker, 1935); Ruari McLean, *Victorian Publishers' Book-Bindings in Cloth and Leather* (London: Gordon Fraser, 1974); and Joseph W. Rogers, "The Rise of American Edition Binding," *Bookbinding in America,* ed. Hellmut Lehmann-Haupt, rev. ed. (New York: Bowker, 1967). Carter points out that the assumption by publishers of binding design affected "the delicately adjusted balance of financial responsibility for a finished book. It . . . threw back on the publisher a function of book production which had hitherto lain in the province of the retailer" (*Publisher's Cloth* 11).

3. McLean 12.

4. While not all publishers chose to design house styles, by the mid-nineteenth century uniform bindings had become common for a substantial part of most editions (Carter, *Origins* 6). Carter has suggested of the decade following 1850 that it "may fairly claim not only the achievement of supremacy for publisher's cloth, but even the title of its golden age" (*Publisher's Cloth* 34).

5. I use "house style" restrictively throughout this essay to refer only to binding design, although the phrase is often used more generally to refer to the entire design and format of a book—typesetting, punctuation, spelling, and the like.

6. G. Thomas Tanselle, "A Description of Descriptive Bibliography," *Studies in Bibliography* 45 (1992): 4. Tanselle continues: "Presumably many readers do recognize or would quickly do so if they gave thought to the matter that the design of any book is worthy of study as a reflection of the taste of its time, as an indication of the statures of the author and genre represented in it, and as a clue to the nature of the audience expected for it. They would then assume that specialized studies of these matters must exist. . . . In the first of these assumptions they would be correct, but not in the second" (4).

7. See Phyllis Franklin, "Editor's Column," *MLA Newsletter* 24.3 (1992): 3–4.

8. D. F. McKenzie, *Bibliography and the Sociology of Texts* (London: British Library, 1986) 17. For a few examples of recent scholarship that treat the relationship between material and verbal texts, see Crys Armbrust, "Nineteenth-Century Re-Presentations of George Herbert: Publishing History as Critical Embodiment," *Huntington Library Quarterly* 53 (1990); Richard Brodhead, *The School of Hawthorne* (Oxford: Oxford UP, 1986) 48–66; and Cathy Davidson, *Revolution and the Word: The Rise of the Novel in America* (New York: Oxford UP, 1986). Promising that such scholarship will continue to be produced, the American Antiquarian Society has mounted a number of summer seminars (under the aegis of its History of the Book in American Culture program) aimed in part at training scholars of American literature and history in methods for interpreting and describing the material text.

9. Tanselle describes this methodology as "literary sociology," an approach to literary texts "concerned with the physical details that may have affected readers' responses (or that publishers and sometimes authors believed would affect those responses)" ("Textual Criticism and Literary Sociology," *Studies in Bibliography* 44 [1991]: 102). McKenzie outlines a more wide-ranging approach—what he calls "the sociology of texts"—to understanding how "forms effect meaning" (4).

10. McKenzie 14.

11. This impressive list of authors was eventually inherited by one of Ticknor and Fields's successor firms, Houghton, Mifflin. For historical information about Ticknor and Fields, see James C. Austin, *Fields of the Atlantic Monthly: Letters to an Editor, 1861–1870* (San Marino, Calif.: Huntington Library, 1953); Ellen B. Ballou, *The Building of the House: Houghton Mifflin's Formative Years* (Boston: Houghton Mifflin, 1970) 45–55; William Charvat, "James T. Fields and the Beginnings of Book Promotion, 1840–1855," *The Profession of Authorship in America, 1800–1877*, ed. Matthew J. Bruccoli (Columbus: Ohio State UP, 1968); James T. Fields, *Bibliographical Notes and*

Personal Sketches, ed. Annie Adams Fields (Boston: Houghton, Mifflin, 1882) and *Yesterdays with Authors* (Boston: James R. Osgood and Company, 1872); John William Pye, *James T. Fields, Literary Publisher* (Portland, Me.: The Baxter Society, 1987); Warren S. Tryon, *Parnassus Corner: A Life of James T. Fields, Publisher to the Victorians* (Boston: Houghton Mifflin, 1963); Warren S. Tryon and William Charvat, *The Cost Books of Ticknor and Fields* (New York: Bibliographical Society of America, 1949); and Michael Winship, *American Literary Publishing in the Mid-Nineteenth Century: The Business of Ticknor and Fields* (Cambridge: Cambridge UP, 1995).

12. For earlier analyses of these specific house styles, see especially Tryon's brief but suggestive discussions (*Parnassus Corner* 175–77; 228–30), but also Brodhead (55), Pye (16–17; 26–27), and Winship (19–22).

13. For the sake of simplicity, I employ an anachronism. In 1849, "Ticknor and Company" changed its imprint (to acknowledge the two junior partners) to "Ticknor, Reed and Fields." When Reed bowed out in 1854, the firm acquired its most famous name, "Ticknor and Fields," which it kept even after William Ticknor's death in 1864. The firm became "Fields, Osgood" in 1868, and Fields retired from the company in 1871, after which it became "James R. Osgood and Company." In this essay, I refer to the firm from 1848 to 1868 simply as Ticknor and Fields, even though it functioned under three different names during that period.

14. John Olin Eidson, *Tennyson in America: His Reputation and Influence from 1827 to 1858* (Athens, Ga.: U of Georgia P, 1943) 76.

15. Tryon suggests that, "By 1850 the chocolate brown covers, stamped in blind with the delicate, lacy acanthus patterns, front and back, denoted a 'Ticknor book' as surely as did the fine literature printed upon the pages within" (177). Pye notes that, "By the time they published *The Princess* in 1848, the style of binding that would become a trademark of the firm had been fully developed" (16). The brown cover style was not used much beyond the mid-1860s.

16. Pye 17.

17. Reminiscing about Ticknor and Fields in 1915, Henry James wrote, "Publishers' names [in the mid-nineteenth century] had a color and character beyond even those of authors, even those of books themselves" (quoted in Pye 3).

18. Tryon 176.

19. William Dean Howells, *Literary Friends and Acquaintance* (New York: Harper & Brothers, 1911) 41.

20. Quoted in "New Books and New Editions Published by Ticknor, Reed, and Fields," catalogue bound into Alfred Tennyson, *In Memoriam* (Boston: Ticknor, Reed, and Fields, 1850) 14.

21. Pye 17; Tryon 176.

22. Tryon 177. Tryon goes on to point out that, "Fields was frequently

referred to, partly because he published poetry, and partly because his books imitated the English publisher so closely, as 'the American Moxon'" (177). An 1857 notice in *The Knickerbocker*, after praising the "paper, printing, form" of Ticknor and Fields editions, wishes "Success to the Moxons and Murrays of America!" ("Editor's Table," *The Knickerbocker* 50.1 [1857]: 94.)

23. Winship 20.

24. Howells probably had this prestige in mind when he wrote of Ticknor and Fields, "Their imprint was a warrant of quality to the reader and of immortality to the author, so that if I could have had a book issued by them at that day I should now be in the full enjoyment of an undying fame" (13).

25. The color images that accompany Allen's *Victorian Bookbindings: A Pictorial Survey* document the rapidly changing fashions of nineteenth-century bindings, most of which "can . . . be dated to within a few years by their cloth and by their style of decoration" (1). On dating cloth bindings, see also John Carter, *Binding Variants in English Publishing, 1820–1900* (London: Constable, 1932) and Rogers 160.

26. Opposite the title page in the first volume of the Ticknor and Fields De Quincey series, a notice reads: "It is the intention of the Publishers to issue, at intervals, a complete collection of Mr. De Quincey's Writings, uniform with this volume." Since the uniform binding was the typical brown cover, in this case there can be no distinction between a uniform style and a house style. And since the De Quincey collection turned out to be quite popular, the house style got a boost in recognizability by being associated with this prestigious edition.

27. On his title pages, Osgood typically made mention of the fact that his firm was "Late Ticknor & Fields, and Fields, Osgood, & Co." This statement appeared directly below his own imprint, "James R. Osgood and Company."

28. *Ancient Spanish Ballads,* translated by J. G. Lockhart and published in 1856 by Whittemore, Niles, and Hall, is another close imitation of the brown cover binding, though the blind-stamped designs on the front and back covers differ. The imitation is particularly notable because Thomas Niles, a partner in the publishing house, had previously clerked for Ticknor and Fields for more than fifteen years, and thus presumably had been educated as to the promotional value of book bindings. For one of his first publications, Niles stole a march on his former employer by publishing De Quincey's *Klosterheim* (1855) before Ticknor and Fields could bring the book out in their De Quincey series. Niles's firm also imitated the Ticknor and Fields blue and gold format I discuss below when it published *Poems* by Charles Swain in 1857. Shortly after the demise of Whittemore, Niles, and Hall in 1858, Ticknor and Fields brought out its own edition of Lockhart's *Ballads.* For information about Niles, see Raymond L. Kilgour, *Messrs. Roberts Brothers, Publishers* (Ann Arbor: U of Michigan P, 1952).

29. Nathaniel Parker Willis, letter to James T. Fields, 6 April 1849 (Hunt-

ington Library FI 4884). Willis's letters are reproduced by permission of the Huntington Library.

30. Nathaniel Parker Willis, letter to James T. Fields, 27 June 1853 (Huntington Library FI 4880).

31. While Ticknor and Fields was developing its house style, the firm was also including extensive lists of its publications *in* its publications. On both the outside and the inside, the Ticknor and Fields book had become an advertisement, converting the book, in Richard Brodhead's formulation, "from marketed object to marketing act" (55).

32. In the early 1850s, the London firm of Routledge published pocket editions of several American poets, including Holmes, Longfellow, and Lowell. These books were bound in blue cloth with gold ornamentation and edges. They probably served as direct models for Ticknor and Fields's blue and gold design. Pye notes that in 1853 "Routledge had produced a book of poems by John Greenleaf Whittier in a handsome, but compact format. This became the forerunner of Ticknor and Fields's now famous 32mo Blue and Gold series" (26). For further information on the origin of the blue and gold format, see "Boston," *Round Table* 1.9 (1864): 140–41.

33. In 1842, Ticknor and Company became the first American publisher to remunerate Tennyson for an American edition of his work, an unnecessary gesture given the absence of international copyright at that time. Later Ticknor and Fields became Tennyson's official American publisher, and they subsequently printed an excerpt from Tennyson's letter of authorization in all their editions of his poetry: "It is my wish that with Messrs. Ticknor and Fields alone the right of publishing my books in America should rest." (See, for instance, *The Poetical Works of Alfred Tennyson* [Boston: Ticknor and Fields, 1856] iii.)

34. Winship 21.

35. New York *Daily Tribune* 20 June 1856: 3.

36. *Putnam's Monthly* July 1856: 98.

37. "Editor's Table," *The Knickerbocker* July 1857: 94.

38. "Antique Building, Corner of School and Washington Streets," *Ballou's Pictorial* 21 February 1857: 1.

39. Houghton, even though he designed "the size of page and paper" for the blue and golds ("Boston" 140), nonetheless preferred bindings "as plain & simple as the dress of a Quaker maiden" (Ballou 55).

40. Quoted in Tryon 229.

41. John Greenleaf Whittier, *The Letters of John Greenleaf Whittier*, ed. John B. Pickard, vol. 2 (Cambridge, Mass.: Harvard UP, 1975). "Fields quickly prepared to place the rest of his authors in the new format. Before he was done he had published forty-one titles in fifty-seven volumes" (Tryon 229).

42. Oliver Wendell Holmes, *The Poems of Oliver Wendell Holmes* (Boston: Ticknor and Fields, 1862) iii.

43. Bayard Taylor, *The Poems of Bayard Taylor* (Boston: Ticknor and Fields, 1856) [i].

44. Pye 26.

45. Tryon 229–30; Pye 27. An author writing for the *Round Table* in 1864 suggests that these other firms worked to some extent in collaboration with Ticknor and Fields: "Messrs. T. & F.'s list now numbers some thirty-six volumes, and about an equal number of volumes has been issued by other publishers jointly, though not always with the Riverside imprint. Appleton, Francis, Miller, and recently, in conjunction with T. & F., Mr. Putnam, have issued popular books in this shape. By an understanding too, with the origina-tors of the style, Little, Brown & Co. have put into it several of the poets from their annotated [British Poets] series, which being all of them acknowledged classics, and the authors no longer living, they form a companionable link between the favorites of the hour and those whose position is secured from the past" ("Boston" 140). The collaboration between Ticknor and Fields and Putnam resulted in the joint reissue in blue and gold of Washington Irving's *The Sketch-Book of Geoffrey Crayon* (1864), a book that bore both publishers' names on the title page and that associated yet another prominent American writer with Ticknor and Fields.

46. Edmund Clarence Stedman provides an example of "blue and gold" as a generic term. Writing to Richard Henry Stoddard in 1863, he notes that he has just received Thomas Bailey Aldrich's new *Poems,* published in New York by Carleton in a blue and gold format. Stedman comments: "I don't like Blue and Gold in so large type; it looks too much like cheap gilt children's books" (*Life and Letters of Edmund Clarence Stedman,* ed. Laura Stedman and George M. Gould, vol. 1 [New York: Moffat, Yard, 1910] 308). (This comment has often been taken incorrectly to refer directly to Ticknor and Fields's blue and golds, not the Carleton imitation; see Tryon 229, Ballou 54, and Pye 27.) A writer for the *Round Table* also uses "blue and gold" generically at the same time that he argues for the superiority of Ticknor and Fields's bindings and books: "several publishers in New York and Philadelphia have issued some very cheap imita-tions of this 'blue and gold' style, which has hardly, however, affected the character of the originals with buyers of any discrimination. They have rather damaged their own reputation by attempts to foist upon the unsuspecting the spurious for the genuine" ("Boston" 140).

47. Gerald Massey, *Poems* (Boston: James R. Osgood, 1872) v.

48. Little, Brown had initiated a "British Poets" series, edited by Francis J. Child, in 1853 (see *One Hundred Years of Publishing, 1837–1937* [Boston: Little, Brown, 1937] 27; "Boston" 140–41). Texts from this series became the basis for the "Pocket Edition of the Poets, in Blue and Gold."

49. Charvat 76–78.

50. Tryon 160. On Fields's promotional efforts and abilities, see Brodhead (48–66), Charvat, and Tryon (178–204). Brodhead argues that Fields's promo-

tional inventions "include the production features he found to stamp on his books, features that both mark them off as separate from other books and confer on them an air of distinction—features like the Ticknor and Fields format of conspicuously good paper and handsome brown boards, promising that what is inside is serious and well-made; or like the Ticknor and Fields imprint itself, which came, through its association with 'quality' authors, to create the presumption of quality in the books it adorned" (55).

51. While I am arguing that cloth bindings functioned as a kind of advertisement for the publishing firm, it should be noted that books issued by Ticknor and Fields in wrappers (paper covers) often had literal advertisements printed on them. For instance, some copies of Whittier's *Leaves from Margaret Smith's Journal* (1849) in wrappers feature advertisements on the outside back cover for Oliver Wendell Holmes's *Poems*. Advertisements on wrappers predate the advent of edition binding and may be considered precursors to the binding practices I trace here.

52. Tryon 175.

53. Ronald Zboray, "Antebellum Reading and the Ironies of Technological Innovation," *American Quarterly* 40 (1988): 74.

Literature in Newsprint: Antebellum Family Newspapers and the Uses of Reading

AMY M. THOMAS

R EADERS OF THE 15 SEPTEMBER 1852 issue of the *Spirit of the Age*, a family newspaper published in Raleigh, North Carolina, perhaps recognized their thoughts about the merits of subscribing to the *Age* in a dialogue contained in the fictional story "Please Stop My Paper":

> "What do you get for your money? A large, closely printed useful sheet; giving you the news of the week, a large amount of miscellaneous reading—philosophical and grave, and humorous—And you can afford one dollar and a half for such a paper a whole year."
>
> "On second thought, I perceive that a good newspaper is about the cheapest thing a man can have. He gets more reading for his money than he can in any other way."[1]

The points advanced here explain the success of the *Age*, one of the best-selling North Carolina newspapers during the 1850s, and of its genre, the numerous weekly publications that flourished after 1825, presenting the eclectic contents of magazines in a newspaper format.[2] The *Age*, like the untitled publication under discussion in "Please Stop My Paper," provided readers with the news and with "philosophical, grave, and humorous" reading material. These varied contents made a family newspaper a "useful sheet" because they fulfilled so many purposes for reading, such as entertainment, moral and intellectual enhancement, and information about local and national communities. All of these needs could be met for $1.50 a year, a lower subscription rate than that of weekly newspapers and monthly magazines in the period, thus offering the reader "more reading for his money."

The low cost of family newspapers was made possible by the economical newsprint format.[3] Yet as the argument of "Please Stop My Paper" implied, a family paper's format could also alienate readers who equated "cheapness" of form with the quality of the publication's contents. "Please Stop My Paper" sought to break this equation by constructing the cheap paper as valuable and useful, giving readers a large amount of high-quality reading material at a low cost. This fictional representation mirrored the actual work that family newspaper editors had to do in order to build a diverse readership for their publications: editors constructed the appearance of family newspapers to embody the value and usefulness of their contents.

The *Spirit of the Age* serves as a useful case study for exploring the relationship between a publication's appearance and readers' purposes for reading. Its high circulation during the 1850s suggests that it was supported by a large base of diverse readers. The paper itself provides two types of evidence for its popularity: the *Age*'s material appearance and contents were revised throughout the 1850s in order to attract new readers; and the paper's editor, Alexander Gorman, used his editorial column to promote these changes and to shape readers' conception of the paper and themselves as readers. Though using self-promotion strategies available to all editors, Gorman was particularly adept at understanding the power of the paper's material appearance to convey to readers a sense of the "usefulness" of its contents.

Ideally, this study would begin with an analysis of readers' responses to the *Age*. Unfortunately, I have not found any private reader records and must attempt to reconstruct reader responses through an analysis of the publication, its contents, appearance, and Gorman's commentary.[4] Current research on mass media "uses and gratifications" provides a conceptual framework for discussing the uses of reading fulfilled by antebellum family newspapers.[5] Numerous studies have shown a variety of motivations for reading. For example, A. Carlos Ruotolo questioned newspaper readers about their motives for reading, suggesting such possible factors as companionship, learning about one's self and environment, confirmation of one's beliefs, social connections, and enjoyment.[6] Each reader reported a combination of motives that clustered to create a dominant orientation or reader "type." Instrumental readers used "the newspaper to get information to be used as a tool for daily living"; opinion makers sought "information to form and compare opinions"; pleasure readers defined newspaper reading "as an enjoyable habitual activity"; ego boosters read "as a means to enhance their self-image"; and scanners read for all of these motives.[7]

Complementing Ruotolo's study, Payne, Severn, and Dozier examined the relationship between readers' motivations and different types of publications. Hypothesizing that a publication's contents determined the motives a reader could fulfill, Payne and his colleagues interviewed readers of two different types of publications, a trade magazine targeted to a specialized professional audience and a general-audience consumer magazine. Trade magazine readers reported stronger motivations for reading to gain information about their environment and to enable them to engage in social interactions than the consumer magazine readers; consumer magazine readers had stronger motivations for entertainment and companionship than trade magazine readers.[8]

These results confirmed the researchers' hypotheses, and they concluded that the "uses of particular media types can be predicted from the content of the medium."[9] However, when reader results are examined not simply to confirm the hypotheses, they suggest that reader motivations are more complex: though trade magazine readers rated information gathering their strongest motive for reading, they also reported reading for pleasure; so, too, consumer magazine readers who read primarily for pleasure also reported reading to gain information for their own use and for use in interacting with others.[10] The motivation patterns of these readers, similar to those of Ruotolo's "scanners," suggest that motivations determined how readers used a publication's content rather than content determining use.

Focusing on readers' social motivations for reading, many researchers have explored the relationship between local newspaper reading and a reader's sense of community ties, hypothesizing that "subscription to and use of media is related to individuals' identity with and attachment to their communities."[11] The study by Viswanath and others of the relationship between community ties and newspaper use in a rural Midwest town found a strong correlation between community involvement and local newspaper subscription: subscribers were more active in voluntary organizations and community politics.[12] Further, people who had networks of friends in the community also had higher rates of local newspaper subscription than respondents lacking such networks. Subscribing to a local newspaper provides readers with information about their community, which creates the foundation for social interaction through their personal networks and, in turn, affects their self-conception or identity as a member of that particular community.

Family newspapers offered antebellum readers an economical way to fulfill these diverse motives for reading. Throughout the 1850s, the *Age*'s annual subscription price remained $1.50, with a fifty-cent discount for "clubs" of five or more subscribers. Other weekly North Carolina newspapers typically charged two dollars for a year's subscription, and northern monthly magazines such as *Harper's* and *Godey's Lady's Book* charged two or three dollars. The history of newspaper and magazine publishing in antebellum North Carolina testifies to the power of economics in affecting readership. The 1850 census reported that North Carolina had the highest rate of illiteracy of any state, and its publishers struggled to create supportive audiences.[13] As Guion Johnson noted, "Of the many newspapers and periodicals established in North Carolina from the opening of the century to the beginning of the Civil War, few lived longer than fifteen or twenty years."[14] Specialized publications, no matter their subject, found it difficult to develop and sustain a large readership. The only literary magazine to publish for any length of time in antebellum North Carolina was the *University of North Carolina Magazine;* established in 1844, it went out of print after one volume, resumed publication in 1852, but failed again when the Civil War began.[15] Temperance journals fared no better, and though many were founded, all were short lived.[16]

Begun as a temperance journal, the *Age* was soon transformed into a family newspaper in an effort to expand its readership. In September 1848, Alexander Gorman and J. B. Whitaker purchased the *Family Visitor,* a "miscellaneous and Temperance newspaper," published in Raleigh, North Carolina.[17] Born in 1814, Gorman learned the newspaper business while working as a printer and foreman for the *Raleigh Register,* one of the state's oldest and most prestigious newspapers.[18] He became the sole proprietor of the *Family Visitor* in June 1849 and reorganized the paper as the *Spirit of the Age: A Family Newspaper— Devoted to Temperance, Morality, Literature, Agriculture, and General Intelligence.* By July 1852, Gorman boasted that the *Age*'s circulation was twice that of any North Carolina newspaper.[19] However, at the end of the same year, the *Age* faced the loss of a key part of its readership: the North Carolina Sons of Temperance, who had adopted the *Age* as their official paper, began to experience a membership decline.[20] Gorman decided to forestall this threatened loss of readers by expanding the *Age*'s appeal to general readers. Gorman kept the *Age*'s multipurpose contents intact but lessened their temperance focus, occasionally adding a new feature or column, and he preserved the paper's general appearance while making occasional changes to show that the paper was "keeping up with the spirit of the age."[21] His efforts to expand the *Age*'s general readership succeeded, and the paper maintained a high circulation until he sold it in 1864 to pursue interests in other publications.[22]

Even a cursory glance at a copy of the *Spirit of the Age* enables a viewer to experience instantly the powerful appeal of family newspapers. The large size of this "useful sheet," measuring 18 by 24^1/$_2$inches (in comparison to today's *New York Times* of 13^1/$_2$ by 22^1/$_2$), created a format whose openness was inviting to readers. Its four seven-column pages were packed with rich contents, yet at the same time it was a manageable form, unlike the mammoth weeklies whose four-foot page length made it impossible for the reader to hold the text and read it.[23] Readers could quickly scan the contents to determine what was of interest, and the varied lengths of the columns, from two inches to half a page, accommodated readers' varying time and energy for reading. Turning to a favorite feature was easy inasmuch as the *Age*'s editor maintained the paper's basic layout throughout the 1850s; Gorman continually refined the paper's appearance but never dramatically altered the layout, perhaps because he recognized the importance of readers feeling that they were reading a familiar text.

The openness and invitation created by the format was enhanced by the paper's mix of type fonts, which suited the paper's eclectic contents and the diverse readers who could find them of interest. The title appeared in striking black letter type (similar in appearance to today's gothic). This was an eye-catching choice, as most daily and weekly North Carolina newspapers used a plain roman font for their mastheads. This special font embodied the exceptional nature of the "spirit of the age." Yet lest these connotations lead some readers to feel that the paper was intended for an elite audience, a roman font was used in other masthead items including for the volume and issue numbers, place of publication, and date, thereby emphasizing the practical nature of the paper's contents. This blend of fonts appeared throughout the paper, creating a sense of balanced contents, elevated but not elite, useful but not ordinary. The paper's subtitle—"A Family Newspaper Devoted to Temperance, Morality, Literature, Agriculture, and General Intelligence"—reinforced this feeling of democracy of contents and readership as each aspect of the "spirit of the age" affirmed readers' different interests, tastes, and purposes for reading. Finally, this feeling was enhanced simply by the publication's newsprint format, itself a democratic form suggesting that the age's spirit was accessible to and shaped by all people. Readers who were neither familiar nor comfortable with "literary" reading in books and would have found newsprint a welcoming format, while readers suspicious of newsprint's cheapness would have been reassured by the "elevated" aspects of the *Age*'s appearance.

Literary columns dominated the paper's front page, announcing that this was not simply a "news" paper. Throughout the *Age*'s history, literature maintained this prominent position, emphasized by the absence of advertising on the front page.[24] While literature's front-page location suggests that it was crucial for attracting readers, Gorman realized that he could not take for granted readers' respect for a genre whose corrupting powers were still being debated in the culture at large. A 1 April 1857 *Age* column titled "Cheap Literature" responded to critics of fiction:

> They seem to regard cheapness as being synonymous with inferiority. But the one is not consequent upon the other, by any means. . . . Our own *Spirit of the Age*, by its very cheapness, has carried the first ray of light and knowledge into many an obscure and darkened mind, from whence will yet issue a light and glory that will electrify earth and heaven. Bless God for cheap literature.

Gorman presented literature in the *Age* in ways that embodied its "superior" nature. Every issue contained "Choice Literature," works reprinted from other periodicals, and "Original" papers or stories written especially for the *Age*. Using the same mix of fonts as that of the masthead, the literary columns reflected visually the nature of their contents: the headings appeared in black letter type, suggesting literature's moral and intellectual character, while the roman used for authors' names and titles of works emphasized literature's practical nature. So, too, the sense that readers could use this literature in their everyday lives was reinforced by the newsprint format in which it appeared.

And this was exactly what the content of the "moral-toned" literature published in the *Age* did, providing its readers with countless opportunities for moral, spiritual, and intellectual growth.[25] For example, many of the works published in the 5 July 1854 issue explored the theme of developing fortitude of character. The concluding chapter of "Horace West; or, The Effects of 'One, and the First Glass,' " depicted the moral recovery of the title character, whose life had been destroyed by the single drink that led to his obsession with alcohol. His fortunes changed when he met a Son of Temperance, and as the story concluded he was reunited with his wife and young child. "Pulpit Eloquence," excerpts from a sermon by Dr. H. B. Bascomb, discussed the unwavering commitment of early preachers, who "shrank from no trial or investigation of their cause." A sketch titled "Life's Pictures" portrayed a woman whose desire to acquire material possessions like those of her neighbors caused her to lose her "moral balance": "To a certain degree, emulation is beneficial, but when it is perverted, it brings sorrow instead of joy—adversity instead of prosperity."[26] These diverse genres of literature fulfilled readers' desires for self-enhancement, affirmed their values, and at the same time entertained.

Though these needs for reading could be met by countless literary publications, the *Age* satisfied another need that could only be met by publications targeted to a local rather than a national audience: affirming readers' identities as members of a particular community and region. Gorman appealed to these reader needs not through the content but through the presentation of the *Age*'s literature. The content of the literature published in "Choice" and "Original" columns was almost interchangeable; occasionally "original" works were set in the South, but they did not present a uniquely southern interpretation of subject matter and themes.

Instead Gorman appealed to readers' identities as southerners by promoting southern literature, particularly by local authors: "In presenting this no. of the Spirit of the Age to our numerous readers, it is with pride and pleasure that we refer to its many *original* articles of sterling worth and interest."[27] Emphasizing the "local" nature of the original literature, Gorman asked his readers to contribute their writing to the *Age:* "We want well-written Stories, Essays, Familiar letters and Communications generally, for our columns. Ladies and Gentlemen, let us hear from you."[28]

In striking contrast to this extensive promotion, "choice" literature was published in the *Age* without notice. Most of the "choice" works were anonymous, and in the few instances that the work of a nationally known author appeared in the *Age*, Gorman never mentioned these works in his editorial column.[29] Many editors during this period, such as the *New York Ledger*'s Robert Bonner, used authors' national reputations to attract readers.[30] Gorman was unequivocally uninterested in such tactics; rather, the promotional rhetoric of his editorial columns worked to inculcate a sense of regional value and to appeal to readers' regional identification.

Yet the presence of the "Choice Literature" column also demonstrates that Gorman knew his readers valued the work of northern authors and that he must publish such works in order to satisfy their desire to keep up with the "national" literary scene.[31] He met this need and at the same time preserved readers' regional identifications by choosing "Choice Literature" selections that were neutral in their subject matter and themes. For example, the 2 July 1856 issue reprinted an excerpt from Irving's *Life of Washington* which described General Washington settling a snowball fight between northern and southern soldiers during the Revolutionary War. An unusual and amusing example of Gorman's nod to readers' desire for northern literature occurred in 2 January 1852's "Poet's Corner": the lead piece, "By Anthropos" and written for the *Age,* was followed by a notice about the arrival of "the long promised poem of Longfellow." The editor did not seem to have awaited its arrival as anxiously as some of his readers, stating, "We have not yet found time to read it, but we perceive it opens beautifully."[32] Gorman then obliged Longfellow fans by reprinting a section of the poem. Occasionally literature about the South was reprinted in "Choice Literature," and these pieces raise interesting questions about the effect of region on a reader's interpretation of a work. "Zeph. Hopkins' Experience," reprinted from Boston's *Flag of Our Union,* was set in New Orleans and used dialect as the source of its humor. Southern readers may have responded to the dialect with a sense of pride in the richness of their colloquial language and humor, though the "original" northern readers may have interpreted the dialect as proof of southerners' lack of education and culture.

Readers' needs for community identity were also satisfied by the other features of the *Age,* particularly the news. Each issue reported on local, state, national, and international news, enabling readers to feel connected to each of these different communities. For example, the 7 September 1853 issue contained a "Local Items" column that reported on a Raleigh town meeting and on construction plans for two paper mills to be built on the nearby Neuse River. National news items, such as the passage of a prohibition law in Michigan, reinforced readers' shared sense of identity with a national "community," while other national news items strengthened readers' sectional identity as southerners. Slavery issues appeared in the news more in the second half of the 1850s as political tensions surrounding this issue increased. For example, the 2 July 1856 issue carried a news update about the bitter conflict in Kansas, and the 3 September 1856 issue discussed the activities of the antislavery "Black Republicans" in Congress. However, the proslavery bias of such accounts did not prevent the publication of news items criticizing the inhumane treatment of slaves. The 5 July 1854 issue carried a news item about a man who had been sentenced for beating a slave woman when he was drunk. The balancing of such news items suggests that Gorman sought to present news coverage that would appeal to readers' diverse political beliefs.[33] Finally, the *Age*, as did other papers then and even now, provided readers with entertaining, strange-but-true news stories, such as an account of the unusual death of a woman in Camden, New Jersey, who died kneeling in prayer in church.[34]

Other columns provided readers with information necessary for living their daily lives. The "Agriculture" column contained information ranging from practical daily concerns such as "To Make Hard Candles of Soft Tallow" to larger concerns such as strategies for forming a County Agricultural Society.[35] "Prices Current" reported on the central trade markets for the region: Raleigh, Wilmington, Petersburg, Fayetteville, Norfolk, and New York. "Marriage and Death Notices" informed readers about community members' lives. The paper's advertisements supplied readers with consumer information about products ranging from books to patent medicines, and advertisements for such things as academies also informed readers about the institutions in their community. "Humorous" reprinted jokes and tales, in most cases demonstrating the power of the contemporary moment in defining and creating humor. "Receipts for the Age" listed the names of people who had begun or renewed their subscriptions, helping create a sense of community for readers by enabling them to see who else read and supported the paper.

The content of these columns appealed to different types of readers and to an individual reader's disparate interests. The only columns in the *Age* targeted to a specific group were the "Ladies Department" and "Editress's Department."[36] These departments "inculcate[d] a spirit of intellectual excellence and literary superiority among the Females of the South" by providing them with readings ranging from moral essays such as "To the Social Circle: Sabbath Musings" to historical essays such as "Jessie Brown," about the humanitarian labors of a Scotswoman during a war in India.[37] The Ladies and Editress's departments were added in 1856 as part of a campaign to increase subscriptions; in addition to creating columns tailored to the women readers' specific needs, Gorman also began to publish more women authors in the literary columns.

Creation of the "Ladies" and "Editress's" departments are just two instances of the small but numerous changes that Gorman made in the *Age* during the 1850s in order to attract new readers. He complemented these changes with editorial commentary intended to shape readers' conception of the *Age* and of themselves as readers. Gorman used his editorial columns to reinforce the different needs for reading the *Age* could fulfill. He targeted readers' desires to affirm their multilayered community identities—local, regional, sectional—in columns announcing changes in the paper's material appearance. The *Age*'s layout and type were revised annually to show that the paper was "keeping up with the spirit of the age;" Gorman announced the impending changes weeks in advance and then made a special note of their first appearance: "Our next number will appear in new dress and on new type, and will present an appearance for neatness of execution unsurpassed by any paper in the State."[38] Holding up the *Age*'s "neatness of appearance" as a mirror of its superior quality as a North Carolina newspaper, Gorman sought to foster readers' pride in their locally produced paper.

He extended these arguments by reinforcing readers' self-conceptions as North Carolinians: "We think our paper presents an appearance equal to any in the South, in every respect; and we intend to keep it so; and improve upon it from time to time, as our Patrons will encourage and sustain us."[39] Having established the *Age*'s superiority as a southern publication, Gorman targeted his readers' sectional identities, arguing that the *Age* was the equal to any northern publication: "Reader! Peruse this number of the *Age* carefully, and tell us if it is not equal to the Northern papers that are so extensively extolled and patronized by Southern men."[40] He matched his praise of the *Age*'s value with attacks on southerners' disloyal support of northern publications, a strategy commonly employed by southern editors to increase their readership: "If the *Age* was published in New York or Philadelphia, we should have twenty or thirty thousand subscribers, and at least two thirds of them would be from Southern states—Will you not support a good paper at home?"[41] He urged readers from all southern states to support the *Age* as a "Southern Literary and Temperance journal."[42]

Gorman affirmed other reader motivations in editorial columns that promoted the uses of the paper's diverse contents:

> If you want something in the way of pleasant entertaining matter, read the interesting articles—"Leaves from Memory"—"Uncle Joshua's Dream"—and the historical story of your favorite, "Will Willowill." Does something of a more didactic character suit your taste better, ponder over the sage remarks of "Dikos"—the stirring appeals from the vigorous pen of "Invincible"—and the discriminating dissertation of "T," from Elizabeth City—all original articles, by North Carolina writers too. You will find enough in the "Humorous" to give spice and zest to the entertainment—and don't forget the Editor's columns.[43]

As he catalogued the issue's contents, from the humorous to the didactic, he simultaneously linked them to uses for reading, from entertainment to moral enhancement.

In another promotion Gorman paired types of reading material with types of readers:

> [The *Age*] not only has paramount claims upon the Temperance public, but also on the *Ladies*, for it contains much that will interest and instruct them, having many very able and accomplished Female writers who contribute to its columns weekly. For the *Family Circle*, it is an entertaining companion, interesting to the *Children* as well as those of riper years. To the lovers of pure and chaste Southern *Literature*, it especially commends itself. The *Farmer* will always find reliable accounts of the markets, and much valuable information concerning the management of his farm. The *Mechanic* frequently much of great importance to him; and the *General Reader* a faithful report of the current News of the Day. The Paper is strictly neutral in Religion and Politics, and no denomination or party (except the abolitionists) are assailed through its columns.[44]

This column depicted images of ideal readers, categories with which actual readers may have desired to identify: becoming a reader of the *Age* would lead to "membership" in one of these designated groups. The readers constructed in this passage were not limited to a particular socioeconomic class, age, occupation, gender, or political party. Though abolitionists were warned that their political views would be "assailed," they were not excluded as a category of reader. Every type of reader would find her or his needs met through the *Age*'s columns.

Through his editorial commentary, Gorman sought to shape readers' conceptions of the *Age* and of themselves as readers by reinforcing their diverse needs for reading and the ability of the *Age* to meet them. His commentary worked in combination with changes in the *Age*'s contents and appearance to attract and sustain a diverse readership; the *Age* maintained a high circulation until Gorman sold it in 1864, and it continued publication until 1895.[45] The factors that contributed to the success of the *Age* and similar publications also provide a model for deepening our understanding of antebellum literature and its readers. Studies such as Jane Tompkins's *Sensational Designs* and Cathy N. Davidson's *Revolution and the Word* have transformed our understanding of nineteenth-century literature by examining the literature readers read and the ways in which their interpretations were shaped by historical context.[46] A parallel body of work, perhaps best exemplified by Barbara Sicherman's studies of Victorian women readers, begins with readers instead of texts, examining how nineteenth-century readers read and used their reading.[47] The factor that can link these two fields of scholarship is one that both have overlooked: a text's material appearance. Family newspapers demonstrate that a publication's material appearance embodies the uses of its contents; in turn, a reader's interpretation of content is affected by their needs for reading. The interrelationship between appearance and the uses of reading that led to the success of family papers like the *Spirit of the Age* needs to be considered for every type of publication, for all formats affect a reader's response to and use of a text.

❧ NOTES ❧

Support for this study was provided by the Stephen Botein Fellowship of the American Antiquarian Society.

1. "Please Stop My Paper," *Spirit of the Age* 15 September 1852: 3.

2. Related publications were literary weeklies such as the *New York Ledger;* sporting weeklies such as the *Spirit of the Times;* and religious publications such as the Methodist *Christian Advocate.* Although these publications contained news, the dominance of non-news contents led catalogers and print historians to classify them as "periodicals" rather than newspapers. The way in which these publications have been classified has made it difficult to examine the connections between appearance, content, and reading uses because their categorization itself denies those connections.

3. The low cost of family papers was made possible by improvements in printing technology. Power presses were not used in North Carolina until 1852. When Gorman announced the change in the paper's format he also an-

nounced that he had purchased a power press. Michael Schudson notes in *Discovering the News: A Social History of American Newspapers* (New York: Basic Books, 1978) that many newspaper publishers had incorporated steam-powered presses by the 1840s (32). However, as Frank Luther Mott observed in *American Journalism* (New York: Macmillan, 1962), most country weeklies were produced on handpresses well into the midcentury, lacking the capital and number of subscribers to support the new printing technologies (295, 316). While these new technologies enabled Boston and New York weekly papers to increase their size during the 1850s to six or eight pages, Gorman's market could not support such a paper, and he used the new power press to increase the size of his paper's four pages, from $15^1/_2 \times 22^1/_2$ inches in 1851 to $18 \times 24^1/_2$ inches in October 1853, making it one of the largest in the state. Guion Johnson, in *Antebellum North Carolina: A Social History* (Chapel Hill: U of North Carolina P, 1937), notes that North Carolina newspapers were typically four pages in length, and that the first eight-page paper was published in January 1859 (779).

4. Gorman did not publish letters to the editor in the *Age*. The "Editor's Correspondence" column published letters concerning the Sons of Temperance's local chapters. Gorman dropped this column in 1853, one of many changes to increase the paper's appeal to general readers.

This essay grows out of a larger study of newspaper and periodical readers in Henderson, North Carolina, in 1857. The U.S. postal records for the town show that the *Age* had the second highest number of subscribers for weekly publications (the first in the town was a Methodist publication, the *North Carolina Christian Advocate*). While many readers subscribed to northern titles, the majority of readers preferred regional publications. The *Age* readers that I have been able to locate in the 1860 census came from a range of classes, ages, and occupations, suggesting that the publication appealed to a diverse group of readers.

5. For an overview of uses and gratifications research, see Philip Palmgreen, Lawrence Wenner, and Karl Rosengren, "Uses and Gratifications Research: The Past Ten Years," *Media Gratifications Research: Current Perspectives*, ed. Karl Rosengren, Lawrence Wenner, and Philip Palmgreen (Beverly Hills, Calif.: Sage, 1985) 11–40.

6. Earlier uses and gratifications studies focused on two motivations, pleasure and gaining information about the environment. Ruotolo questioned readers about fifteen different motivations.

7. A. Carlos Ruotolo, "A Typology of Newspaper Readers," *Journalism Quarterly* 65 (1988): 128–29.

8. Gregg A. Payne, Jessica J. H. Severn, and David M. Dozier, "Uses and Gratifications Motives as Indicators of Magazine Readership," *Journalism Quarterly* 65 (1988): 912.

9. Payne, Severn, and Dozier 913.

10. Readers were asked to rate motives on a scale of 1 to 3—"not at all" "some," and "very much." By focusing only on what type of publication received the highest motivational score, Payne, Severn, and Dozier overlook the significance of the lower scores in other categories. Table 2 on page 913 reports the motivational rankings by type of publication.

11. Kasisomayajula Viswanath, John R. Finnegan, Jr., Brenda Rooney, and John Potter, "Community Ties in a Rural Midwest Community and Use of Newspapers and Cable Television," *Journalism Quarterly* 67 (1990): 899. For an overview of research on community ties, see Keith R. Stamm, "Community Ties and Media Use," *Critical Studies in Mass Communication* 5 (1988): 357–61.

12. Viswanath et al. 906–7.

13. Johnson 805.

14. Johnson 804.

15. The *University of North Carolina Magazine* resumed publication in 1878 (Johnson 797–98).

16. Johnson 804. In her discussion of antebellum North Carolina publications, Guion Johnson classifies the *Age* as a temperance journal, failing to note that its longevity was due to its multilevel contents and readership.

17. Johnson 803.

18. William S. Powell, *Dictionary of North Carolina Biography*, 5 vols. (Chapel Hill: U of North Carolina P, 1986) 2:321.

19. *Spirit of the Age* 21 July: 2. The unnamed editor's column always appeared on page 2 of the paper. Subsequent references to material from the *Age* will always be from the paper's second page unless otherwise noted. Gorman did not provide a specific circulation number to substantiate his boast, but in the 8 September 1852 issue he reported the *Age's* circulation as 4,300 and, on 1 March 1854, as 5,000.

20. The Sons of Temperance provided a solid readership base for the *Age* in its early years. Daniel Whitener, in *Prohibition in North Carolina, 1715–1945* (Chapel Hill: U of North Carolina P, 1945) states that North Carolina Sons of Temperance membership peaked in 1851 at twelve thousand, dropping to ten thousand at the end of 1852; membership continued to decline as the decade progressed, and in 1860 there were four thousand members (30–33). Though this pool of readers declined, it still provided the *Age* with a solid number of subscribers that Gorman sought to supplement with general readers.

21. The only department to be cut was "Editor's Correspondence," which had been used to publish the proceedings of Sons of Temperance chapters. During important times in the temperance movement, Gorman increased coverage of temperance issues. He also used the paper's growing general readership to sustain the interest of temperance readers; he reminded temperance readers that if they wanted it to reflect their concerns, they must support it. Gorman made such appeals at the "local" level, addressing individual

readers in such columns, and at times he made such appeals at the institutional level, at the North Carolina grand division meeting of the Sons of Temperance.

22. Powell 2:321. In January 1864 Gorman purchased the semiweekly *State Journal* (Raleigh) and began publishing it as the *Daily Confederate* on 26 January 1864. Gorman sold the *Age* in March 1864, a choice suggesting that his goals had changed and could be accomplished more effectively by different means; providing people with news of the war became his main concern, and this could not be accomplished through the medium of the family paper. William S. Powell has noted that the *Daily Confederate* "demonstrated complete devotion to the Confederate cause," and Gorman devoted himself to it until his sudden death on 24 January 1865 (2:322).

23. Frank Luther Mott, *A History of American Magazines, 1741–1850* (Cambridge: Harvard UP, 1957) 358–63.

24. Most four-page papers placed advertising on the front page (Mott, *Journalism* 298).

25. In *Novels, Readers, and Reviewers: Responses to Fiction in Antebellum America* (Ithaca: Cornell UP, 1984), Nina Baym notes that antebellum reviewers evaluated fiction with a "moral" tone as superior to that with a "morbid" tone (173–95). The literary and moral values enforced by reviewers in literary magazines Baym examined were also embodied in the literature of this weekly family paper.

26. *Spirit of the Age* 5 July 1854: 1.

27. *Spirit of the Age* 2 January 1852.

28. *Spirit of the Age* 3 September 1856.

29. Though for the most part the nationally known authors were northern, the publication of the prominent southern author Caroline Lee Hentz's story "The Two Sisters and the Two Uncles" in the 3 September 1856 issue received no special notice.

30. Frank Luther Mott, *A History of American Magazines, 1850–1865* (Cambridge: Harvard UP, 1957) 356–63.

31. Gorman also accommodated readers' interest in northern publications by offering reduced rates for readers who combined their subscription to the *Age* with *Harper's, Graham's, Peterson's,* or *Godey's.* Such ads ran in the 5 July 1854, 2 July 1856, and 16 July 1856 issues.

32. *Spirit of the Age* 2 January 1852: 4.

33. In "*Frank Leslie's Illustrated Newspaper* and *Harper's Weekly:* Innovation and Imitation in Nineteenth-Century American Pictorial Reporting," *Journal of Popular Culture* 23 (1990): 81–111, Andrea Pearson states that the editors of both publications hesitated to express their support for the Union or the Confederacy because they did not want to offend any of their readers, particularly their southern subscribers (88).

34. *Spirit of the Age* 5 July 1854: 3.

35. *Spirit of the Age* 17 May 1857: 4, 7 September 1853: 4.

36. The Ladies Department appeared in some 1851 issues of the paper but was discontinued until it reappeared in 1856.

37. *Spirit of the Age* 5 September 1855, 13 May 1857, 10 March 1858.

38. *Spirit of the Age* 31 August 1853.

39. *Spirit of the Age* 5 September 1855.

40. *Spirit of the Age* 16 March 1853.

41. *Spirit of the Age* 23 November 1853; Mott, *Magazines 1850–1865* 107–8.

42. Each issue of the paper listed new subscribers and subscription renewals. The list of out-of-town subscribers advertised the paper's wide appeal and helped to substantiate its claim to be the family paper of the South.

43. *Spirit of the Age* 16 March 1853.

44. *Spirit of the Age* 18 June 1856.

45. Powell 2:321. In 1876, the title of the *Age* was changed to *The Good Templar,* and it became the official paper of the North Carolina Good Templars, a national temperance organization. It was reincarnated under its original title in 1881, the product of the merger of two temperance papers, *Friend of Temperance* and *The Good Templar.* The *Age* continued to be published until 1895 (Whitener 55, 112).

46. Cathy N. Davidson, *Revolution and the Word: The Rise of the Novel in America* (New York: Oxford UP, 1986), and Jane P. Tompkins, *Sensational Designs: The Cultural Work of American Fiction, 1790–1860* (New York: Oxford UP, 1985).

47. Barbara Sicherman, "Sense and Sensibility: A Case Study of Women's Reading in Late-Victorian America," *Reading in America: Literature & Social History,* ed. Cathy N. Davidson (Baltimore: Johns Hopkins UP, 1989) 201–25, and "Reading and Ambition: M. Carey Thomas and Female Heroism," *American Quarterly* 45 (1993): 73–103.

Manufacturing Intellectual Equipment: The Tauchnitz Edition of The Marble Faun

SUSAN S. WILLIAMS

W HEN NATHANIEL HAWTHORNE FINISHED writing *The Marble Faun* in 1859, he declared it his "best Romance," although he also acknowledged that there might be "some points where it is open to assault."[1] Readers of this work have long found many such points of assault, focusing on its diffuse execution, overly conventionalized characters, formal incoherence, and general "defeat" of romance.[2] When the work was first published, criticism centered specifically on the ending. "Few can be satisfied with the concluding chapters, for the reason that nothing is really concluded," Edwin Whipple wrote in the *Atlantic,* a point later echoed most trenchantly by Henry James, who wrote that "the story straggles and wanders, is dropped and taken up again, and towards the close lapses into an almost fatal vagueness."[3] More recent critics, taking the work's formal failings for granted, have worked to explain *why* they occurred, pointing to the constraints Hawthorne felt as a self-consciously "high art" writer, his profound ambivalence about his aesthetic sensibilities, his regrets and anxieties about his past works, and the personal pain surrounding the illness of his daughter.[4]

If the critical reception of *The Marble Faun* has never been wholly positive, however, the popular reception has been even more mixed. One of the great paradoxes of American literary history is that the most unread of Hawthorne's works in our own time was the most popular in his. This popularity stemmed largely from its vivid and detailed descriptions of Italian landscapes and art: precisely those guidebook qualities (lifted almost verbatim from Hawthorne's notebooks) that make it seem to fail as a romance. James, even as he criticized the ending, recognized its success in the national and international market. "It has probably become," he wrote, "the most popular of Hawthorne's four novels. It is part of the intellectual equipment of the Anglo-Saxon visitor to Rome, and is read by every English-speaking traveller who arrives there, who has been there, or who expects to go."[5] Hawthorne's editors continued to stress these guidebook qualities well into the twentieth century. In 1923, Charles Curtis Bigelow introduced the work with an apparent (though unacknowledged) allusion to James, noting that "no English-speaking traveller intent upon visiting Rome ever fails to read the book, for it has become a necessary part of his mental equipment and a preparatory text-book to an appreciation of 'The Eternal City.'"[6] And in 1958, Maxwell Geismar called *The Marble Faun* the "best guidebook to Italy, if not a pocket guide to European culture." Indeed, "it is rather as though Dostoevski had written a Baedecker."[7]

Although *The Marble Faun* was published in several editions in both England and America in 1860, its international success was largely attributable to its publication by the Leipzig publisher Bernhard Tauchnitz. Hawthorne's son Julian wrote in his biography that *The Marble Faun* "is perhaps the most widely read of all Hawthorne's works, owing to its extensive circulation in Rome in the Tauchnitz edition."[8] Although it was originally issued as part of Tauchnitz's series of English and American authors, Italian booksellers encouraged their customers to distinguish it from that series by embellishing it with photographs and binding it in sumptuous leather vellum. These extra-illustrated copies not only gave *The Marble Faun* particular access into the tourist market but also guaranteed success in that market by making the book into a personalized souvenir as well as a guidebook. For American tourists the Tauchnitz *Marble Faun* presented a particular attraction. Buying it, they could simultaneously support an American author and acquire a foreign souvenir; the same work of fiction that they could enjoy while traveling could also memorialize those travels once they returned home.

In this essay I want to examine the implications of the Tauchnitz edition for our understanding of the ways in which book production and packaging affected the reception of *The Marble Faun*. When readers inserted particular photographs into the text and wrote captions for them, they found a concrete way to participate in the construction of *The Marble Faun*. Critics have long seen this text as demanding particular attention from its readers, who must picture various works of art, decide between competing interpretations of various characters and events, and make sense of an ending that Hawthorne insisted be left ambiguous. For this reason, as Jonathan Auerbach puts it, the act of reading itself becomes "a process of sightseeing which offers the reader room to move about [the text]."[9] The participation invited by the Tauchnitz *Marble Faun*, however, extended well beyond the text itself, and well beyond Hawthorne's authorial control: the booksellers and readers who began the practice of extra-illustration also helped construct *The Marble Faun* as a guidebook and a souvenir. *The Marble Faun* became a piece of "intellectual equipment" not only because of Hawthorne's descriptions of Rome but also because of the way in which the Tauchnitz edition was marketed and received: a reception that ultimately becomes interlocked with the logic of tourism at work in nineteenth-century America.

By the late 1850s, when Hawthorne began writing *The Marble Faun*, he was already established as a serious and important American author. But if Hawthorne was already well established, the Tauchnitz firm was equally so; indeed, the growth of the Tauchnitz firm closely paralleled that of Hawthorne as an established author. Bernhard Tauchnitz founded his publishing firm in 1837, the same year that Hawthorne published *Twice-Told Tales;* in 1860, the year that Hawthorne published *The Marble Faun*, Tauchnitz was celebrating the publication of the five-hundredth volume in his "Collection of British Authors," a profitable series of reprints that, despite its title, included works by both British and American authors. (It was not until 1930 that the Tauchnitz firm officially changed the designation to "Collection of British and American Authors.")

Tauchnitz had early recognized that there was great demand for inexpensive editions of American and British authors on the continent, and he quickly cornered the market. His base in Leipzig put him at the geographic center of the continental book trade, a trade facilitated by a rapidly expanding network of railway lines after 1839. From this base, he distributed books not only to Europe but also to the United States, Africa, and the Near East.[10] He also took advantage of advances in stereotyping that enabled him to cut costs by publishing multiple impressions of a work from a single stereotype plate; by 1887 his firm had on hand a stock of over a million stereotype plates and matrices.[11] The volume of his list enabled him to undersell his competition, creating an early antecedent to paperback series of "classic" authors such as those produced by Penguin or Pocket Books.[12] As early as 1849, a newspaper in Washington, D.C., reported that "this country is now flooded with German reprints, in English, of the standard classics of our tongue, which are sold at so cheap a rate as not only to force from the market English editions, but to compete successfully even with the American." Since these editions "[are] printed on fine and white paper, and with a beautiful type," the article continued, "they compare at infinite advantage with the bad editions of the best authors, with which booksellers and the reading portion of the American people have too long been content."[13] Tauchnitz's influence also created concern that American booksellers might be pushed out of the market. As an editorial in New York's *American Review* put it, "When Germany does all our publishing and printing, England all our manufacturing; when France makes our hats and shoes, and the English philosophers regulate our politics, what an intellectual, happy, shrewd, and prosperous people we shall be!"[14]

Tauchnitz's geographic location, use of technological advances, and marketing savvy clearly helped contribute to his success in the international market. But he also distinguished himself by being one of the few publishers who paid his authors to grant him contractual authority to reprint their works. Since there were not yet formal conventions governing international copyright, he, like other European publishers, could easily have reprinted works without authorial permission. But in 1843, he sent out a circular to the most well-known British authors of the time, announcing his policy of paying them for the right to reprint. "I, as well as any other publisher in Germany, have at present the right to embark in such undertakings without any permission from the authors," he stated. Nevertheless, he sought permission out of a "wish" to make a "first step" toward "an extension of the rights of copyright, and to publish my editions in accordance with those rights."[15] And once he began this practice, he kept his promise to make regular payments to his authors; in January 1864, for instance, Tauchnitz sent Hawthorne a payment of $120 for the Tauchnitz edition of *The Scarlet Letter*, a book that had been published more than a decade earlier.[16]

Having paid his authors for the right to reprint, Tauchnitz was able to sell books bearing the designation "author's edition," "authorized edition," or "copyright edition," imprints that distinguished his editions from the rampant unauthorized and pirated editions with which he competed in the market.[17] Thus, when he wanted to celebrate the publication of two thousand volumes in his series, he was able to issue a special edition of Henry Morley's *Of English Literature in the Reign of Victoria* that included a frontispiece bearing facsimiles of the signatures of all of his contemporary authors. This frontispiece not only displayed the diverse pantheon of Tauchnitz authors (Hawthorne's signature is between that of Bret Harte and Sir Arthur Helps) but also documented Tauchnitz's respect for the rights of those authors. Since the facsimiles of the signatures were "photographed from [the authors'] correspondence and agreements with Baron Tauchnitz," they testified to these authors' approval of the Tauchnitz enterprise.[18]

Writers who authorized their works to be reprinted by Tauchnitz received not only monetary payment but also, in Tauchnitz's view, international prestige. This emphasis on literary promotion is particularly clear in his preface to *Five Centuries of the English Language and Literature,* the five-hundredth volume of his British Library. "As a German-Saxon," he wrote, "it gave me particular pleasure to promote the literary interest of my Anglo-Saxon cousins, by rendering English literature as universally known as possible beyond the limits of the British Empire."[19] For this reason, an invitation to be a "Tauchnitz author" was an invitation both to extend one's market and to gain international fame. Thus, when Hawthorne received a proposal from Tauchnitz to publish *The Scarlet Letter,* his wife, Sophia, wrote that "all the world is on its knees at his feet and he is fast becoming Crowned King in the realm of Letter and Genius."[20]

Tauchnitz worked hard to recognize such "kings"; his governing principle, as the managing director of the firm later put it, was "to bring awareness of a book deemed worthy of propagation to a completely new circle of admirers." Such a project clearly advanced the cause of British imperialism. Even as Tauchnitz marketed his books to the growing numbers of English speakers traveling on the continent, he also sought to appeal to non-native English speakers who were interested in consuming English culture. In this respect, the Tauchnitz edition was "a mediator of the intellectual products of a great nation for foreign countries" that sought to create a "representative collection" of

"English literature of the moment."[21] As such a mediator, Tauchnitz succeeded "in joining care for the higher interests of Literature with the diffusion of much healthy intellectual amusement."[22]

Tauchnitz's attempts to diffuse "healthy intellectual amusement" led him to establish a list of authors that cut across not only national boundaries but also ones of genre and cultural taste. Even as he focused on books that he "deemed worthy of propagation," he also offered books "worthy" only because of "the principle of *vox populi*," books that demanded "attention for the one reason that [they] obtained a paying readership of 100,000 English people, in contradiction to criticism."[23] Thus, within the Tauchnitz catalog one could find Milton's *Poetical Works* as well as Susan Warner's *Queechy;* and Sterne's *Tristram Shandy* as well as Collins's *The Woman in White.* The series eventually included works of natural history, the Bible, and various dictionaries, ensuring that the European traveler could, as Tighe Hopkins put it in 1901, "send to the nearest bookseller's with a moderate certainty of getting for one-and-eightpence the book, of whatever kind, that he had forgotten to slip into his bag on starting from home."[24] When the Tauchnitz firm ceased publication in 1943, it had published 5,300 volumes in more than forty million copies: a massive list that has been catalogued by William Todd and Ann Bowden in their bibliography *Tauchnitz International Editions in English.*

All of the Tauchnitz editions were issued in printed wrappers and were generally of a standard length (eighteen gatherings of 288 pages) and given a particular number within the series.[25] Even as Tauchnitz recognized the difference between books receiving critical acclaim and popular books endorsed by "the principle of *vox populi*," he published those books in a series that, in format and price, did not differentiate between "literature" and popular writing. Thus, in 1860, when Tauchnitz published *Transformation* (the English title of *The Marble Faun*) in two volumes as numbers 515 and 516 of his series, he also published a variety of other works, including poems by Coleridge and Tennyson; plays by Bulwer Lytton; and novels by Maria Susanna Cummins, Charles Lever, and Dinah Craik as well as by Eliot, Scott, and Dickens.[26]

Consistent with Tauchnitz's policy regarding authorial rights, *Transformation* appeared on this list only after Tauchnitz had received permission to reprint it through agreements with Hawthorne and his British publisher, Smith, Elder and Company. Details about this contract are sketchy, but we know that Tauchnitz wrote to Hawthorne in January 1864, reporting that *Transformation* "was considered as an English book and I made an agreement about it signed by you and Messrs Smith Elder & Co."[27] Smith, Elder had already paid Hawthorne six hundred pounds for the rights to publish the book; Hawthorne provided them with his manuscript from which to set the type, stipulating that they would then send advance sheets to his American publishers, Ticknor and Fields. In order to protect copyright, these British and American editions were supposed to be issued simultaneously, although in fact the English edition appeared a week before the American one.[28] The Tauchnitz edition appeared only a few months after these initial American and British editions.

Tauchnitz clearly had a large role from the beginning in distributing *The Marble Faun* to an international market. Yet his role as publisher was conceived along quite different lines than that of Ticknor and Fields or Smith, Elder. Whereas Tauchnitz aimed to include the whole range, or "representative collection," of authors writing in English, these firms prided themselves on cultivating particular writers and producing books that were commensurate with high cultural status. Ticknor and Fields, in particular, early began to advertise Hawthorne's work in ways that predicted its success and to arrange reviews that would emphasize his importance as an American author.[29] Prior to their publication of the first American edition of *The Marble Faun* on 7 March 1860, for instance, they had already ordered three printings and proudly announced in advertisements that advance orders had almost depleted the first printing. This promotion was a success; they sold 14,500 copies of the book in its first year, more than the total American sales of any of Hawthorne's previous romances.[30]

Smith, Elder, who had negotiated with Fields to publish *The Marble Faun* in England, similarly courted and promoted prominent authors such as Ruskin, Hardy, and Thackeray. A few months before *Transformation* was published, George Smith had also taken over publishing *Cornhill Magazine,* in which he showcased the work of his house authors just as Ticknor and Fields did in the *Atlantic Monthly*. And like Fields, Smith was known for the lavish dinners he gave for his writers and other visiting literati. Indeed, soon after the publication of *Transformation,* Smith wanted to give such a dinner for Hawthorne and introduce him to the contributors to *Cornhill,* but Hawthorne declined, saying that he was "tired to death of dinners."[31] Although Tauchnitz respected authorial rights and had his own critical standards, he was less concerned with the aura of literary celebrity than with creating a literary empire that included everything from classic works by Chaucer, Shakespeare, and Milton to the most recent sensation novel.[32] For this reason, his publication of *The Marble Faun* was, rather than a much-heralded publishing event, simply another item in a long series by a wide range of authors.

Eventually, however, *The Marble Faun* began to stand out within this series, as Italian booksellers worked to convert it from an inexpensive reprint into a valuable souvenir, a book that one would want not only to read but to keep as a memento. Specifically, these booksellers rebound copies of *The Marble Faun*, substituting ornate white vellum, often with gold tooling, for the cloth wrappers in which the books first arrived. They then inserted albumen prints or photographs of the scenes Hawthorne described; if customers did not like these ready-made versions, they could also purchase loose photographs from separate displays and insert them into the book. Many of these illustrations corresponded to scenes described in the book, although customers could also personalize their books by choosing scenes of particular meaning to them. The sellers also occasionally bound into the books photographs provided by the customers themselves.[33] Sometimes, customers presented their own books for rebinding. One reader, for instance, inscribed her Tauchnitz edition of *The Marble Faun* as being purchased in Rome in February 1867 and then "bound in Rome" in January 1870.[34]

This reader's delay in rebinding the book is not surprising: although the first Tauchnitz edition of *The Marble Faun* was issued in 1860, the practice of inserting albumen prints or photographs into ornately bound and extra-illustrated souvenir sets probably did not begin until about 1868. This practice continued throughout the nineteenth century, although it is difficult to date copies exactly since Tauchnitz made a practice of leaving the original imprint date on the title page of all subsequent impressions of his books.

These souvenir sets are particularly fascinating because each is distinct; no two contain exactly the same group or number of photographs. Certain works of art explicitly mentioned in the work tend to be placed near their description: thus, for instance, the portrait of Beatrice Cenci formerly attributed to Guido Reni (Figure 1) always appears in chapter 7 ("Beatrice"), just as Guido's painting of St. Michael and the Devil is always in chapter 20 ("The Burial Chant"). Other Roman landmarks, such as the Temple of Minerva or the statue of Marcus Aurelius, appear in some copies but not in others. Some copies include photographs featuring scenes of everyday life, such as a

1. Portrait of Beatrice Cenci, Palazzo Barberini, Rome. Formerly attributed to Guido Reni; now attributed to Elisabetta Sirani, ca. 1660. Tipped into *The Marble Faun* beside a description of the portrait. Courtesy, William Charvat Collection of American Fiction at the Ohio State University Libraries.

baker's shop or a portrait of a Roman policeman (Figure 2), while others include only works of art. Among the photographs frequently added to *The Marble Faun* is one of Hawthorne himself, based on the often-reproduced "Bright-Motley" pose taken in England in 1860.[35] Most copies of the book have between fifty and a hundred photographs, although some contain more than two hundred.[36]

2. Roman policeman, ca. 1870. Tipped into *The Marble Faun* beside a description of the inefficacy of the police in searching for Hilda, who has disappeared from Rome. Courtesy, Peabody Essex Museum, Salem, Mass.

The Marble Faun was not the only book in Tauchnitz's collection to become extra-illustrated as a travelogue: Macaulay's *Lays of Ancient Rome*, Bulwer Lytton's *Last Days of Pompeii*, and Eliot's *Romola* were also embellished in this way. All of these works were sufficiently popular to require that their stereotype plates be reset at least once, and in the case of Hawthorne and Macaulay, four times.[37] Yet *The Marble Faun* was the most frequently extra-illustrated book in the series. *The National Union Catalog* lists twenty-nine institutional locations for Hawthorne in the United States alone, twelve more than for *Romola*, the second most frequently extra-illustrated book. The fact that these souvenir sets are so widely dispersed attests to their popularity among American tourists.[38]

The second half of the nineteenth century saw a proliferation in the number of photographically illustrated books. Although the daguerreotype could be copied only through engravings, after about 1860 it became common for original albumen prints to be trimmed and pasted into book volumes, usually on separate unfolded leaves glued (in publishing parlance, "tipped in") at the spine of the book. In 1879, these prints began to give way to photogravures, which were based on carbon prints and provided a richer range of tones than the albumen prints. In the United States alone there were perhaps as many as three thousand photographically illustrated books published during the period between 1844 and 1914, ranging from Putnam's *Homes of American Statesmen* to an edition of *Rip van Winkle* featuring theatrical photographs by Joseph Sarony. During this period there were also increasing numbers of photographically illustrated travel books, especially those reporting on travel for exploration or within the British empire. In the 1860s, for instance, the British publisher Alfred William Bennett issued a series of travel books, including William and Mary Howitt's *Ruined Abbeys and Castles of Great Britain and Ireland*. In the 1870s Sampson Low, Marston and Searle published lavishly illustrated editions of William Bradford's *The Arctic Regions* as well as of P. H. Emerson's *Life and Landscape on the Norfolk Broads* and *Pictures of East Anglian Life*.[39]

In encouraging readers to extra-illustrate *The Marble Faun*, Italian booksellers were continuing this proliferation of photographically illustrated travel books. Yet the unique appeal of this practice lay in its production of a personalized souvenir, a book that would reflect the tourist's particular experiences in Rome. A copy of *The Marble Faun* could thus also bear some resemblance to the family photograph album, which was first patented in 1861; both enabled their owners to display photographs of personal significance. Furthermore, these personal souvenirs were available to any tourist in Rome. To be sure, these extra-illustrations and bindings made the book more expensive: one purchaser of the Tauchnitz *Marble Faun* noted that the book itself cost four lire, the bindings twenty, and the hundred photographs twenty-five lire.[40] One could choose fewer photographs, however, and reduce the price, so that the extra-illustrated copies were not prohibitively expensive.

Even as the extra-illustrated *Marble Faun* enabled tourists to create a personalized souvenir, it also enabled them to participate in a practice that had originally been available only to elite private collectors. During the nineteenth century such collectors frequently extra-illustrated their books in order to display their taste and collecting skills as well as to increase the value of the books. One such collector, making what he termed a "plea for bibliomania," recognized that his fellow collectors were "generally men of culture" who bore "a small proportion to the mass of the population." Yet in privately illustrating their books, these cultured men were motivated not only by "the love they [had] for the beautiful" but also by a "passion" for "speculation." And the rewards of such speculation could be great: in 1866 Thomas Morrell sold for two thousand dollars a copy of Washington Irving's *Life of George Washington* that he had extra-illustrated with 1,100 prints, including 145 portraits of Washington.[41]

Tourists who extra-illustrated their Tauchnitz *Marble Fauns* also increased the value of the books, albeit on a much smaller scale. Ultimately, however, their practice not only helped to democratize what had been an elite activity but also encouraged Houghton, Mifflin and Company—the successors to Ticknor and Fields—to produce a uniform illustrated edition of *The Marble Faun*. In 1889, the firm issued a two-volume edition of the book, complete with fifty photogravures, in cloth with gilt-edged pages. A full vellum binding in a boxed set was also available. At the same time, Houghton, Mifflin issued a special "large-paper edition" on laid paper, limited to 150 copies.[42] Although the practice of customizing individual copies of *The Marble Faun* continued, the publisher believed there was now an audience for a more uniform illustrated edition.

In the advertisement contained within the book itself, Houghton, Mifflin explicitly identified this edition as continuing the tradition of illustration begun in Rome. "[I]t early became the custom of visitors to Italy to collect photographs of the statues, paintings, and buildings referred to in the romance, and to interleave the book with them," the advertisement notes. Yet Houghton, Mifflin, having "taken the hint from this well-established custom," undertook to provide higher quality photographs than those available in Florence or Rome. "Great care has been taken by the publishers in the choice of photographs, and their selection is not a mere repetition of the dealer's choice," the advertisement claims. "Every traveller knows that there is a wide difference between the best and poorest of these photographs, and no pains have been spared to obtain the best made directly from the objects themselves."[43] According to this advertisement, Hawthorne continues to deserve the best quality edition, with "no pains spared." The souvenir tradition associated with the Tauchnitz *Marble Faun* here merges with the high-art tradition established by Ticknor and Fields to create, as the advertisement puts it, "a valuable record of the past as well as a pleasure to the eye."

In this 1889 edition, individual extra-illustration had given way to a mass-marketed illustrated edition that enabled readers to participate in armchair travel without ever leaving home. At the same time, the clarity of the photogravures and gilt edges of this edition marked it, like the extra-illustrated Tauchnitz copies, as a work of art: a book to be treasured as well as read. To be sure, the elite continued to extra-illustrate Hawthorne's works in ways that could never be mass-marketed: one New York collector overwhelmed the text of *The English Notebook* by tipping in three hundred portraits and views, while a Boston collector inserted 383 illustrations into his copy of Julian Hawthorne's *Nathaniel Hawthorne and His Wife*.[44] Yet the 1889 *Marble Faun* enabled even middle-class Americans to own an amply illustrated edition, one that was explicitly designed to compete with copies ready-made by Italian booksellers. The ideal was still for readers to choose their own photographs, but when this was not possible the 1889 edition offered a quality substitute. "It is at once a cheapening of a pretty fancy when the trader steps in to do for the indolent or ignorant what the intelligent enthusiast does for himself," the *Atlantic Monthly* claimed in a review of the book; "but the change from the photographer's or bookseller's clumsy extension of The Marble Faun to the publisher's edition, in which all the arts of bookmaking were studied with patience and nice attention to detail, was one worth making, and the result was notable for the good taste which marked it throughout."[45]

The fact that Houghton, Mifflin attempted to reproduce the souvenir copies of *The Marble Faun* in an illustrated standard edition attests to the way in which the Tauchnitz edition had influenced conceptions of the text. Although it was part of a series of inexpensive reprints of British and American authors, the book's Italian sales had converted it into a treasured and unique souvenir. At the same time, this souvenir tradition converted a literary romance into a guidebook that also functioned as a work of art. Although the text is concerned with the difficulty of seeing art "correctly" and the potential "emptiness of picture galleries," readers had increasingly come to use the book itself as a kind of portable gallery. For this reason, it seems clear that the history of the Tauchnitz edition needs to be considered in any account not only of the publishing history of *The Marble Faun* but also of the reception of the text itself.

In order to speculate about the influence of the Tauchnitz edition on the reception of *The Marble Faun*, we must first think about its status as a guidebook or piece of "intellectual equipment." For Henry James, a person of highly cultivated aesthetic sensibilities, dependence on such "equipment" may have seemed to mark the aesthetic limitations of ordinary tourists who used it to structure their Italian journeys. Yet the proliferation of travel guides in the nineteenth century testifies to the fact that it was mandatory to do some preparation before travelling.[46] As Henry Tuckerman put it in 1839, "the only worthy pleasures peculiar to Europe, are those of taste, and . . . to enjoy these, a certain preparedness is requisite."[47] Such preparation enabled tourists to recover some sense of the history and significance of the sites that they visited, thereby compensating for their own sense of belatedness in the face of Italian ruins.[48] Even if tourists could never fully recover the original, historical meanings of what Hawthorne's character Kenyon calls "a heap of worthless fragments," they could nevertheless begin to write their own story through the process of travel itself.[49] "The Prometheus of the present day is needed rather to animate statues than to make them," Julia Ward Howe wrote in 1868.[50] For a tourist to read *The Marble Faun* as a guidebook was to begin to engage in this Promethean task.

In this sense, we might think of Hawthorne himself as the first, and most ideal, reader of *The Marble Faun*. He wrote *The Marble Faun* in part to alleviate his own anxieties about his aesthetic sensibilities, to prove that he could experience art as deeply and fully as any cultured person should. In his journals of this period he vacillates between referring to himself as a "Goth" in need of aesthetic training and wondering why one should want to undertake such training, complaining that "there is something forced, if not feigned, in our tastes for pictures of old Italian schools."[51] Hawthorne's own experience reading guidebooks had taught him that descriptions of tourist sights often diminished one's appreciation of the real thing; their idealized presentations made it impossible to experience the original in an unmediated way. As he put it in his journal in 1858, "I have come . . . to the conclusion, that there was a better St. Peter's in my mind, before I came to Rome, than the real one turns out to be. The reality is a failure."[52]

Yet in *The Marble Faun,* Hawthorne himself contributed to the creation of a "better St. Peter's" as he provided elaborate pictorial descriptions of papal and ancient Rome. In revising the manuscript, he writes in the preface, he "was somewhat surprised to see the extent to which he had introduced descriptions of various Italian objects, antique, pictorial, and statuesque." But his surprise resulted from the fact that he had been so receptive to Italian culture: "[T]hese things fill the mind, everywhere in Italy, and especially in Rome, and cannot easily be kept from flowing out upon the page."[53] In presenting these descriptions, Hawthorne wanted to find a way to create an original experience of them: an experience that was a literary rather than visual one.

In creating these literary representations of artworks, Hawthorne animated them by replicating and doubling them in the characters in the novel. Hilda is the subject of a portrait that many viewers think is of Guido's Beatrice Cenci; she is a copy of an "original" work of art. The bust of Donatello that Kenyon sculpts seems to many spectators to be "an unsuccessful attempt towards copying the features of the Faun of Praxiteles."[54] Donatello is thus both a model for and a replica of the Faun. In addition, the mysterious model who haunts Miriam looks like the figure of the demon in Guido's sketch for the painting of the Archangel Michael in the Church of the Cappuccini.

Through such doublings, Hawthorne imagines what it would mean to erase the frame of a work of art and have it not hanging on a museum wall but alive in a walking replica of the original. He also animates works of art by telling stories about them. Hilda, the copy of Beatrice, loves Kenyon; Donatello, the copy of Marble Faun, loves Miriam; and so on. Late in the novel, Hawthorne explicitly attributes the origins of his own narrative to the experience of looking at Kenyon's sculpted bust of Donatello. "It was the contemplation of this imperfect portrait of Donatello that originally interested us in his history, and impelled us to elicit from Kenyon what he knew of his friend's adventures."[55] As in the tradition of ekphrastic poetry, a work of the visual arts compels the writer to construct a narrative about it. And this narrative, to return to Julia Ward Howe's terms, does the Promethean work of animating statues.

If Hawthorne wrote *The Marble Faun* in part to animate and enrich his own experiences of Rome, readers' accounts testify to his success in animating them for others as well. For tourists "who wished to be thought elect," as William Dean Howells put it, *The Marble Faun* became nothing less than an "aesthetic handbook" that needed to be not only consulted but "deeply read." Such readers "devoutly looked up all the places mentioned in it, which were important for being mentioned; though some places such as the Tarpeian Rock, the Forum, the Capitoline Museum, and the Villa Borghese might secondarily have their historical or artistic interest." In this view, Hawthorne's Rome was more "important," more present, than ancient or papal Rome, and original sights were interesting precisely because Hawthorne had described them. Such "elect" tourists "devoutly" worshipped Hawthorne rather than a past more distantly removed from them, establishing what Howells calls a "citizenship in that Rome of the imagination which is greater than any material Rome."[56] By encouraging such citizenship, *The Marble Faun* contributed to what Dean MacCannell terms the "sight sacralization" of Rome; certain sights became sacred, or worthy of special—even devout—attention, because they had already been reproduced in Hawthorne's text. And it is such reproduction, according to MacCannell, "that is most responsible for getting the tourist in motion on his journey to find the real thing."[57] As an "aesthetic handbook," then, *The Marble Faun* both inspired readers to visit certain sights and mediated their experience once they arrived there.

At times, however, the "real thing" was a disappointment, as Hawthorne's description proved to be more compelling than the actual sight. Thus when Howells visited the Tarpeian Rock, the scene of the mysterious model's murder, "it seemed but a shallow gulf compared to that in our fancy. We were somewhat disappointed; but then Niagara disappoints one; and as for Mont Blanc. . . ."[58] Like Hawthorne, who concluded that "there was a better St. Peter's in my mind, before I came to Rome, than the real one turns out to be," Howells recognized that his "Rome of the imagination" could render anticlimactic his experience of the original.

If Howells found it difficult to reconcile his imaginary Rome with the material one, however, other tourists found that their reading of

The Marble Faun enhanced their experience of the real thing by creating certain associations with particular sights. Thus, for instance, Marion Harland's visit to the Piazza del Popolo was enhanced by Hawthorne's "thrilling" reminder that its obelisk " 'supplied one of the recollections which Moses and the Israelites bore from Egypt into the desert.' " Yet Harland was even more impressed by Hawthorne's ability to unite "the historical and the imaginative," a blending that enables one to recollect, "in the same instant, that the parapet by which he is standing is the one over which Kenyon and Hilda watched the enigmatical pantomime of Miriam and the Model beside the 'four-fold fountain' at the base of the obelisk."[59] Even as Harland replicates the elision of history and fiction that Hawthorne produced in *The Marble Faun,* she also responds to the scene precisely because of Hawthorne's "subtle and delicate genius" in describing it.

In 1871 a writer in *Scribner's Monthly* reported similar experiences visiting "scenes from the Marble Faun." Unlike Howells, this writer found that Hawthorne's descriptions perfectly echoed his perception of the experiences of the actual scenes. In looking down the Via Portoghese, for instance, this writer saw Hilda's tower:

> —square, grim, and battlemented, as Hawthorne had described it. On the summit is the shrine of the Virgin, with its attendant lamp. Immediately below the battlements is a small window, which, on the day when I discovered the tower, was half-draped with a white curtain which Hilda's fair hands might have looped up. The white doves were 'skimming, fluttering, and wheeling about the topmost height of the tower,' and nothing was wanting to complete the scene but the delicate figure of Hilda herself, leaning out of the window and calling her feathered companions to their morning meal.[60]

This description again collapses the distinction between fantasy and material reality, as the writer sees a white curtain that Hilda herself might have touched. At the same time, his visit collapses the historical disjunction between author and reader; his emphasis on the accuracy of Hawthorne's description reveals his uncanny sense that he is looking at the same tower that Hawthorne himself had seen. Although his visit to the tower is itself motivated by his reading of *The Marble Faun,* that reading also enables him to take pleasure in visiting an imaginary Rome inhabited by Hilda and by Hawthorne.

Another reader of Hawthorne, Louise Chandler Moulton, reported encountering a similar pleasure when she went to the grounds of the

Villa Borghese. While there she engaged in a quiet reverie in which she imagined seeing Miriam and Donatello "where the sun sifts through the young green leaves." Indeed, she found that Miriam's "human, deep-souled beauty" and Donatello's "fantastic grace are the only things here that cannot change," since they are "immortally beyond the reach of the effacing years."[61] Moulton thus uses fiction to counteract the sense of loss embodied in the scene, taking solace in the status of Miriam and Donatello as characters living outside of time. Just as the writer in *Scribner's* had imagined Hilda always hovering just behind the curtain, so too does Moulton imagine Miriam and Donatello dancing just beyond the green leaves.

In describing Miriam and Donatello as immortal figures of the imagination, Moulton echoes Hawthorne's own understanding of romance. Despite the realistic descriptions in *The Marble Faun*, Hawthorne defined it, like his other works, as a romance that had no specific correspondence to reality. As he put it in the preface, he "proposed to himself merely to write a fanciful story, evolving a thoughtful moral, and did not purpose attempting a portraiture of Italian manners and character." Indeed, he found Italy appealing precisely because it was conducive to the "poetic or fairy precinct" of romance, a precinct "where actualities would not be so terribly insisted upon, as they are, and must needs be, in America."[62] On the grounds of the Villa Borghese, Moulton discovers just such a fairy precinct, a place of "enchanted glades" where the "sunbeams dance with the shadows."[63]

The very accuracy of Hawthorne's descriptions, however, made some readers focus on the "actualities" in *The Marble Faun* rather than its fanciful story. Thus, when T. B. Aldrich reported his visit to the catacombs of the Cappuccini in 1883, he cited Hawthorne as an authoritative source. "'There is no disagreeable scent,' says the author of The Marble Faun, describing this place, 'such as might have been expected from the decay of so many holy persons, in whatever odor of sanctity they may have taken their departure.'"[64] Aldrich, who concurs with Hawthorne's findings, again collapses the historical distance between Hawthorne and himself, but in this case only to emphasize the realism of *The Marble Faun*. In this respect, he anticipated the experience of Edmund Wilson, who would later report being "in a position to recognize the perfect accuracy of Hawthorne's description of the effect of modern Rome on a Protestant Anglo-Saxon."[65]

The illustrated editions of *The Marble Faun* further emphasized the "perfect accuracy" of the text, since readers could compare Haw-

Hilda's Tower.

3. "Hilda's Tower." Photograph of medieval tower in the Via Portoghese, Rome, with hand-written caption identifying it with the fictional character in *The Marble Faun.* Courtesy, American Antiquarian Society.

thorne's descriptions not only to their actual visit to a given site but also to a photograph tipped in beside the description itself. Thus, for instance, a photograph of Hilda's Tower or Donatello's Tower (Figures 3–4) was a reminder that places in the "Rome of the imagination" were based on actual sites. Carol Shloss speculates that such photographs served as "visual clues given in the real world, which guided the reader in imagining the author's fantasy."[66] Yet such clues were also antithetical to Hawthorne's notion of romance. Even as a photograph labeled

Donatello's Tower.

4. "Donatello's Tower." Photograph of actual tower, probably at the Villa Montauto outside Florence, with hand-written caption identifying it with the fictional character in _The Marble Faun._ Courtesy, American Antiquarian Society.

"Hilda's Tower" mixed a fictional character with a real place, it also insisted on the "actuality" of that place. And such an actuality encouraged readers to explore the material Rome as well as an imaginary one: to look for "the balloon of experience" tied to the earth, in James's phrase, rather than the "disconnected and uncontrolled experience" that comes when the romancer cuts the cable.[67]

Hawthorne's own stake in such disconnected experience was so strong that in his letters he insisted that one could not find a photograph of the "real" Marble Faun, the statue by Praxiteles that had given him the idea for the opening scene of the novel. "There are photographs, stereoscopic and otherwise, of another Faun, which is almost identical with the hero of my Romance, though only an inferior repetition of it. My Faun is in the Capitol; the other, in the Vatican. The genuine statue has never been photographed, on account, I suppose, of its standing in a bad light. The photograph of the Vatican Faun supplies its place very well, except as to the face, which is greatly inferior."[68] Since the Capitoline Faun was not photographed in the nineteenth century, the photographs added to the Tauchnitz *Marble Faun* were of the Vatican Faun. Not only was this the "wrong" Faun, but it was also frequently photographed with fig leaves, whereas the statue Hawthorne saw was completely nude.[69] For Hawthorne to have depicted a statue that could not be photographed was consistent with his notions of romance, however; to have no photograph of the original statue was to avoid the terrible insistence on "actualities" that he laments in America.

Although the practice of extra-illustrating the Tauchnitz edition did not begin until after Hawthorne's death, Hawthorne's emphasis on romance and the irreproducibility of the Faun suggests that he would not have been satisfied with the illustrations. Indeed, his friend John Lothrop Motley had joked in a letter that "nothing less than an illustrated edition, with a large gallows on the last page, with Donatello in the most pensile of attitudes . . . would prove satisfactory" for readers who insisted on making *The Marble Faun* into "an everyday novel." Hawthorne replied that he was gratified to have a "Gentle Reader" who understood so well "the way in which my Romance ought to be taken" and that "these beer-sodden English beefeaters do not know how to read a Romance."[70] Such "beefeaters" were presumably also the readers who wished for an illustrated edition; lacking the imagination to read romance, illustrations would help anchor them in the everyday world.

Given this dismissive attitude, Hawthorne would probably have been gratified by readers such as Louise Chandler Moulton who could envision Hawthorne's timeless figures of romance without the aid of photographs. Indeed, when Moulton purchased her requisite Tauchnitz edition, she illustrated it only with a photograph of Hawthorne, as if the reproductions of the "enchanted glades" she had seen and read about would ruin their magic. At the same time, she took pains to mark the book as a special souvenir; her copy, bound in white vellum, has her initials embossed in gold on the front.[71] Her appreciation of the book as a romance did not stop her from wanting to memorialize her own trip with this artifact from the "real" Rome.

It is this artifactual quality of the Tauchnitz *Marble Faun* that may, in the end, have made it more compatible with Hawthorne's notions of romance than he might have imagined. If the photographs of the Marble Faun in these copies are wrong, in the sense that they are not the Faun that Hawthorne had in mind, then they inherently resist any "realistic" correlation between picture and text. Nor is the Faun the only photograph that breaks the conventions of realism. Many of them, such as a photograph of an Italian senator that has been dated to 1865, are clearly anachronistic, taken after Hawthorne's death.[72] On one hand, such anachronisms show that the material book must always be tied to the historical moment in which it is produced, while romance itself can aspire to be an ahistorical "fairy precinct." At the same time, they suggest that these photographs are not images for "beer-sodden beefeaters" to take at face value but rather testimonies to readers' own attempts to create their own narrative of what Hawthorne calls the "dreamy character of the present."[73] Just as Hawthorne created the romance of *The Marble Faun* as a response to his experiences as a tourist, so too could readers create their own romance of travel by selecting illustrations that evoked memories of their present-day experiences.

By choosing the photographs they wanted to tip into their books, readers could literally insert themselves into the novel; some of the images show people—possibly the tourist/readers themselves—posing in front of various sites (Figure 5). Readers also occasionally colored in the photographs by hand, penciled in captions and put reproductions of several paintings on one page to create a collage (Figures 6–7). Such participation created an interplay between text and image. The paintings in Figure 7, for example, are all self-portraits of artists taken from the Uffizi Gallery in Florence. The owners of this particular *Marble Faun,* Ann and Sarah B. Bartlett, placed these reproductions beside a

5. Unidentified man, possibly the owner of the book, in a Roman cemetery. Tipped-in frontispiece to *The Marble Faun*. Courtesy, William Charvat Collection of American Fiction at the Ohio State University Libraries.

6. Photograph of Roman soldiers, tipped into *The Marble Faun* and hand painted, probably by the owner of the book, with orange and yellow. Courtesy, Peabody Essex Museum, Salem, Mass.

7. Page from *The Marble Faun* with reproductions of self-portraits of painters in the Uffizi Gallery, Florence. Paintings are by (clockwise from top left) Leonardo da Vinci (1452–1519), Carlo Dolci (1616–1686), Elisabeth Vigée-Lebrun (1755–1842), and Raphael (1483–1520). Courtesy, Peabody Essex Museum, Salem, Mass.

passage in which Donatello views Miriam's self-portrait. In the passage, Hawthorne alludes to the Uffizi's famous collection of self-portraits and notes the ability of these images to reveal hidden "traits" and "expressions" (*CMF* 49). By juxtaposing portraits by Leonardo, Raphael, and other Masters with the description of Miriam's portrait, the Bartletts made an implicit connection not only between real and fictional works of art, but also between Miriam's abilities and those of highly revered painters.

Even as these paintings provided a commentary on Hawthorne's text, they also enabled the Bartletts to personalize their copy of *The Marble Faun*, since no other copy would have this particular grouping of portraits. Another copy of the Tauchnitz *Marble Faun* at the American Antiquarian Society is inscribed "Mabel Blake, Rome, May 15, 1888, who inserted the photos." To own *The Marble Faun*, in these cases, was also to help create its form, to participate in its artifice by tipping in "real" scenes. Given this participation, it is not surprising that these Tauchnitz copies frequently contain other mementos, such as pressed flowers, between their pages.

In 1892, Daniel Tredwell summarized the attraction of such readerly participation in his monograph on extra-illustration. "Reader, are you an illustrator?" he asked.

> You, undoubtedly, have some purpose in illustrating a book. It is in a sense either to annotate and interpret the text through the means of additional graceful, contemporaneous prints; or to animate the subject-matter of the book, exemplify the incidents, manners, and customs, by a reinforcement of portraiture, drawings, sketches, autograph letters, or anything that may add graphic force to the subject-matter of the book; or to decorate and embellish the work from an artistic point of view, regardless of the above facts; or to gratify a personal vanity and a desire to possess that which no one else can obtain; or for the pleasure derived from coauthorship in the work in having added something which enhances its literary and artistic merit.[74]

In the case of the Tauchnitz *Marble Faun*, this "coauthorship" was not only between writer and reader but also between bookseller and reader, as readers chose illustrations primarily from those available from the bookseller. At the same time, these illustrations served to "animate" the *Marble Faun* itself, providing another way for readers to interpret the text.

Tredwell also warned that extra-illustration could be carried too far and knew that "a beautiful text is entirely lost sight of in the wilderness of illustration." Instead, "in a properly illustrated book the print is no greater expounder or illustrator of the text than the text is of the print."[75] Although some extra-illustrated copies of the Tauchnitz *Marble Faun* do threaten to overwhelm the text, in many some of the tipped-in leaves are left blank, inviting readers to provide a mental picture if not an actual one, or to add another photograph later. A reader could also write on these blank pages, a conceit that Elia Peattie explores in "On a Blank Leaf in 'The Marble Faun,'" a poem published in the *Century Magazine* in 1891. Although the title of the poem is ambiguous—the poem could literally be written on the leaf or could be about the leaf—the blank leaf itself seems to evoke a "poetic precinct" for this author. The poet addresses her verse to a lover who reminds her of Donatello: "'T was something in your eyes—I swear it, friend, / For you seemed part of a stream, and wood, and field. / I've watched your soul grow young!" Having watched this growing youth, however, the poet does not want her lover to suffer the knowledge of experience:

> Oh, learn no wisdom, for that may bring grief;
> And love no woman, for 't will sure bring pain;
>   Be Donatello still!
> Believe me, friend, this learning is a thief,
> And where it thrives the simple joys are slain.
>   Ah, drink your fill
> Of sky and hill, of sun and wind and sea;
> Be thou my faun, but I no Miriam to thee.[76]

The poet has here created a fantasy based on her identification with characters in *The Marble Faun,* an identification she emphasizes by imagining the poem as being inscribed in the book itself. At the same time, by publishing this poem in a mass-produced magazine, Peattie converts a personal response to the book into a public expression.

In the preface to *The Marble Faun,* Hawthorne laments the loss of his "Gentle, Kind, Benevolent, Indulgent, and most Beloved and Honoured Reader," who, he fears, has withdrawn to "the Paradise of Gentle Readers" and is no longer visible to "the great Eye of the Public."[77] The Tauchnitz editions of *The Marble Faun,* however, seem to have appealed to sympathetic readers, readers who participated in the construction of the text by tipping in and coloring photographs, adding other mementos, and, in the case of Elia Peattie, literally writing themselves into its blank pages. These readers' own investment in the book—both personal and financial—increased their benevolence toward it. In a sense, it was not only Hawthorne's book but theirs as well.

In 1887, the editor John Torrey Morse captured this personal identification with the book in a letter to Houghton, Mifflin. He was in Rome and "of course am reading, for about the tenth time, the Marble Faun. Naturally I am seized with the desire to get as full a set of photographs to illustrate it, as I can; & I like to make *my own* selection. Also I would like to have the volumes bound here in the famous Roman vellum, so that the whole thing may be as *local* as possible."[78] The photographs and binding create a "local" souvenir for Morse, while his selection of them makes it "his own." Morse requests that Houghton, Mifflin send him an unbound copy of *The Marble Faun* for this purpose, but he is clearly following a tradition established with the Tauchnitz edition: the same tradition that Houghton, Mifflin would draw on two years later in publishing its own deluxe illustrated edition. The fatedness of Morse's practice testifies to its frequency: to tip in illustrations is now a "natural desire."

The creation of this "natural desire" suggests that to look at a photograph is not fully to experience a work of art or a tourist sight, just as to read a book is not fully to comprehend it. A full response requires the creation of the reader's own narrative. This narrative, which we might also term a romance of travel, enabled Louise Chandler Moulton to see Miriam and Donatello sitting with her at the Villa Borghese, and William Dean Howells to visit the Tarpeian Rock and imagine the sublime gulf into which the model plunged. It is also a narrative such as that created by readers who inserted their own photographs, flowers, and poetry into their souvenir copies of *The Marble Faun*. Readers of *The Marble Faun* had to work to draw their own conclusions about the text. But this textual engagement did not itself wholly constitute their use of the text, as they also worked to use it as a guidebook that both shaped and reflected their personal experiences of Rome.

Although Hawthorne had himself worried that guidebooks had diminished his experience of the real thing, his own text—especially in its extra-illustrated copies—testifies to the way in which "intellectual equipment" can enhance, rather than diminish, one's travel experience. First, it inaugurates the process of "sight sacralization" that inspires tourists to travel; to read about and see a picture of Hilda's tower makes one want to visit the actual place. Second, it provides readers with a way to authenticate their travel by noting the accuracy of a written description or imagining a literary character hovering around the corner. Third, this very process of reading and touring provides travelers with activities through which they can structure their leisure time. In the case of the Tauchnitz *Marble Faun,* these activities gave way to even more concrete pursuits, as readers tipped in and hand-colored the photographs, and wrote captions, and even poems, on the blank pages. These concrete pursuits not only gave tourists a way to ennoble their leisure by converting it into a kind of productive work but also enabled these readers to use *The Marble Faun* to help organize their own experience of travel.[79]

Such readers did not, in the end, use the book prescriptively but rather imaginatively: focusing, through the illustrations, on certain tourist sights and artworks over others, and sympathizing with certain characters but not with others. In this regard, it is important that Elia Peattie, in her poem comparing her lover to Donatello, rejects the part of Miriam for herself. Miriam's fate does not have to be her own. In this way, romance enables readers to develop a context for their own experience as tourists and to create a romance of travel based on their own original experiences, albeit experiences constructed in part by the tourist industry that recognized the importance of creating a personalized, yet also mass-produced, souvenir.

To think about historical readers requires us to be open to various forms of reading: forms that, in the case of the Tauchnitz *Marble Faun,* lead not only to a desire to follow a plot but also a desire to extend the act of reading to the social realm, as one visits the "real" places inhabited by fictional characters, chooses photographs that memorialize both the experiences of those characters and one's own experiences in a foreign place, and converts the book itself into a work of art. If the Tauchnitz *Marble Faun* was a piece of "intellectual equipment," then, it was a piece manufactured not only by Tauchnitz and his Italian booksellers but also by the readers who worked to make it into a lasting souvenir.

∾ NOTES ∾

I would like to thank Irmgard Schopen for her research assistance and Michele Moylan, Joel Pfister, Stephen Rachman, Lane Stiles, William Stowe, Michael Winship, Thomas Woodson, and the members of the Ohio Early

American History and Culture Seminar for their helpful suggestions on earlier versions of this essay.

1. Nathaniel Hawthorne, "To James T. Fields," 17 Nov. 1859, letter 1050 of *The Letters, 1857–1864,* ed. Thomas Woodson, James A. Rubino, L. Neal Smith, and Norman Holmes Pearson, vol. 18 of *The Centenary Edition of the Works of Nathaniel Hawthorne* (Columbus: Ohio State UP, 1987) 200.

2. I take this last phrase from the title of Richard Millington's chapter on *The Marble Faun* in *Practicing Romance: Narrative Form and Cultural Engagement in Hawthorne's Fiction* (Princeton: Princeton UP, 1988) 177–206.

3. Edwin Whipple, rev. of *The Marble Faun, Atlantic Monthly* 5 (1860): 622; Henry James, *Hawthorne* (1879; Ithaca: Cornell UP, 1956) 134.

4. I am thinking here in particular of Richard H. Brodhead, *The School of Hawthorne* (New York: Oxford UP, 1986) 67–80; Rita K. Gollin, "Hawthorne and the Anxiety of Aesthetic Response," *Centennial Review* 28/29 (1984–85): 94–104; Millington 177–206; and T. Walter Herbert, *Dearest Beloved: The Hawthornes and the Making of the Middle-Class Family* (Berkeley: U of California P, 1993) 215–72.

5. James, *Hawthorne* 131.

6. Charles Curtis Bigelow, introductory note, *The Marble Faun,* vol. 9 of *The Works of Nathaniel Hawthorne* (New York: Bigelow, Brown, 1923) iv.

7. Maxwell Geismar, introduction, *The Marble Faun* (New York: Washington Square P, 1958) vi. For an overview of critical editions of *The Marble Faun,* see David B. Kesterson, "*The Marble Faun*" and "Checklist," *Essex Institute Historical Collections* 127 (1991): 69–87, 96–99.

8. Julian Hawthorne, *Nathaniel Hawthorne and His Wife,* 2 vols. (Boston, 1885) 2:171.

9. Jonathan Auerbach, "Executing the Model: Painting, Sculpture, and Romance-Writing in Hawthorne's *The Marble Faun,*" *ELH* 47 (1980): 106.

10. Although his editions were legally contraband in England, many were smuggled there as well. As one British publisher wrote, "[L]et us suppose that there has always been a recording angel perched up aloft on every steamboat, who has taken note of the contents of every passenger's baggage, and to count the number of smuggled Tauchnitz volumes; how many scores of thousands of these contraband luxuries would that recording spirit have had to report to have crossed the Channel and found homes in respectable libraries?" (Edward Marston, *After Work: Fragments from the Workshop of an Old Publisher* [London: William Heinemann, 1904] 114–15.) See also Ann Wilsher, "The Tauchnitz 'Marble Faun,'" *History of Photography* 4 (1980): 62; and William Todd and Ann Bowden, *Tauchnitz International Editions in English, 1841–1955* (New York: Bibliographical Society of America, 1988) 190–91.

11. Todd and Bowden viii.

12. For further discussion of such series, see William B. Todd, "Books in

Series," in *Collectible Books: Some New Paths,* ed. Jean Peters (New York and London: R. R. Bowker, 1979) 7–26.

13. *The Republic* 12 July 1849: 1, reprinted in Todd and Bowden 907.

14. *American Review* August 1849: 216, quoted in Todd and Bowden 908. For further documentation of Tauchnitz's agents in New York, see Robert E. Cazden, *A Social History of the German Book Trade in America to the Civil War* (Columbia, S.C.: Camden House, 1984) 170, 431.

15. Quoted in Todd and Bowden 4; Tighe Hopkins, "'The Tauchnitz' Edition: The Story of a Popular Publisher," *The Pall Mall Magazine* 25 (1901): 198; and Simon Nowell-Smith, *International Copyright Law and the Publisher in the Reign of Queen Victoria* (Oxford: Clarendon P, 1968) 43. Other firms, such as Baudry and Galignani in Paris and Friedrich Fleischer in Leipzig, had already begun successfully publishing reprints, though not with the authors' permission. See Todd and Bowden 3; Karl H. Pressler, "The Tauchnitz Edition: Beginning and End of a Famous Series," *Publishing History* 6 (1980): 65; and Nowell-Smith 41–42.

16. Bernhard Tauchnitz, letter to Nathaniel Hawthorne, 9 Jan. 1864, Houghton Library, Harvard University, cited in Claude M. Simpson, introduction, *The Marble Faun,* vol. 4 of *The Centenary Edition of the Works of Nathaniel Hawthorne* (Columbus: Ohio State UP, 1968) xxx [hereafter cited as "*CMF*"].

17. Nowell-Smith 44–45.

18. Henry Morley, *Of English Literature in the Reign of Victoria* (Leipzig, 1881) i.

19. Quoted in Todd and Bowden vii.

20. Sophia Hawthorne, "To Louisa Hawthorne," 1 Dec. 1851, letter 526 of *The Letters, 1843–1853,* 16:511. In making this conclusion Sophia also mentions British editions of several of Hawthorne's works, as well as a translation of *The Scarlet Letter* from Prussia.

21. [Curt Otto, J.D.], *Der Verlag Bernhard Tauchnitz 1937–1912* (Leipzig: Tauchnitz Verlag, 1912) 25–26, quoted in Todd and Bowden 119–20.

22. Morley x.

23. *Der Verlag Bernhard Tauchnitz,* quoted in Todd and Bowden 120.

24. Hopkins 199.

25. Todd and Bowden 123.

26. Although the Tauchnitz edition continued to be published under the title *Transformation,* for the sake of clarity in this essay I refer to it by Hawthorne's preferred American title.

27. Bernhard Tauchnitz, letter to Nathaniel Hawthorne, 9 Jan. 1864, in the Houghton Library, Harvard University; cited by Simpson, introduction, *CMF* xxx.

28. *CMF* xxiv; C. E. Frazer Clark, Jr., *Nathaniel Hawthorne: A Descriptive Bibliography* (Pittsburgh: U of Pittsburgh P, 1978) 245.

29. For an overview of Ticknor and Fields's promotional techniques, see Brodhead 54–58. For a more specific case study of these promotional techniques, see Scott E. Casper, "The Two Lives of Franklin Pierce: Hawthorne, Political Culture, and the Literary Market," *American Literary History* 5 (Summer 1993): 203–30.

30. See Simpson, introduction, *CMF* xxix.

31. Nathaniel Hawthorne, "To Una Hawthorne," 25 May 1860, letter 1101 of *The Letters, 1857–1864* 293. For information about Smith and Elder see the detailed notes in this volume on pp. 281 and 294.

32. Todd and Bowden viii.

33. William B. Todd, "Firma Tauchnitz: A Further Investigation," *Publishing History* 2 (1977): 14–15; Clark 254.

34. This inscription, made by Fannie L. Fiske, is in an illustrated edition of the Tauchnitz *Marble Faun* now in the Ohio State University Library.

35. For a discussion of this pose and its various incarnations, see Rita K. Gollin, *Portraits of Nathaniel Hawthorne* (Dekalb: Northern Illinois UP, 1983) 55–63. Carol Shloss suggests that the presence of this photograph may indicate "the author's collusion in the enterprise," since he would have had to give Tauchnitz the picture (*In Visible Light: Photography and the American Writer, 1840–1940* [New York: Oxford UP, 1987] 39). But this assertion is unlikely, given the fact that the illustrated editions did not appear until after Hawthorne's death and that Tauchnitz himself was not responsible for the illustrations.

36. This information is based on my examination of Tauchnitz editions of *The Marble Faun* in the Charvat Collection of the Ohio State University Library, the American Antiquarian Society, and the Peabody Essex Museum.

37. Todd and Bowden 123–24.

38. Todd and Bowden, while citing this fact, also warn that the *National Union Catalog* "cannot be regarded as a reliable index of popularity" (197). At the same time, the comparison to other Tauchnitz editions such as *Romola* seems instructive.

39. For more detailed descriptions of photographically illustrated books and the processes used to produce them, see Lucien Goldschmidt and Weston J. Naef, *The Truthful Lens: A Survey of the Photographically Illustrated Book, 1844–1914* (New York: Grolier Club, 1980); John B. Cameron and William B. Becker, *Photography's Beginnings: A Visual History* (Albuquerque: U of New Mexico P, 1989); Stuart Bennett, "Photography as Book Illustration, 1839–1900," in *Collectible Books* 152–76; Lois Olcott Price, "The Development of Photomechanical Book Illustration," in *The American Illustrated Book in the Nineteenth Century*, ed. Gerald W. R. Ward (Winterthur, Del.: Henry Francis du Pont Winterthur Museum, 1987) 233–56; and Rolf H. Krauss, "Travel Reports and Photography in Early Photographically Illustrated Books," *History of Photography* 3 (1979): 15–30.

40. Goldschmidt and Naef 204.

41. Daniel M. Tredwell, *A Monograph on Privately Illustrated Books: A Plea for Bibliomania* (Flatbush, Long Island, 1892) 54–55, 138.

42. Clark 256.

43. Advertisement, *The Marble Faun or the Romance of Monte Beni*, 2 vols. (Boston, 1889) 1:ii. For further details on this edition, see Clark 256; also Simpson, introduction, *CMF* xxx.

44. Tredwell 150, 262.

45. "Holiday Books," *Atlantic Monthly* 67 (1891): 123.

46. The scope of these accounts is suggested by Harold F. Smith, who lists almost three hundred travel works written by Americans before 1900 in *American Travellers Abroad: A Bibliography of Accounts Published before 1900* (Carbondale: Southern Illinois UP, 1969).

47. Henry T. Tuckerman, *Isabel; or Sicily* (Philadelphia, 1839) 15.

48. See Robert H. Byer, who argues that tourists were "seeking in guidebooks, or copies, or in each other a substitute for the authority and sublimely legible presence of the orator's discourse" ("Words, Monuments, Beholders: The Visual Arts in Hawthorne's *The Marble Faun,*" in *American Iconology*, ed. David C. Miller [New Haven: Yale UP, 1993] 171).

49. *CMF* 424.

50. Julia Ward Howe, *From the Oak to the Olive: A Plain Record of a Pleasant Journey* (Boston, 1868) 64.

51. Nathaniel Hawthorne, *The French and Italian Notebooks*, ed. Thomas Woodson, vol. 14 of *The Centenary Edition of the Works of Nathaniel Hawthorne* 115.

52. *The French and Italian Notebooks* 136.

53. *CMF* 3.

54. *CMF* 381.

55. *CMF* 381.

56. William Dean Howells, *Roman Holidays and Others* (New York: Harper and Brothers, 1908) 226–27.

57. Dean MacCannell, *The Tourist* (New York: Schocken, 1976) 45.

58. William Dean Howells, *Italian Journeys* (New York, 1867) 162–63.

59. Marion Harland, *Loiterings in Pleasant Paths* (New York, 1880) 218.

60. "Scenes from The Marble Faun," *Scribner's Monthly* 2 (1871): 493.

61. Louise Chandler Moulton, *Lazy Tours in Spain and Elsewhere* (Boston, 1898) 103.

62. *CMF* 3.

63. Moulton 103.

64. T. B. Aldrich, *From Ponkapog to Pesth* (Boston, 1883) 27.

65. Edmund Wilson, *Europe without Baedeker* (New York: Farrar, Straus and Giroux, 1966) 212.

66. Shloss 40.

67. Henry James, *The Art of the Novel* (New York: Charles Scribner's, 1934) 34.

68. Nathaniel Hawthorne, "To Henry A. Bright, 5 May 1860, letter 1092 of *The Letters, 1857–1864* 276.

69. Todd gives an accounting of nine copies of *The Marble Faun*, noting that in two photographs the Faun is completely exposed, in two partially covered, and in five completely covered ("Firma Tauchnitz" 15).

70. Nathaniel Hawthorne, "To John Lothrop Motley," 1 April 1860, letter 1082 of *The Letters, 1857–1864* 256. Motley's letter to Hawthorne, dated 29 March 1860, is quoted in the note on p. 258.

71. Moulton's copy of *The Marble Faun* is now in the first-editions collection of the American Antiquarian Society.

72. Wilsher 64.

73. *CMF* 6–7.

74. Tredwell 430–31.

75. Tredwell 436–37.

76. Elia W. Peattie, "On a Blank Leaf in 'The Marble Faun,'" *Century Magazine* 42 (1891): 847.

77. *CMF* 2.

78. John Torrey Morse, letter to Houghton, Mifflin and Co., 28 Dec. 1887, Houghton, Mifflin and Co. Papers, bMS Am 1925 (1282), Houghton Library, Harvard University. This letter is cited here by permission of the Houghton Library, Harvard University. I am grateful to Scott Casper for bringing it to my attention.

79. On the connection between leisure and work, see William W. Stowe, *Going Abroad: European Travel in Nineteenth-Century American Culture* (Princeton: Princeton UP, 1994).

Finding His Mark:
Twain's The Innocents Abroad
as a Subscription Book

NANCY COOK

❧ I. ❧

M ARK T WAIN'S STATUS AS A classic American author has
come about, in part, because of his own efforts at self-fashioning,
which are inextricably linked to his mode of writing for the subscription book trade. His first major book, *The Innocents Abroad*, was shaped
by its production, promotion, and sales as a subscription book. Mark
Twain represents the author as *maker* of books, one who performs a
number of tasks throughout the publication process. In addition to
writing, he managed many editorial and promotional tasks, all which
served to enhance the status and reputation of Mark Twain as much as
the book itself. A "Mark Twain" style emerged and subsumed the
substance of any particular text. *The Innocents Abroad*, then, displayed
the ascendancy of style over substance both within and outside the text,
for textual strategies were mirrored by the very process of publishing
the subscription book.[1]

In this chapter I would like to suggest how the publication of *The
Innocents Abroad* as a subscription book both shaped and conditioned
Mark Twain's development as a successful writer, and to intimate how
the experience of reading *The Innocents Abroad* as a subscription book
might differ significantly from a reading of other editions. Consequently, I refer throughout the essay to the first edition, published by
the American Publishing Company of Hartford, Connecticut, in 1869.

Readers of the works of Mark Twain in editions such as the Harper and Brothers "Author's National Edition," or the Penguin Classics, or even some of the Iowa-California scholarly editions, read books that differ radically from the books Twain's contemporaries read. The publication process itself produces uniformity: the corporate logo, colors, design, and size of Penguin books label them as "classics," and their introductions or afterwords by noted scholars place them within the context of literary history. In the Penguin editions, such disparate authors as Longfellow, Emerson, Hawthorne, Cooper, Stowe, Melville, Barnum, and Twain can snuggle uniformly on American literature's own shelf of classics.

Comparing first editions, however, one would immediately have recognized a profound difference. Longfellow's and Hawthorne's books might have seemed indistinguishable, bound as they both were in the plain brown cloth that served as a trademark of understated highbrow quality for Ticknor and Fields—the publishers who, according to legend, came quietly knocking at the artist's door, politely inquiring if he had a manuscript he might care to show. But Barnum's and Twain's books looked considerably different. They were bigger, fatter, gaudier, and copiously illustrated. Subscription publishers often printed on cheap paper, crammed pages with text and small margins, and filled the back matter with ads. When placed next to a copy of Longfellow, they were discernibly mismatched.

Books as well as texts suggest, beckon, even posit an audience, and subscription books offered themselves as a very different kind of attraction. In this massive study of American book publishing, John Tebbel defined subscription books as generally "those for which a definite market is created, before or after publication, by soliciting individual orders."[2] But in the latter half of the nineteenth century, the method was associated with a particular style of solicitation. One bookman recalls: "In my bookhood [*sic*], the predominating plan of selling books was through the army of book agents numbering many thousands who skirmished through every city, town, and hamlet, armed with prospectuses showing various styles of binding and containing persuasive testimonials to back up the carefully memorized sales arguments of the solicitors."[3]

Early in his career, Mark Twain allied himself with the subscription publishing method and put armies of canvassers to work hawking his wares. His success as an author depended in large part on his ability to reimagine the role of the author in America, to situate himself firmly within a book marketplace and to break down the idea of authorship as a phase of production discrete from publishing and promotion. His success not only brought him fame and fortune but also changed the way in which many readers approached and read his books, as well as how they perceived his status as an American author.

In 1867 Twain embarked on a tour of Europe and the Holy Land aboard a luxury steamer named the *Quaker City*. His expenses had been paid by a newspaper, the *Daily Alta California,* and Twain agreed to send back dispatches for publication. Twain was not the only journalist aboard, however: several other passengers dispatched correspondence for publication in the States. By the time the *Quaker City* returned in the fall of 1867, the passengers had become minor celebrities and the voyage was well known.

In the preface to *The Innocents Abroad* Mark Twain made a kind of contract with his reader, offering a "record of a pleasure-trip," one that was distinctive because it suggested to the reader "how *he* would be likely to see Europe and the East if he looked at them with his own eyes instead of the eyes of those who travelled in those countries before him," and a book "written honestly" if perhaps not "wisely" (v). Despite this irony—for in fact readers were dependent upon Mark Twain's eyes—Twain worked immediately to distinguish himself from "those who travelled in those countries before him," and suggested a special relation between himself and his readers. In doing so Twain amended the contract he had already made with Elisha Bliss, Jr., adding restrictions to the kind of book he had agreed to make.

When Bliss initially wrote to Twain, he indicated only that the American Publishing Company was "desirous of obtaining from you a work of some kind, perhaps compiled from your letters from the East, &c., with such interesting additions as may be proper."[4] Twain answered indicating that he was interested and asking Bliss for more details. Bliss replied:

> We think we see clearly that the book would sell; a *humorous* work, that is to say, a work *humorously inclined* we believe it, and Richardson's work [*sic*] we think owe a good deal of their popularity to their *spicy* nature. The first thing then is, will you *make* a book? For material we should suggest your collected letters, *revamped and worked* over and all the other matter you can command.[5]

Bliss's letter directed Mark Twain as to what "sells," and pointedly asked not that Mark Twain *write* a book but that he "*make*" one. Bliss expanded this idea, indicating that the making of a book was a process of compilation and revamping, even commanding material, rather than one of composing. Mark Twain's writing process in fact followed Bliss's advice, and this determined the character of the artifact that resulted.

Bliss's expectations were clarified in the formal contract between them, though it was not prepared until several months later. The contract demanded that "Clemens" provide the publisher with a "manuscript properly prepared & written to make an Octavo volume of at least 500 pages," that the publisher "shall have the exclusive use of sd [*sic*] Manuscript & right to publish the same & that he [Clemens] will not use the same in any other manner, or any part of it or of its contained matter," that the subject was "to be the trip of the 'Quaker City to the Holy Land,'" that "Clemens is to give all necessary time & attention to the reading of proofs & correting [*sic*] the same if necessary & to all other matters connected with the bringing out of the Book usually done by Authors & to do all in his power to promote the sale of the work."[6]

The contract defined the term "author" in terms of the subscription book business. He should be able to provide, according to accepted standards of preparation, a lengthy manuscript. He sold the publisher "exclusive" use of his material, which was on a subject agreed to by contract. The interest of the publisher, and presumably of the buyers, was topical—that is, the subject must be the already well-publicized voyage of the *Quaker City*. Moreover, as an author, Clemens was responsible for seeing the book through publication. Under the terms of this contract, he could not abandon the project after completion of the manuscript, as he had apparently done with *The Celebrated Jumping Frog*.[7] Most importantly, an author was required to "do all in his power to promote the sale of the work." Apparently both author and publisher assumed that Samuel L. Clemens would produce and promote this work as "Mark Twain," though the pseudonym is never mentioned.

The notion of the sovereign artist has been undermined here. Elisha Bliss was no James T. Fields, who, according to legend, politely cajoled Nathaniel Hawthorne to extract a hidden masterpiece from his bureau drawer, then published it as *The Scarlet Letter*. Though the publishers Ticknor and Fields were very aware of the literary marketplace, literary historians have tended to promote the apocryphal legend, not the market-oriented fact. In the Fields-Hawthorne model of literary history, the writer's work was represented as a masterpiece: a remote, even Platonic product untainted by market concerns.[8] Elisha Bliss, on the other hand, contracted with Mark Twain to make literary piece work.

Not perceived as a potential masterpiece, *The Innocents Abroad* was instead a product remarkably responsive to the shape proposed for it by the market, as conceived by Bliss. It was written to order, just as the subscription books produced from the text were later printed, and then bound to order, only after the canvassers had sold a sufficient number. The logic of distinct or discrete phases—author to text to publisher to public—has been broken, and a complex feedback loop has been substituted for it.

∿ **2.** ∿

The American Publishing Company suggested in an ad seeking to recruit canvassers that nearly everyone had already heard of Mark Twain, and thus prospects would be eager to buy his "new" book. Mark Twain had achieved a degree of fame from his ubiquity in American newspapers and his relentless lecture tours. Even his most rural readers had access to national news and literature by means of wide distribution of urban newspapers, or through exchanges that appeared in local papers. Moreover, Mark Twain lectured in many places on the lyceum circuits, coursed by speakers as diverse as Emerson, Thomas Nast, Petroleum V. Nasby, and Elizabeth Cady Stanton. Thus, Americans with the requisite money and leisure time, even those outside urban centers, had access to a range of cultural activities. The potential market for a book by Mark Twain was enormous and varied.

In addition to offering "One large and Exceedingly Handsome Volume of Over 650 Octavo Pages, profusely adorned with 234 beautiful, spirited, and appropriate engravings," the American Publishing Company suggested myriad other selling points for *The Innocents Abroad,* including the reputation of Mark Twain himself.[9] In the ad mentioned above, placed to recruit canvassers for *The Innocents Abroad,* the publishers presumed that Mark Twain's name not only spoke for itself but incorporated a number of identifiable qualities:

BOOK AGENTS WANTED
to sell
MARK TWAIN'S NEW BOOK
Who has not heard of him? Who has not laughed over his quaint sayings and queer ideas? Who has not fairly succumbed to his racy anecdotes and melted under his pathetic stories? Who has not thrilled with his fine descriptions, acknowledged the keenness of his satire and admired the frank and daring openness of his word?

The ad posited a Mark Twain who was already successful and whose "new" book had been eagerly awaited. Canvassers, the ad suggested, would not have much selling to do, for the name "Mark Twain" would do the selling for them. The approach was rather bold since for most of his potential audience this was Mark Twain's first *book*, given that *The Celebrated Jumping Frog* had not had a large press run nor been reviewed widely. Moreover, the ad placed its readers on the defensive, for after reading such copy, who would have admitted to an ignorance of Mark Twain's work? The ad continued:

THE INNOCENTS ABROAD,
or the
NEW PILGRIM'S PROGRESS,
is the quintessence of himself, the condensation and concentration of all his powers. No stoicism can withstand its gentility and humor. No prejudices destroy the effect of his truthful delineation of the follies or fulnes [*sic*] of life and society. It is the most readable, enjoyable, laughable, yet valuable book printed for years. It will be the most popular.

50,000 *volumes printed in advance and now ready for distribution by Agents* to whom liberal terms, and free territory will be given. Apply to
AMERICAN PUBLISHING CO.
HARTFORD, CONN.[10]

The language of the ad suggested that to buy the book was somehow to buy Mark Twain, for the book offered not so much a travel narrative, as "the quintessence of himself, the condensation and concentration of all his powers." Readers were powerless before him; they had to follow his lead, for the book lay at the top of the heap, and the name "Mark Twain" should have topped everyone's list. Thus, although the appeal was broad (and contradictory), promising the "quaint" and the "queer," "racy anecdotes," "pathetic stories," "fine descriptions," "satire," "gentility and humor," truth and value, the book cohered under the inscription "Mark Twain." Furthermore, the ad campaign corresponded to the relentless valuation of the persona over the narrative that occurred within the text itself.

Agents worked on a commission basis, and the recruitment ads played on the speculative possibilities of canvassing. An ad placed in a Hartford newspaper announced that one agent received "$100 in Gold" as a premium for selling large quantities of *The Innocents Abroad*. Agents "constantly" reported taking as many as "74 orders in one day," as at least one agent in Rochester apparently did. In addition to "the largest commissions," "extra premiums" such as "$100 in Gold" awaited the prospective canvasser.[11] While the promises made by the American Publishing Company might have been inflated, for it was unlikely that many canvassers took "74 orders in one day," nevertheless the ad assured would-be sales agents that the money itself was not. The company offered premiums in gold, not greenbacks.

Canvassers were offered "free territory" in which to stake their claims, with no claim jumping sanctioned by the company. But just as in Mark Twain's mining camps, even free territory was worthless unless worked, and since some territories were richer than others, claim jumping occurred with some regularity.[12] Moreover, the language of inflation functioned as more than just a recruitment tool of the publishers, for canvassers themselves could inflate book prices by selling the higher-priced bindings. The promotion and subsequent inflation of both Mark Twain's reputation and his book began as soon as Bliss and Twain opened discussion in December 1867. Twain began to plug the book in his private letters, he continued to incorporate *Quaker City* anecdotes into many of his lectures, and he continued to encourage newspaper stories and interviews for promotional purposes. While in California securing the rights to his letters from the *Alta California* and revising the *Innocents Abroad* manuscript, Twain lectured on Europe and the Holy Land, which allowed him to test his material while at the same time it offered previews of the coming book to prospective purchasers.

When Twain returned to the East in the summer of 1868, he made preparations for the 1868–69 lecture season. He decided to continue to use material from the *Quaker City* excursion rather than his proven Sandwich Islands material, a choice that recognized the promotional aspect of his contract with Bliss. Starting in Cleveland in November, Twain first delivered his lecture "The American Vandal Abroad." His friend and fellow *Quaker City* traveler, Mary Mason Fairbanks, puffed his performance in her husband's newspaper, the *Cleveland Herald*, and Twain was off to a good start. Between November and the end of the season in the spring of 1869, Mark Twain traveled extensively, delivering dozens of lectures throughout Ohio, Pennsylvania, New York, New Jersey, Michigan, Indiana, Illinois, Iowa, and Wisconsin. While lecturing he plugged *The Innocents Abroad* both in large cities—Chicago, Pittsburgh, Cleveland—and in small towns such as Tecumseh, Michigan, and Ottawa, Illinois.

The lyceum circuit made certain demands. Program committees wanted to provide audiences a break from the spate of didactic lectures offered by scores of clergymen and "professors" on the circuit, but they did not want mere humor. To be successful, Mark Twain was obliged to entertain and amuse, but he also needed to provide some instruction, perhaps even offer a moral.

All this he did. As Twain wrote in a letter to Mary Mason Fairbanks, he offered audiences:

> the hideous statue of a *skinned man* in the Cathedral ('twill make you shudder) . . . then some more description; the Acropolis, the Parthenon & then, Athens by moonlight . . . then the *moral* of the lecture, which is Let the Vandal continue to travel—it liberalizes him & makes a better man of him (though the moral is an entirely gratuitous contribution & will be a clear gain to the societies employing me, for it isn't deduced from anything there is in the lecture)—& *then*, we close with a starchy & a high-toned glimpse at each of the most imposing pictures we saw— Gibraltar . . . the Pyramids, Damascus, &c—fireworks, you know— then, finis. . . . Of course, scattered all through, are the most preposterous yarns, & all that sort of thing. But I *think* it will *entertain* an audience, this lecture.[13]

The lecture allowed Mark Twain to show his range, convincing both lyceum committees and prospective book buyers that he was more than a humorist. In the lecture he tried strategies similar to those employed in the book. The lecture, then, offered a trial run to test the success of his methods of composition and suggested strategies for the successful promotion of the book itself. His romantic description of the Sphinx proved particularly popular, and Bliss, realizing the popularity of the passage, had it inserted into later printings of the salesman's dummy for *The Innocents Abroad*.

Newspaper notices and reviews of his lectures helped Twain build his reputation, making the bravado of the ad's "Who has not heard of him?" a little less ridiculous, but he realized that more could be done to capitalize on his touring. While in Chicago he wrote to Frank Bliss, Elisha's son and the treasurer of the American Publishing Company: "Why don't you issue prospectuses and startling advertisements now while I am stirring the bowels of these communities? I have big houses—and more invitations to lecture than I can fill."[14] The feedback circuit seemed to be functioning, but it might have been even more efficient. The issue became one of volume, of critical mass: how many times could a single lecture, or one trip, be used to the mutual benefit of Twain and his employers? It seems as if nothing less than ubiquity would do.

In this scheme publicity ideally worked within a circuit of mutual benefit for lecture and book alike. In one example from a Toledo newspaper where the strategy worked, the reviewer observed: "Much of the humor contained in the book is already familiar to those who have heard Mr. Clemens lecture, but the lecture did not tell the half."[15] With an eye always toward self-promotion, Mark Twain reprinted this notice in his own newspaper, the Buffalo, New York, *Express*. Audiences at the lectures received an oral presentation of the prospectus as well as the suggestion that the book would not only confirm their initial delight but would also offer them additional pleasure. The newspaper pieces assured them that their good opinion of Mark Twain was shared; if they bought the book they would not be disappointed. Each bit of publicity built on earlier ones; each performance supported another. The separate spheres of composition, production, and sales have been blurred.

No doubt book sales benefited from the notices the voyage of the *Quaker City* had received earlier. Having been clipped or "exchanged," these appeared in newspapers throughout the country. The American Publishing Company prepared promotional copy for journalists in hopes that newspapers would seize upon the publication of *The Innocents Abroad* as a continuation of the previous stories, in hopes that Mark Twain's lecture series had kept him newsworthy, and to help that overworked class of workers, the newspaper editor. Twain scholar Leon Dickinson has noted that these advertising leaflets and broadsides became the company's chief promotional device. It sent out six-by-twenty inch sheets containing five press notices for *The Innocents Abroad* to newspaper editors throughout the country. That copy included this comment: "Knowing well that the pressure of business detail upon an Editor often renders it extremely inconvenient for him to devote the time necessary to the proper preparation of Book Reviews, we have copied portions of several notices of our new book from leading journals."[16] Not surprising, the quoted passages represented only portions of the original reviews; unfavorable comments were simply excised.

The marketing strategy represented the system at its most efficient. Harried editors sometimes used these ready-made reviews, but they had already been pared down to their essential message, which of course was "buy the book." With any luck, the complete broadside versions appeared in newspapers, which in turn would be clipped, and the wholly good, wholly manufactured review might be recycled indefinitely. In his role as newspaper editor, Mark Twain certainly saved himself trouble in finding new material for the Buffalo *Express,* for he used the publication of his own book as the subject of several items, including a notice that the book had received some twelve hundred newspaper notices. Since subscription publishers rarely bought advertising for any of their titles and almost never sent out review copies to newspapers or periodicals, these "news" items stirred up interest in their books for little cash outlay.[17] This method of marketing not only helped sell the book but also kept Mark Twain himself in the news, where his name remained throughout his life.

Publicity spawned more publicity in a seemingly endless cycle of better notices. Even after the book was a proven success, Twain used his regular column in the nationally circulated *Galaxy* to keep the book's title before the public. He included humorous bits about canvassers' encounters with prospects, he published a burlesque bad review, followed by responses to it, and he continued to publish anecdotes that referred either to the book or the trip itself. Once the way for the book's release had been carefully prepared, and after some delay, canvassers, prospectuses in hand, finally were dispatched.

The prospectuses or dummies were distributed to agents before the books became available. Sample bindings, representing a range of prices, often were pasted to the inside covers. Prospectuses usually contained up to about a hundred pages, including fifty or sixty pages of sample text. These samples were added to a table of contents, list of illustrations, sample engravings, advertising, edited reviews, and blank forms for subscription lists. Agents supposedly worked one book at a time for a particular publisher. Each book, then, had two emissaries to the buyer—the canvasser and the prospectus.

When canvassers from the American Publishing Company called on prospective customers in the summer of 1869, they brought an elaborately embossed prospectus for *The Innocents Abroad*—a selection of highlights from the book done up in the standard binding, a slimmer version of the book itself—Mark Twain's first title under their imprint. On the spine, gold-stamped leaves and a garland decoration issued from the letters that announced "*The Innocents Abroad or the New Pilgrim's Progress* by Mark Twain." Just below the author's name and in type only slightly smaller is the word "ILLUSTRATED." The publisher's name appeared prominently, blind-stamped within a large gold-stamped shield. From the spine alone, prospective buyers knew they would get a substantial, well-illustrated volume from a well-established publisher of fine Bibles and popular histories.

1. Cover of the first edition of *The Innocents Abroad*, American Publishing Company, Hartford, Conn., 1869. Courtesy, American Antiquarian Society.

The spine was attractive, but the playful cover of the prospectus invited the customer to buy, for it proclaimed that Twain's book was more than the average trade-press travel book. In an array of different lettering, the gold-stamped title meandered through several illustrations of the exotic sights that presumably signified the adventures lurking within (see Illustration 1). In the first edition, as in the prospectus, Mark Twain's text of *The Innocents Abroad* represented only one element in a high-gloss production.

The title, as done up for the cover of the prospectus and duplicated on the cover of the book itself, made reference to several episodes from the narrative. A mélange of exotic landmarks surrounded the title, including a cathedral dome, an erupting volcano, a structure resembling the Parthenon, and a pyramid fronted by a Sphinx-like statue. On the pyramid, one "pilgrim" slid down a corner, umbrella first, while two figures appeared on its face: one figure was in the act of inscribing his name, having accomplished "MARK TWAI," as another arrested his progress. Just below them rested the Sphinx, whose face bore a strong resemblance to George Washington.

The cover illustration offered a preview of the narrative within, including a few rather elaborate jokes or puns. As one looked at it one had "seen the elephant," common American slang a century or so ago for seeing life or the world, "especially the underside of the world."[18] Although in the text Mark Twain railed against "the vandals" who left

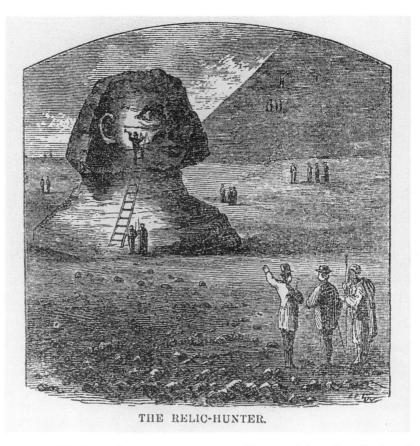

THE RELIC-HUNTER.

2. Image of the Sphinx from *The Innocents Abroad.* Photograph from the collection of Nancy Cook.

their names but took souvenirs, the cover pictured Twain himself as the vandal. And although illustrations within the book showed a conventional, relatively realistic representation of the Sphinx, on the cover the Sphinx looked like George Washington.[19] The image might have suggested, especially to Americans, that the readers' own cultural icons would be taken along when they traveled abroad, at least as the guest of Mark Twain. Imagined a little differently here, the Old World became, in a sense, an analog of the American frontier; that is, it became a place for adventure where inhibitions were cast off, where a man could make his mark. As Mark Twain's illustrated vandalism of the pyramid suggested, whether explorers or pilgrims, Americans appropriated and named for themselves what they "discovered." (For a comparison of the Sphinx compare Illustrations 2 and 3 with Illustration 1.)

PYRAMIDS AND SPHYNX.

3. Image of the Sphinx from *The Innocents Abroad*. Photograph from the collection of Nancy Cook.

General readers should immediately have recognized George Washington, an icon of American culture. Placed in front of the scrawling Mark Twain on the pyramid, Washington's image taunted the vandal with his superior visibility, even without the benefit of his written name. More telling, Washington's visage vandalized the standard post-card image of the nineteenth-century Holy Land. Retrospectively, readers may have found that the cover illustration with the figure scrawling "MARK TWAI . . . " and George Washington as the Sphinx undercut the sentimentality of Twain's often-quoted meditation on the Sphinx, which came near the very end of *The Innocents Abroad*. In the cover illustration both George Washington's face and the scribbling vandal intruded in a way that corresponded to the vandal's intrusion into Twain's reverie, which occurred during the Sphinx section of the narrative. As the vandal, Mark Twain's image underscored his ambiguous role as traveler and scribbler, rendering ironic those moments in the text when Twain seemed most reverent.

After waxing sentimentally, and at length, on the "majestic" Sphinx, which "was gazing out over the ocean of Time . . . thinking . . . of joy and sorrow, the life and death, the grandeur and decay, of five thousand slow revolving years," Twain added: "While we stood looking, a wart, or an excrescence of some kind, appeared on the jaw of the Sphinx. We heard the familiar clink of a hammer, and understood the case at once."[20] Twain's sentimental musings were interrupted by one of his fellow pilgrims, the American vandal abroad. Thus, the clever cover art might have offered readers of the first edition access to the complexity and even duplicity of Twain's recollections of the Sphinx, a reading coincident with Twain's comments to Mary Mason Fairbanks quoted earlier. All this is missed, of course, by readers of modern editions such as those from Penguin or Signet Classics.

Even, or especially here, it was the *American* who made his mark on the "eternal figure of stone," with no mention of the vandal Napoleon, whose cannons cost the Sphinx its nose.[21] Napoleon, George Washington, even Mark Twain himself remained absent *as vandals* in the descriptive prose of the text, yet, as the cover and other illustrations asserted, each has refashioned the Sphinx. The visual and verbal images of vandals and a marred Sphinx were important, I think, for they illustrated one series of power relations at work throughout *The Innocents Abroad* in particular, and throughout Twain's travel writing generally.[22] To the degree that readers found the cover illustration charming and legible, they were encouraged to see themselves as powerful, inscribing Americans—in other words, like Mark Twain.

The spine and cover of both the prospectus and first edition of *The Innocents Abroad* indeed implied that inscription (especially in terms of appropriating the foreign for one's own purposes) had been emphasized before the narrative formally began. Before readers knew anything of the narrative, they knew the author of it. His name had been repeated on spine and cover; his initials appeared on the cover in several parts of the illustration; he rode the camel and scaled the gilt pyramids on the cover, asserting his place among the icons of Old World travel. Moreover, the irreverent tone suggested by the illustrations set this travel book apart from the scores of others in the marketplace. The book as material artifact showed one way in which Mark Twain, with the aid of his publisher, negotiated for authority, marketability, and celebrity. Although it began with the voyage of the *Quaker City* and the publicity that pleasure trip garnered, those qualities became inscribed and came to fruition in the composition, publication, and promotion of *The Innocents Abroad,* a book sold only by subscription. His success in these endeavors, moreover, situated Mark Twain within a cultural and economic marketplace vastly different from the place he occupies today.

Buyers of the American Publishing Company product found that the book was no less manipulative than the prospectus, for the front matter was identical. Once readers opened the cover, but before they began to read the narrative itself, they encountered further signs; so that by the time readers got to the first chapter, their expectations and relation to the text had been guided. Two facing full-page engravings materialized first, separated by a tissue guard (see Illustrations 4 and 5). The engraving on the left, titled "*Quaker City* in a Storm" ("Steamship in a Storm" in some copies), gloomily countered the irreverent and playful cover illustration. Twain made much of the pilgrim's stormy passage and corresponding seasickness in the early chapters of the book.

During the book's production Mark Twain felt that he was not yet well enough known to merit the usual steel-engraved frontispiece portrait, so, as he wrote his friend Mary Mason Fairbanks, "I refused—I hate the effrontery of shoving the pictures of nobodies under people's noses in that way, after the fashion of quacks and negro minstrels. Told them to make a handsome *wood* engraving of the Quaker City in a storm, instead."[23] Twain may have felt that at least at the outset, *The Quaker City* and its landmark voyage were as well known, or even better known than he was, but their notoriety was due in large measure to his own efforts. By replacing the usual author's portrait with the images of the ship, the book announced itself as a travel book; moreover, a stormy sea suggested something beyond the usual guidebook fare, perhaps even romantic adventure. In the same letter to Mary Mason Fairbanks, Twain discussed possible titles for the book:

> I want a name that is *striking, comprehensive, & out of the common order*— Something not worn & hackneyed, & not commonplace. I had chosen "The New Pilgrim's Progress," but it is thought that many dull people will shudder at that, as at least taking the name of a consecrated book in vain & perhaps burlesquing it, within. I have thought of "The Irruption of the Jonathans—*Or*, the Modern Pilgrim's Progress"—you see the second title can remain, if I only precede it with something that will *let it down easy*.[24]

The prospective titles Twain mentioned are telling, for they indicated important aspects of his thinking.

In selecting "The New Pilgrim's Progress," he proclaimed that his book would not be of the modest sort, with a few mildly humorous rebukes of gullible tourists and sham holy sights; others had already published that sort of travel book. Rather Twain aimed his burlesque

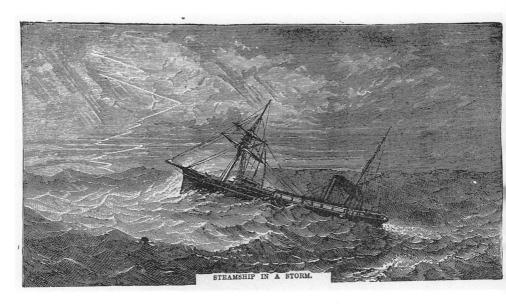

STEAMSHIP IN A STORM.

4. Frontispiece, alternately titled " *Quaker City* in a Storm," from *The Innocents Abroad.* Photograph from the collection of Nancy Cook.

high, ready to tilt at the classic texts of Christianity as well as its most pious acolytes. As a New World pilgrim, Twain offered humorous critiques of various Old World customs.

Twain's second suggestion, the two-part title, added a more obvious opposition between New and Old Worlds, an opposition that would have had currency in popular culture. "The Irruption of the Jonathans" undercut the piety of a pilgrimage and instead suggested an infestation of unsophisticated American tourists. In 1867 the Civil War was over, many people had money to travel, and hordes of middle-class Americans headed for the Paris Exhibition. The Jonathans, as Americans were often called, indeed had burst upon the European scene. "The Modern Pilgrim's Progress" suggested, as the advertisements for the voyage of the *Quaker City* made clear, that the journey was a pious *pleasure* cruise, a pilgrimage involving not hardship and suffering but comfort, fun, even acquisition, with famous biblical sights as part of the bargain (or alibi). Striving to assert the conventional as well as the irreverent, Mark Twain attempted to situate himself within the marketplace, trying both to attract attention and to avoid alienating any large portion of the reading public. With these goals in mind, quite possibly a standard frontispiece portrait would set too reverent a tone for the narrative that followed.

THE PILGRIM'S VISION.

5. Frontispiece, from *The Innocents Abroad.* Photograph from the collection of Nancy Cook.

The engraving that appeared, however, was titled "Steamship in a Storm" in later printings of *The Innocents Abroad,* and not "*Quaker City* in a Storm." It seemed that Elisha Bliss, Twain's penurious publisher, recycled an engraving he had on hand. As Beverly David noted, "what purported to be the *Quaker City* in Mark Twain's first edition was not the pilgrim's ship at all but a full-page engraving of the *Steamer Wright* which had been engraved for a Bliss publication, *Overland through Asia.*" She added that although Bliss captioned the engraving with an ambiguous title, Twain's suggested caption, "*The Quaker City* in a Storm," remained in the list of illustrations.[25] (One wonders whether the engraving had served even earlier duty.)

The image worked to the degree that it was emblematic, signifying the *idea* of the pleasure excursion (albeit one with more than a hint of adventure or danger), for it failed as an image of a particular ship on a particular voyage. Perhaps intuitively Bliss understood that few readers would care about the accuracy of the image; rather, it was the text that provided significance, even meaning, to the image. Likewise, from the outset Mark Twain's interpretation of the voyage and not the voyage itself was the subject of *The Innocents Abroad.*

When readers lifted the tissue curtain that separated the two engravings, "The Pilgrim's Vision" was revealed on the right. In this engraving a group of men loafed on deck smoking, while above them in the clouds images of the exotic emerged, not unlike those on the cover. Here, however, there was no humor, merely dreamlike images of mountains and towers, pyramids and camels, the Sphinx (now without Washington's face), an elephant, a gondola, and horsemen. The sea was calm. Significantly, no ladies appeared in the scene. The men were relaxed, dreaming of the treasures and adventures that awaited them, and their vision excluded women (see Illustration 5). Indeed, readers might have expected that, for the most part, the lady pilgrims would be spared from ridicule or misadventure. And although Mark Twain made *The Innocents Abroad* tame enough to be read by women, even children, it promised a view of a man's world. In a sense, the work allowed the ladies to lift the tissue veil and see what the men did when they were off by themselves.

Apparently Bliss had suggested the idea for this illustration, as Twain recalled in a letter to him: "remember your idea about it before?—What they *expected* to see—and what they *did* see?"[26] Turned toward the sky as they were, however, the pilgrims could not see the opposite engraving with its stormy sea. And though one loomed in the clouds, these innocents had not yet "seen the elephant." In the presentation of *two* versions of the ship, readers might have sensed that this book was more than a mere guidebook or the usual travel narrative. The two illustrations, set opposite each other as they were, suggested tension between the ideal and the real; yet Bliss's choice of subject matter in "The Pilgrim's Vision," along with its placement after rather than before "Steamship in a Storm," collapsed or at least confused the distinction between the ideal and real that both publisher and author seemed to desire. In the order in which they appear in the text, they suggested that the "Pilgrim's Vision" had weathered the storm if not the narrative itself. At the outset, then, the book set up a series of complex, sometimes contradictory expectations, many of which are lost to the modern reader. Through the text of *The Innocents Abroad*, readers needed to negotiate the gap between the two engravings, the space occupied by the tissue veil. And readers would find that, contrary to claims that Mark Twain made in his preface, the tissue was not transparent.

The title page followed, offering "descriptions of countries, nations, incidents and adventures, as they appeared to the Author," rather common pronouncements for a travel book. Readers found another attraction announced: "TWO HUNDRED AND THIRTY-FOUR ILLUSTRATIONS," an asset emphasized by salespeople and reviewers alike. Readers learned that Mark Twain was the pen name for Samuel L. Clemens and that the book was sold by "subscription only, and not for sale in the bookstores." Here the pen name "Mark Twain" offered no anonymity for the author, for his real name was listed immediately below it. The author, it suggested, was no patrician, hiding behind a pen name when publishing popular literature, but a man who wanted to be known twice over—as the "wild humorist of the Pacific Slope" and as Samuel L. Clemens, Victorian "Man of Feeling." In claiming authorship as Mark Twain (Samuel L. Clemens), he set himself apart from other humorists of his day, such as Petroleum V. Nasby (D. R. Locke), whose real name remained more obscured from public view.

As if to underscore the variety and pleasure that awaited, a five-page list of illustrations, followed by an eight-page table of contents, completed the front matter. Like most books published by subscription, *The Innocents Abroad* asserted its weight and value through its standard front matter. Before the first chapter began, Mark Twain had inscribed his text materially, legally, commercially, visually, and sentimentally. Readers of either prospectus or narrative had been conditioned to accept the work as new, amusing, instructive, and materially impressive. Everything cohered to announce that *The Innocents Abroad* was an impressive book and that its author was impressive too.

The visual and typographical apparatuses, as well as the literary discourses of the preface, not only offered a preview of the narrative but also proffered evidence of a distinctive way of looking *and* a distinctive narrative voice—as marked by tones of parody, sentiment, and matter-of-factness. More importantly, the front matter presented to readers a public—that is, a saleable—persona.

One of the strong selling points was the profusion of illustrations. Among the various types of illustrations in *The Innocents Abroad*, one deserved special notice in relation to the business of selling the book. Conventional, realistic illustrations taken from photographs, post-cards, and the like helped sell the book generally as an *illustrated* one, but it was particularly the numerous caricatures of the author that sold Mark Twain. Mark Twain first appeared in caricature on the cover of *The Innocents Abroad*, teasing readers and prospective buyers with the irreverence of his persona, but the caricatures within sold readers on the book as humorous autobiography rather than informational travel narrative.

The American Publishing Company wanted its readers to accept, at least nominally, that the book was both. Therefore, the image of Mark Twain appeared in various degrees of exaggeration but always with at least one signature element: either his checkered trousers, his tousled hair, a particular style of hat, or his bushy mustache identified him to readers as the author of the text and, as presented in many of the more humorous illustrations, as the author of his own misfortune. Mark Twain in caricature surfaced frequently and discernibly throughout *The Innocents Abroad*. In fact, Frank Bliss claimed: "One of the charms of 'Innocents' pictures was that people could see how *MT* looked in an awkward situation."[27] (For examples of the range of representations of Mark Twain, see illustrations #6, #7, and #8.) Reviewers were quick to comment on the size of *The Innocents Abroad*, as well as other attributes (its profuse illustrations, for example) that announced it as a subscrip-tion volume. Even reviewers who praised the book took jabs at the subscription method of publication. Bret Harte joked that "the book has that intrinsic worth of bigness and durability which commends itself to the rural economist, who likes to get a material return for his money."[28] Harte's comment suggested differences in kinds of ac-quisitiveness, with the "rural economist" confusing bulk with quality.

"POET LARIAT."

6. Caricature of Mark Twain, from *The Innocents Abroad.* Photograph from the collection of Nancy Cook.

But *The Innocents Abroad* spoke to a large audience, in part because it acknowledged the acquisitiveness of the nation, eager to acquire culture, even to cart it home in the form of relics, as many of the pilgrims did *including* Mark Twain. (Though he makes fun of the "vandals" in his text, apparently Twain could not resist bringing home one of those stone faces that glared up at him from the moonlit Acropolis.)

Since Twain recycled much of the material that appeared in newspapers and magazines—the Buffalo *Express,* the *Galaxy,* the *Atlantic Monthly*—into his subscription books, we might assume that readers of periodical literature and readers of subscription books shared interests if not identities. In all probability buyers of *The Innocents Abroad* were like Mark Twain in many ways. They were upwardly mobile and acquisitive. The book displayed Mark Twain prominently between its covers, and buyers displayed *The Innocents Abroad* prominently in their

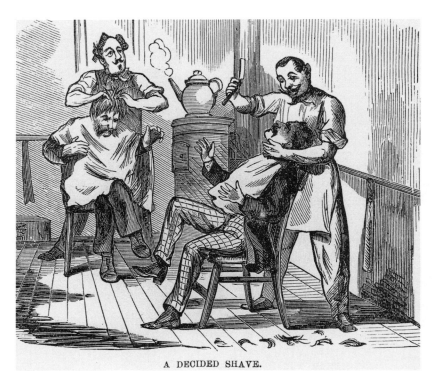

A DECIDED SHAVE.

7. Caricature of Mark Twain, from *The Innocents Abroad*. Photograph from the collection of Nancy Cook.

parlors. These buyers established Mark Twain as a successful writer, and that success in turn gained him access to high-brow magazines such as the *Atlantic* as well as to better rates from those magazines for his work.

Subscription publishing in Mark Twain's time evoked a complex web of processes, a network of promotion for profit, where each link in the chain, each person from production to reader, was important, if sometimes invisible. All this worked to sell the author in order to sell the book to the salespeople who would then sell it to the readers. Like the structure of dependency set up in the nursery rhyme, this *was* the house that Mark built. *The Innocents Abroad,* inclusive of its composition, production, marketing, and sales, represented both the interdependence of a house of cards and the structure of a set of Chinese boxes. The strategies at work within the text as functions of its composition were duplicated in and coordinated with the book's publication history.

The methods Mark Twain employed at this crossroads in his career served him well. By 1896, Twain was negotiating with both Harper and

RETURN IN WAR-PAINT.

8. Caricature of Mark Twain, from *The Innocents Abroad*. Photograph from the collection of Nancy Cook.

Brothers and the American Publishing Company for uniform sets of his collected works. Within his lifetime he managed to achieve success in magazines, newspapers, trade publication, and subscription book publication. He lived to see his books offered in a range of standard editions, with and without illustrations. Through his careful manipulation of his persona throughout all stages of book production, Mark Twain made himself a classic American author.

Though often reviled or at least disdained, subscription publishing, and Mark Twain's enormous success with the method, may have had far-reaching consequences for the profession of authorship in America. Subscription book buyers supported a market that promoted *American* authors in a time when most failed to make a living in the profession.[29] A writer for the *American Bookseller* quotes William Dean Howells, evidently with some dismay:

> The present subscription system is the development of one of the oldest methods of publication, if not the first, and if we continue without an international copyright law it may be the refuge and the hope of literature with us. When the cheap reprints have made it more and more difficult to publish copyright works, for which the publisher pays the author, at a living profit, they may be glad to invoke the aid of the despised book agent who carried literature from door to door.[30]

No doubt Howells at least obliquely defended his friend Mark Twain here, but he also recast the buyer of subscription works as a patron of the arts, thereby allowing for authorship as a profession in America, a profession that Howells and many others felt was under siege.

Though many of his contemporaries might have bristled at Howells's application of the term "literature" to subscription books, few could have argued that the subscription book industry was not a haven for American writers. In a period when America was flooded with foreign literature, subscription publishers offered a wide array of books about American topics, usually by American writers. Popular topics within the subscription trade included: American history, especially the Civil War; American historical figures, especially presidents and military heroes; American commerce, especially "how to succeed" books; American agriculture; American phenomena such as Mormonism, Indian captivity, exploration in the American West; travel and exploration by Americans; and American humor. In fact, of all publishers in the United States, as a group the subscription publishers did more to promote and support the idea of nationalism, both in subject and authorship, than any other type of publisher. It could be argued that subscription publishers did more to make America a legitimate subject for publication than all the so-called "classic" American authors—Irving, Cooper, Hawthorne, Melville, Whitman—combined. In this vein buyers of subscription books bought American culture, and in doing so they became patrons of American artists and made Mark Twain a household name; however their status as patrons is somewhat paradoxical, for they achieved that stature by privileging the book over the text.

∿ NOTES ∿

1. For discussion of the composition of *The Innocents Abroad,* see, among others, Nancy S. Cook, "Marketing Mark Twain, or, Samuel Clemens and the Selling of *The Innocents Abroad,*" diss., State U of New York at Buffalo, 1991; Leon T. Dickinson, "Mark Twain's Revisions in Writing *The Innocents Abroad,*" *American Literature* 19 (May 1947): 139–57; Dewey Ganzel, *Mark Twain Abroad: The Cruise of The Quaker City* (Chicago: U of Chicago P, 1968); Robert Hirst, "The Making of *The Innocents Abroad,*" diss., U of California–Berkeley, 1975; and Thomas Asa Tenney, "Mark Twain's Early Travels and the Travel Tradition in Literature," diss., U of Pennsylvania, 1971. For a full discussion of the mirroring process between composition and publication, see Cook.

2. Tebbel quotes Frank E. Compton from his *Subscription Books* (fourth of the R. R. Bowker Memorial Lectures [New York: New York Public Library, 1939]) in "The Bowker Lectures on Book Publishing" (New York: The Typophiles, 1943) 107. Tebbel's characterization and brief history of subscription publishing in America is in his *A History of Book Publishing in the United States,* 2 vols. (New York: R. R. Bowker, 1975) 2:511–34.

3. From Hubert Hungerford, *How Publishers Win* (Washington, D.C.: Ransdell, Inc., 1931) 281, as quoted in Donald Sheehan, *This Was Publishing: A Chronicle of the Book Trade in the Gilded Age* (Bloomington: Indiana UP, 1952) 190.

4. Mark Twain, *Mark Twain's Letters: Volume 2 1867–1868,* ed. Harriet Elinor Smith and Richard Bucci (Berkeley: U of California P, 1990), letter of 21 November 1867, 120.

5. Twain, *Letters* (24 December 1867) 162; emphasis in original. Bliss refers to the popular books by Albert Deane Richardson. The American Publishing Company had done well with Richardson's *The Secret Service, the Field, the Dungeon, and the Escape* (1865) and *Beyond the Mississippi* (1867).

6. Twain, *Letters* 421–22.

7. Twain had complained to Bret Harte that the *Jumping Frog* was "full of

damnable errors of grammar & deadly inconsistencies of spelling in the Frog sketch because I was away & did not read the proofs—but be a friend & say nothing about these things" (1 May 1867, *Letters* 39).

8. Within the last few years, many fine books and articles have helped scholars to reconsider the demands of the marketplace and the myths of authorship in nineteenth-century America. One might speculate that earlier literary critics and historians, in an effort to bolster the merits of domestic authors, underplayed market considerations in favor of a romantic conception of authorship. Though Ticknor and Fields concerned itself with the marketplace, the legend has remained attractive.

The prestige associated with high-brow publishers and their authors and the myths of romantically defined authorship have hindered studies of more popular writers, such as those published by the American Publishing Company. Many authors who published by subscription have been excised from recent reference works, and archival material is scarce.

9. From *The Innocents Abroad* salesman's dummy, 1869, at the American Antiquarian Society (AAS), Worcester, Mass. The dummy duplicates parts of the first edition, including its cover and front matter. Salesmen's dummies vary, however, and my research has included an examination of only the one in the AAS collection.

10. This ad is from the (Hartford) *Connecticut Courant*, 31 July 1869, and is reproduced in Leon T. Dickinson, "Marketing a Best Seller: Mark Twain's *Innocents Abroad*," in *Papers of the Bibliographical Society of America* 41, no. 2 (1947): 113. Some of the type is unclear in Dickinson's reproduction, and I have assumed the following to be correct transcriptions: "follies," "fulnes," and "50,000."

11. Ad in the *Connecticut Courant*, 13 November 1869, quoted in Dickinson, "Marketing a Best Seller" 113.

12. In an account of her experiences, one book agent discussed "claim jumping" at length. See Mrs. J. W. Likins, *Six Years Experience as a Book Agent in California: Including My Trip from New York to San Francisco via Nicaragua* (San Francisco: Women's Union Book and Job Printing Office, 1874).

13. Mark Twain, *Mark Twain to Mrs. Fairbanks*, ed. Dixon Wecter (San Marino, Calif.: Huntington Library, 1949) 43–46.

14. 7 January 1869 in *Mark Twain's Letters to His Publishers 1867–1894*, ed. Hamlin Hill (Berkeley: U of California P, 1967) 17.

15. The review, which originally appeared in the *Toledo* (Ohio) *Commercial*, was reprinted in the Buffalo, N.Y., *Express*, 9 October 1869, and quoted in Dickinson, "Marketing a Best Seller" 117.

16. Dickinson, "Marketing a Best Seller" 116.

17. Though subscription publishers often chose not to run book advertisements in newspapers, they did advertise. Often titles of new and forthcoming

books appeared in newspaper ads that solicited canvassers. Subscription books publishers used their ads to serve more than one purpose.

18. William S. Walsh, *Handy-Book of Literary Curiosities* (Philadelphia: J. P. Lippincott, 1911).

19. This may be some veiled allusion to a connection between George Washington and Freemasonry, for Twain was a Mason at the time of publication.

20. Twain, *The Innocents Abroad* 628–30.

21. Twain, *The Innocents Abroad* 629.

22. These power relations are discussed at length in Cook, but the important point here is that for readers who examined the visual material of the book, what often lingered, over and above any images of Europe or the Holy Land, was an image and a sense of Mark Twain. They received emphatically Mark Twain's Europe, not (as he promised in his preface) what Europe would be if seen through their own eyes. Hence, Mark Twain had it both ways: readers remembered Mark Twain and, paradoxically, allowed him to stand in for them, to be their eyes in the Old World.

23. Twain, *Mark Twain to Mrs. Fairbanks* 84.

24. Twain, *Mark Twain to Mrs. Fairbanks* 84.

25. In Beverly R. David, *Mark Twain and His Illustrators* (Troy, N.Y.: Whitson, 1986) 53. David, citing Hamlin Hill, explains the disparity in titles this way: "This engraving had not been completed by early June. The illustrators had left and time had run out. Bliss reached conveniently into his pile of available electros for a handy engraving of a ship. What purported to be the *Quaker City* in Mark Twain's first edition was not the pilgrim's ship at all but a full-page engraving of the *Steamer Wright* which had been engraved for a Bliss publication, *Overland through Asia,* and would be reused later in *The American Publisher,* a Bliss in-house journal, as 'A STEAMSHIP IN A GALE.' Since the 'List of Illustrations' had already been set up (using Twain's suggested caption, THE QUAKER CITY IN A STORM) the list was not changed. Bliss, however, knowing that it was not the *Quaker City,* provided a more ambiguous caption below the frontispiece print—STEAMSHIP IN A STORM" (53).

After examining both a first edition–first state copy of *The Innocents Abroad* in the collection of the AAS and the Hippocrene Books facsimile reprint, I question David's explanation. Both the AAS copy and the Hippocrene reprint contain an engraving that differs slightly from that found in later imprints. In the early state, the ship more closely resembles the *Quaker City,* having two smokestacks and two side-wheels; in the later state and in an 1875 reprint of Knox's *Overland through Asia,* the ship has only one smokestack and no side-wheels. The sea and sky are exactly the same. Furthermore, in the early states, the engraving is titled "*The Quaker City* in a Storm." Hamlin Hill does not comment on either the alterations made to the engraving or on the substitutions between printings, nor does anyone else whose work I have read.

26. Twain, *Letters to His Publishers* 20.

27. Frank Bliss to Samuel L. Clemens, 27 June 1869, quoted in David 36.

28. Quoted in Frederick Anderson and Kenneth M. Sanderson, eds., *Mark Twain: The Critical Heritage* (London: Routledge and Kegan Paul, 1971) 33.

29. Though subscription publishers did not print American authors exclusively, they did provide many American authors with a way to make a good living as writers. In addition to the potential for high-volume sales and often a healthy royalty, subscription publishing offered a market for recycled material. Many authors made their work pay and pay again through its inclusion in various anthologies. Writers also made money by serving as editors, often doing no real editorial work but rather simply allowing their names to be used for promotional purposes.

30. Marjorie Stafford, "Subscription Book Publishing in the United States, 1865–1930," master's thesis, U of Illinois, 1943, 92. Stafford cites the *American Bookseller* 20 (1 December 1886): 535. The piece from the *American Bookseller* offers a version of Howells's comments from his "The Editors Study" column in *Harper's* (vol. 74, no. 439 [December 1886]: 162) that significantly tones down Howells's defense of subscription publishing. In this column he both quotes his friend Mark Twain and defends the much maligned book agent.

◊

Defining the National Pantheon: The Making of Houghton Mifflin's Biographical Series, 1880–1900

SCOTT E. CASPER

IN FEBRUARY 1901, THE BOSTON publishers Houghton, Mifflin and Company advertised "Our Special Offer Beginning the Twentieth Century." The front of the firm's small brochure featured the images of six eminent American men of letters: Longfellow in the center, encircled by Emerson, Oliver Wendell Holmes, Whittier, Hawthorne, and James Russell Lowell. Inside appeared eleven tiers of similarly bound books: "Houghton, Mifflin & Co.'s Standard Library Editions," two hundred volumes available by subscription on the installment plan for just sixteen dollars a month. These "fine books at low prices" could be "sent on approval if desired" but were "not sold by book stores." The Standard Library Editions included the works of seven Americans (the six on the cover plus Bret Harte), all of whom had been stars in the firm's constellation of authors during their lifetimes. Three British authors—Macaulay, Thackeray, and Dickens—also appeared in this literary firmament, each with more volumes than any American author. And just above Dickens at the base of the advertisement was a series called "American Statesmen. 32 vols."[1] The story of how "American Statesmen" came to be advertised with the works of Dickens, Emerson, Longfellow, and Hawthorne offers a case study in literary repackaging—one that begins twenty years before the dawn of the new century.

In the 1880s and 1890s, Houghton, Mifflin and Company produced two series of biographies, the American Statesmen and the American Men of Letters.[2] Each series possessed a distinctive, readily identifiable appearance: the American Statesmen with its dark blue binding, gold lettering, and band of gold stars across the top of the spine and front cover; the American Men of Letters bound in burgundy and lettered in gold. Each included prominent Americans from the Revolutionary period to the era of the Civil War: the Statesmen from Franklin and Washington to Lincoln and Thaddeus Stevens, the Men of Letters from Franklin and Noah Webster to Emerson, who had just died in 1882. Together, the series offered a national pantheon, a Who's Who of political and literary worthies of the nation's first century, and indeed a biographical history of that century. Houghton, Mifflin marketed the series in precisely this fashion. The American Statesmen, when completed, would present "a thorough sketch of the whole history of the period covered by it"; in the case of the American Men of Letters, "a small shelf of these modest volumes will offer to the reader a fair view of the different phases of our literature."[3] The phrase "our literature" asserted that such a thing existed—that a nation with a relatively short political history and an even shorter literary one had nonetheless acquired a storied past by the 1880s. Moreover, by defining the past, the series could demonstrate America's present literary condition: the quality of these books themselves would testify to the abilities of American historians and critics. Within fifteen years, however, the series' fortunes had diverged: thanks to delinquent authors and poor sales, the American Men of Letters proved a disappointment to the publishers, while the American Statesmen became a commercial success. This divergence led Houghton, Mifflin to its "Special Offer" at the turn of the century, the "Standard Library Edition" of the American Statesmen, now temporarily divorced from the Men of Letters, advertised with the *works*, not the lives, of authors like Emerson, and repackaged for subscription sale. Faced with the success of one series and the failure of the other, Houghton, Mifflin responded to what it recognized as readers' demand.

This twenty-year episode provides a suggestive glimpse at the formation of cultural canons in late-nineteenth-century America. The story of Houghton, Mifflin's biographical series involves more than simply the formation of an American national pantheon that somehow defines the nation by its grand figures of the past. The publishing history of the series reveals not a coordinated program of cultural production but an uncertain and contested process, dependent on the schedules of writers and the desires of readers as well as on the aims of editors or publishers. When Houghton, Mifflin worked with Charles Dudley Warner to begin the American Men of Letters and with John Torrey Morse, Jr., to inaugurate the American Statesmen in 1880 and 1881, the firm and these editors began a process of continual addition and revision that lasted for twenty years. Publishers and editors debated exactly what a "man of letters" or a "statesman" was and who deserved those titles. As the series became recognized publishing entities, Warner, Morse, and the firm also found themselves responding to readers and authors who wanted additional subjects included. What ended up in the series often had not been planned at the outset, as biographical subjects and biographers were added and dropped. Volumes appeared in haphazard order, as authors finished them: the first published volume in the Statesmen series was the life of John Quincy Adams; Washington and Franklin would have to wait for years.

The publishing technique of the "series" served to hide these internal shifts and debates and to present each volume published as a worthy addition to the pantheon simply by virtue of having been included. Material uniformity (in binding, size of volume, typography, frontispieces, and title pages) identified the works as part of a coherent material whole, even when publishers, editors, and authors privately knew that creating the series involved manufacturing coherence out of diversity and, often, confusion. Some authors recognized the "manufactured" quality of the project and argued with the editors and publishers about tailoring their works to meet a publisher's standard form. Others, however, saw the series as an opportunity to gain fame and were more than willing to create works that fit the guidelines—guidelines of size and space as much as of content. Only when Houghton, Mifflin created the Standard Library Edition of the American Statesmen in 1898—with new introductions that connected the volumes to each other, as well as new bindings, typography, and illustrations—did the series become a textual whole.

Equally important, the creation of Houghton, Mifflin's biographical series was firmly rooted in the literary, political, and cultural history of late-Victorian America. Encouraged by the success of Macmillan's pioneering English Men of Letters series in the late 1870s, American publishers rushed to imitate it; the Houghton, Mifflin series, though distinguished for their longevity, were not unique publishing ventures. The 1880s and 1890s were also precisely the cultural moment when many American colleges and universities came to adopt the German model of scholarship that created the academic professions of history and literature, and these series straddled the shift. The series' editors were not academic professionals; nor were most of the men (no women wrote for either series) who wrote the early volumes. But the proportion of academics among the writers increased as the series continued into the 1890s. However, the possibility still existed for a "literary" publishing firm—a firm that had sought to define American literature through its imprints (as Houghton, Mifflin and as its various predecessors, including Ticknor and Fields) for nearly half a century—to try to define a broader cultural pantheon, "a valuable and permanent addition to historical literature, which cannot be displaced by more elaborate historical or biographical writings."[4]

At the same time, these biographies of subjects from an earlier era reflected their authors' own Gilded Age political and literary concerns. Each series offered readers a past with lessons for the present; indeed, despite the diversity of authors who wrote for the American Statesmen and American Men of Letters, several themes united many of the volumes. Overwhelmingly populated by northern subjects and biographers, with token inclusion of the South, the series represented their New England publishers' and editors' vision of the reconstructed United States less than a generation after the Civil War. America's literary "progress" toward postwar realism met with ambivalence from the Men of Letters authors, whose literary history of the nation celebrated antebellum romanticism. The nation's political "progress," according to the Statesmen authors, was founded on Whig principles of orderly democracy—and decidedly not on Jeffersonian or Jacksonian "democracy." The Statesmen volumes, more than the Men of Letters ones, exhibited a shared political sensibility that reflected the genteel reform vision of the Gilded Age. The decline of the series by the early twentieth century coincided with the waning of this vision in an age of "Progressivism" and "Progressive" history that defined both historical progress and historical practice in new ways.

∾ THE VICTORIAN BIOGRAPHICAL ∾ SERIES IN TRANSATLANTIC CONTEXT

The origins of the American Statesmen and American Men of Letters series cannot be understood apart from the transatlantic history of biography in the Victorian era. The foremost antebellum predecessor of Houghton, Mifflin's series was the twenty-five-volume Library of

American Biography (1834–48), edited by Jared Sparks.[5] In commissioning biographies to be prepared especially for the Library, Sparks—the foremost biographer of the Jacksonian era and a former editor of the *North American Review*—envisioned a biographical history of the nation.[6] The series was to include lives of prominent Americans from the earliest colonial settlement through the early republic, to admit at least one subject from each of the original states, and to represent the various arenas in which Americans had gained distinction (hence biographies of the writer Charles Brockden Brown and the scientist David Rittenhouse as well as of political and military figures). The length of each biography depended upon the availability of sources; some volumes contained as many as four biographies, while others consisted of one full-length life. Sparks expended great effort in securing authors competent to write the biographies, either through their historical knowledge or through their regional and familial connections. The initial advertisement for the Library announced that the series "would embrace a perfect history of the country, of its social and political progress, its arts, sciences, literature, and improvements of every kind"—a description not unlike Houghton, Mifflin's for the American Statesmen series a half century later.[7]

The American Statesmen and American Men of Letters series also emerged as part of a reaction against another form of biography: the massive, multivolume "life and letters" that proliferated on both sides of the Atlantic in the Victorian period. By the 1850s, many critics in England and America complained that biographies seemed to be growing beyond their proper proportions. "Lives and letters" told their subjects' histories primarily through correspondence, weaving letters together with a thin narrative thread. Two equally troubling tendencies aroused condemnation. On the one hand, the desire to memorialize and glorify subjects led writers to edit the correspondence, making subjects into impossibly perfect models of behavior and writing. On the other hand, writers could publish too much, admitting uninvited readers into the private chambers of the subject's home. This dilemma led to the dictum that true biography should reveal the "inner man," the individual springs of thought and action that defined the subject's unique "genius." The "inner man" was not necessarily the private man, and neither writing endlessly of daily life nor presenting readers with thousands of letters would necessarily capture him. This mode of biographical criticism placed the highest value on the biographer's own artistry, which (combined with the necessarily "scientific" work of gathering and arranging materials) could bring the subject alive for the reader. This concept of biography, which remains central to the genre to this day, was just in the process of delineation in the mid-nineteenth century, and attacked both the prevalent didactic concept of biography and the plethora of "lives and letters," especially of literary figures.[8] In their emphases on concision and on critical analysis of the subject's actions and writings, the editors in the American Statesmen and American Men of Letters series partook of this critical stance.

The English Men of Letters series, edited by John Morley and published by the London firm of Macmillan, provided the model for both the American Men of Letters and the American Statesmen. Begun in 1878 with Leslie Stephen's *Samuel Johnson*, the English Men of Letters quickly became a literary institution in late-Victorian England, with thirty-six volumes published by 1884. Harper and Brothers of New York contracted with Macmillan to sell the series in the United States, and numerous other firms copied and pirated the volumes. According to F. J. M. Korsten, "after a number of years the series was on the market in a bewildering variety of formats, covers, colours, and titles."[9] Many of the authors of the English Men of Letters volumes were noted literary men, among them Stephen, Anthony Trollope, and Henry James, whose important life of Hawthorne belonged to the series. The authors divided into roughly three groups, based on their positions within the literary criticism of the period: the "freethinkers, rationalists, agnostics, and positivists," who included Morley and Stephen; the "authors from orthodox Anglican circles"; and "the mandarins of literature, often university professors."[10]

John L. Kijinski has suggested that the series, particularly the volumes on writers of prose fiction, represented an attempt to buttress Victorian social order in the face of social unrest and cultural crisis. This endeavor, carried out by educated Victorian "men of letters," would prescribe a reading strategy to the relatively unschooled—a strategy that would instruct on both what and how to read. Morley's project, and that of his contributors, involved explaining what constituted literary value. Authors' lives became models of the bourgeois success ethic, thus validating their works. Those works succeeded to the extent that they balanced realism with respectability, eschewing both coarseness and excessive polemic. "[G]eneral lessons of public virtue" were appropriate to prose fiction; "a concretely political or social critical purpose" was not. Moreover, the treatment of works followed clear lines of gender: "manliness" became "an important characteristic

of works worthy of being placed within the great English tradition."
The series sought to build a canon of English literature, which included writers who treated "universal" themes and excluded those who
dealt in the transitory and the domestic (indeed, no woman of letters
appeared in the first series of volumes). The canonical transcended
"social and historical constraints"—a view that Kijinski identifies with
the editor's and authors' social conservatism, not modernism.[11] In its
attempt to define a national literature through concise, analytical biography, the English Men of Letters became the touchstone for Houghton, Mifflin's series. Indeed, as we shall see, the very genesis of the
American Men of Letters series lay in the relationship between the
English series and an American author, Charles Dudley Warner.

In the wake of Morley's successful series, various American publishers began similar biographical projects in the early 1880s. One 1882 issue
of the *Atlantic Monthly* contained reviews of works in Putnam's "New
Plutarch Series" and Osgood's "American Actor Series," as well as
books in Harper's American printing of the English Men of Letters and
in Houghton, Mifflin's American Men of Letters.[12] Charles Dudley
Warner worked with Henry Holt and Company on a series of American biographies (mostly of colonial leaders and political figures) from
1878 to 1882. And just as Houghton, Mifflin began plans for the American Statesmen and American Men of Letters, both Warner and Morse
noted that the publisher D. Appleton and Company was considering "a
similar Enterprise."[13] None of these other publishers' series achieved
the lasting renown of the Houghton, Mifflin series, but at the outset,
Houghton, Mifflin launched its enterprise into a sea of similar projects.

∾ CREATING HOUGHTON, ∾
MIFFLIN'S SERIES

The American Men of Letters series might never have come into
existence at all had John Morley not rejected Charles Dudley Warner's
biography of Washington Irving for the English Men of Letters. After
Warner wrote an article on Irving for the *Atlantic Monthly* in 1879,
the American publisher G. P. Putnam's Sons expressed interest in expanding it into a full-length volume for a new edition of Irving's
works. William Dean Howells, then editor of the *Atlantic*, suggested to
Warner in December 1879 that he offer it to Morley, whose series had
already become a major project in literary biography and criticism.[14]
Putnam's assured Warner that publishing in the English series would

not threaten its plans; indeed, Putnam's would "appreciate the service that the publication of such a volume would render in reemphasizing, for the present generation, Irving's position in literature."[15] Howells telegraphed Morley, who cabled back on 20 January, "Send Warners Irving. Will gladly consider."[16] Apparently Warner sent some portion of his Irving manuscript and Morley rejected the proposal, for on 12 March 1880, Howells wrote to Warner,

> I am more disgusted than I know how to say at Morley's behavior. His telegram gave every reason to expect a favorable decision, and I am deeply mortified that I ever suggested the matter to you. Of course if you had cut Irving up, and mishandled America generally, your book would have been accepted with acclaim. To think how dull and stupid the greatest number of that series are, and then to think of his rejecting a book that he ought to have gone on his knees to get! I can't express myself.[17]

Howells, of course, had expressed himself—and revealed several layers of connection between the English Men of Letters series and American men of letters, past and present. No matter how he might condemn Morley's "dull and stupid" volumes after the rejection of Warner, Howells—editor of the magazine that carried the banner of American "high" literature in the Gilded Age—had suggested that Warner try to get his book into that very series. And Howells explained the rejection in national terms: if the American Warner had "cut up" his American literary predecessor and "mishandled" the United States, then the presumably Anglocentric Morley might have taken his book (as he had taken James's *Hawthorne*). But this, of course, American men of letters would not do, even to enter the "English" pantheon of literary worthies. What Howells saw as an issue of national chauvinism, Warner interpreted on literary grounds: Morley's "radical agnosticism" would not allow him "to believe in what I prize in Irving," and more importantly the book was "not up to [Morley's] literary or critical standards," because it was "too biographical and too little critical."[18]

Warner was thus left with his *Atlantic* article and George Haven Putnam's interest in the Irving book. But in July Putnam withdrew his offer, citing another, "clumsily written" recent volume on Irving and the announcement that the publisher D. Appleton intended to publish a series called "American Men of Letters" that would include "a biographical study of Irving." Given these two works, "a properly remunerative circulation for a third book" was unlikely, and thus Putnam freed Warner to make other arrangements—perhaps even to contribute his Irving biography to the Appletons' series.[19] Instead, in November 1880, Warner approached Henry Oscar Houghton, who had recently dissolved his connection with James R. Osgood and founded the publishing house of Houghton, Mifflin and Company, with a proposition of his own.[20]

Warner proposed to Houghton a series of "the biographies of American Men of Letters," a name clearly modeled on Morley's. Warner may have intended to model his series on the English Men of Letters— and also to assert the value of American men of letters, given his recent experience with Morley. But Houghton might not have known of Warner's rejection, and proposed a different name: "Why not call it Warner's Biographies, etc. & you will write what you can, & let Aldrich & others to write the remainder?"[21] At this point no series existed, and Houghton left open the possibility that "we can group [Warner's biography of Irving] with your other books if we do not publish the series"—thus creating a standard edition of Warner like the firm's standard editions of other English and American authors.[22] But both Warner and Houghton preferred a biographical series, and by early 1881 Howells, Thomas Bailey Aldrich, and Horace Scudder (all editors or future editors of the *Atlantic Monthly,* the firm's literary magazine) offered their support for the project and suggested possible subjects and biographers. As the project took shape, Houghton asked James T. Fields, the publishing titan who had been a partner in Ticknor and Fields and its successor Fields, Osgood and Company, to serve as general editor of the series. (Apparently Warner at first declined this task.) But Fields withdrew in mid-April and died on 24 April, and the firm approached Warner once again. After some bargaining over the precise duties and compensation of the editor, Warner accepted.[23]

The discussion of the series name revealed much about Warner's and Houghton's concepts of the enterprise and suggested some disagreement over what exactly a "man of letters" was. Clearly Warner sought to create an American counterpart, perhaps even rival, to Morley's English Men of Letters, the biographical institution that by January 1881 had announced James's "Life of Hawthorne."[24] Houghton's first suggestion, "Warner's Biographies," conveyed nothing of the substance of the series and implied that Warner would play a more prominent authorial role than his letters suggest he intended. The publisher wondered whether "American Men of Letters" was broad enough to allow a whole series: "There was in the previous generation such a paucity of them that if we could have a more comprehensive title, it might give us more liberty. What do you think of 'Lives of Eminent Americans?' "[25] Warner envisioned a comprehensive series under the "Men of Letters" title, which he believed "would take in historians, and even some statesmen . . . novelists, poets, etc." Breadth did not mean all-inclusiveness: even if the series would admit more than "novelists and poets," it should remain "a choice and rather charmed circle."[26]

Warner's connection between the choice of subjects and the mode of publishing was also significant. In rejecting Houghton's "Lives of Eminent Americans" as "disagreeable, commonplace, pretentious," he criticized not just this title's excessive breadth but also its resemblance to that of "a bogus subscription book." For an author who had written books for the subscription publishing houses that proliferated in the 1870s, and whose friend Mark Twain had become famous in large part through subscription publishing, this statement meant something. Warner was distinguishing between the gaudiness of subscription-house wares and the elegant simplicity of works associated with Houghton, Mifflin (and its predecessor Ticknor and Fields), the firm that prided itself on its association with the foremost American authors (including Hawthorne, Longfellow, and Thoreau). Subscription firms did publish volumes of biography, but these tended to be fat books with garish bindings, often with titles embossed in gold and black and heavily embellished. Warner clearly wanted something more in keeping with Houghton's editions of the literature itself: small volumes with a minimum of show.

By 22 January 1881, Houghton had acceded to Warner's general idea of the title, but he still ventured that it "would also include women."[27] (Margaret Fuller and Lydia Maria Child were discussed as potential subjects from the outset.) From this point until 19 July, the firm's letters to Warner consistently called the series "American Men and Women of Letters." When Houghton, Mifflin sent a proof copy of its announcement of 6 August to Warner, however, the title read simply "American Men of Letters," returning at last to Warner's original version.[28] It is unclear why "American Men and Women of Letters" gave way finally to Warner's preferred "American Men of Letters." Perhaps the publishers simply agreed to Warner's request or recognized the value of the parallel with Morley's English series. Thus, when the firm announced the series in August 1881, it described "a series of volumes entitled 'American Men of Letters,' using the title as a generic term that may include both sexes."[29]

The double process of selection—picking the "men of letters" who would be the series subjects *and* the "men of letters" who would write their lives—had already begun as Warner and the firm haggled over titles. In February 1881 H. O. Houghton proposed that "a dozen or more very attractive biographies" might compose the series, including (in addition to Warner's life of Irving) "James Fenimore Cooper, Nathaniel Hawthorne, Theodore Parker, Henry D. Thoreau, William Ellery Channing, George Sumner, Washington Allston, Margaret Fuller, Lydia Maria Child, with several others subject, of course, to modifications that may arise."[30] This exclusively northern and largely New England group was expanded slightly by James T. Fields, during his brief editorial tenure, to include lives of Noah Webster (by Horace E. Scudder) and Nathaniel Parker Willis (by Thomas Bailey Aldrich). In addition, Fields hoped to include "the Life of some Southern author, if we could find one of sufficient eminence," perhaps William Gilmore Simms or John Pendleton Kennedy.[31] This suggestion might be construed as an attempt to restore the South to the Union of letters just four years after Reconstruction had ended, or as an attempt to attract southern buyers to the series.

More likely, however, it represented the publishers', Fields's, and Warner's desire "to include the history of American literature in the Lives of those who have been its representative authors"—a goal that led them to formulate a list on historical, as much as literary, grounds.[32] Not only was a southern author (eventually Simms) to be included but also an author from the antislavery movement (Edmund Quincy was eventually chosen over Child, at the suggestion of Sydney Howard Gay, who was to write this volume). Noah Webster represented the literature of the early republic, and after reading Scudder's manuscript Warner recommended that he "interject into the first part something more about the literary, intellectual and social conditions of the New England community in which Webster was born, the state of culture, what the people read, what they learned at school and from the pulpit, their recreations &c, so as to give the genesis of such a man as Noah," and that he include something about the Hartford Wits, even though Webster was not one of them, "as I do not intend to give a volume to any of them separately."[33] (The early chapters of Scudder's published volume reveal that he took Warner's advice.) When a Mr. Todd proposed to write a life of the Hartford Wit Joel Barlow for the series several years later, Warner counseled rejection on the grounds that Barlow "was in letters less representative" than others and that "Mr.

Scudder has paid some attention to Barlow and his period."[34] Similarly, Nathaniel Parker Willis, the influential magazine writer and editor of the antebellum period, merited inclusion for literary-historical reasons rather than for the value of his writings. When the publishers complained that Henry A. Beers's volume on Willis was too long, Warner countered that "the literary class would certainly like to see it all," because

> It must be remembered that the value of this volume is not altogether in Willis, per our series. He had a career, which makes him a very good subject, but he was a trifler and the outcome of his life was trifling. But he represented a phase of our literature which we cannot leave out. For over twenty years the reading public fed a good deal in such sort of stuff as he furnished, and the development of which he was a type is important in our literary history. . . . however thin Willis and his literature was, they really stand for something. We want the series to represent the development of our literature in all its phases.[35]

Some subjects (like Emerson, Poe, and Hawthorne) belonged in the "charmed circle" for their individuality, others for their representativeness. And "our literature" was constituted both by unique individuals and by what might be called literary cultures, like the magazine world of Willis and the antislavery movement of Quincy.

The list of who did not belong also indicates the publishers' and editor's plans. Francis Lieber was merely "a scholar, and a publicist," impossible to "squeeze" into the series.[36] George Sumner, who was part of Houghton's original list, was dropped in 1884 as not "enough of a literary man."[37] If Barlow were included, wrote Houghton, "it would seem to imply the possibility of including a great many second-rate men on the series."[38] Warner's most forceful statement came in 1898, when Houghton, Mifflin proposed Walt Whitman for the series because of "a continuous and permanent interest in him." Of Whitman, Warner asked, "Whatever he is, would you in any way call him a Man of Letters?" Even if Whitman's work displayed "genius in places," he was "an awful *poser*." "If he must go into our Series," concluded Warner, "I should not wish to have him treated by one of his abject worshipers, who repudiates our whole idea of the difference between poetry and prose, in order to admit him among the poets."[39]

Warner's and the publishers' other central concern involved the biographers: finding the right man for each volume and getting him to write the book. Numerous letters between Warner and the firm reveal their idea of what constituted the "right man." First, he needed some familiarity with the subject in question, either through scholarly pursuits or through personal knowledge. Second, he must himself be a "man of letters"—a man possessed of the proper "sympathy" with the subject to represent his works fairly. Third, he had to be a writer of some skill, as evidenced in previous publications. Literary fame was a fourth desirable characteristic: if both the subject and the biographer possessed some renown, the volume might sell better and enhance the reputation of the entire series. Thus Warner and Houghton made great efforts to have Oliver Wendell Holmes write the Emerson volume (and rejoiced when he agreed) and sought in vain for years to induce James Russell Lowell to write Hawthorne and William Dean Howells to write Longfellow.[40]

The original authors were mostly New England men of letters in their fifties and sixties, many of them affiliated with abolitionism and other reform movements: Franklin B. Sanborn (who wrote *Henry David Thoreau*), O. B. Frothingham (*George Ripley*), Thomas Wentworth Higginson (*Margaret Fuller Ossoli*—so named to distinguish it from Julia Ward Howe's contemporaneous biography of Fuller). Among them were one academic, Thomas R. Lounsbury of Yale, a personal friend of Warner who wrote *James Fenimore Cooper,* and George E. Woodberry (*Edgar Allan Poe*), at twenty-nine the youngest author and later a noted literary critic and professor of English literature at Columbia. Over time (and perhaps as academic disciplines became more respected) two professors of history, John Bach McMaster of the University of Pennsylvania and William P. Trent of the University of the South, joined the list of contributors. The shift in authorship from "men of letters" to professional historians and literary critics was never absolute, however. Warner turned to McMaster only after Higginson gave up Benjamin Franklin for Fuller, and to Trent only after the well-known Louisiana novelist George Washington Cable failed to produce a life of William Gilmore Simms. Moreover, several men who wrote for the series in the 1890s resembled the gentleman of letters more than the academic critic. As Kermit Vanderbilt has explained, the academic study of American literature was in its infancy in the 1880s. Moses Coit Tyler had begun his work on colonial and Revolutionary American literature. But few other works existed, even fewer universities offered courses in American literature, and the Modern Language Association, founded in 1883, rarely heard papers on American writings.[41] Academic critics may not have been Warner's first choices to write for the American Men of Letters—but even if they had been, his selection would have been limited.

The American Statesmen series began with similar, but less tortuous, negotiations between editor and publisher over its purpose. John Torrey Morse, Jr., a Harvard graduate who abandoned a legal career to pursue authorship, had written a biography of Alexander Hamilton (1876) and several articles for the *North American Review*. After "reading a volume of Morley's *English Men of Letters* Series," he envisioned a similar series of lives of American statesmen. After the publisher Henry Holt rejected the idea, Morse approached Henry Oscar Houghton in the winter of 1880–81.[42] After Houghton gave preliminary approval to the scheme (no disputes over the title seem to have occurred), Morse began discussing it with potential contributors, including fellow Bostonian men of affairs like his cousin Henry Cabot Lodge and university professors like William Graham Sumner (soon to write *What the Social Classes Owe to Each Other*) and Moses Coit Tyler. But when Morse sent his list of potential subjects to the publishers in April, Houghton, Mifflin objected to many of them, raising the question of what his series was to be.

As Morse summarized the "obvious question of fundamental principle,"

> Shall the series consist of the dozen, or thereabouts, most distinguished names in our history without regard to the amount of attention any one of them may have already rec<u>d</u> from previous writers, & the amount of knowledge which the public generally have concerning any one of them; or shall the effort be to select names less hackneyed in the popular mind, concerning which more that is fresh & novel can be said? Your list chimes well with the former scheme; mine chimes better with the latter. . . . It is a question for whom the series is intended. If for school-boys & school-girls, we should have Washington, Franklin, John Adams, Jefferson, Hamilton, Madison & that ilk; but if for general & adult readers, it is probable that in such brief biographies as we propose to furnish we could add little to their knowledge concerning these men; & should have to depend for success upon a degree of brilliancy & originality in thought & treatment, not perhaps impossible, but which it is highly improbable that we shall secure in more than two or three instances.[43]

Morse's idea resembled what Jared Sparks had intended in the Library of American Biography a half-century earlier: a series that would add to Americans' historical knowledge by treating less-familiar subjects than Washington and Franklin (whose names were apparently not in Morse's initial proposal). To achieve this end, Morse sought "competent hands," often professors of history, to write the volumes, and proposed to give them some latitude in choosing their subjects. Thus Gouverneur Morris, whom Morse had not originally considered a promising subject, became part of his list when "two persons competed eagerly to write about him," and Patrick Henry won a place because Professor Tyler "was quite 'set' upon" him.

The choice of subjects thus involved negotiation and accommodation among Morse, the publishers, and the individual writers. Morse and Houghton agreed upon six subjects—Jefferson, John Quincy Adams, Madison, Calhoun, Clay, and Daniel Webster—although Carl Schurz would likely not complete Clay for some time and potential authors shied away from writing Webster. The publishers seem to have objected most strenuously to less familiar subjects, like Morris, John Randolph, and Timothy Pickering, to which Morse replied that the lack of general knowledge of them was precisely the source of interest. The same applied to James Monroe, whom Morse conceded "was certainly not 'a statesman of great calibre'" but defended on the grounds that "*nothing* has ever been written of him," thus offering "the charm of freshness & novelty." Houghton, Mifflin suggested three names not on Morse's list: Franklin, Hamilton, and John Adams. Morse agreed that all three would be desirable subjects. Nobody had yet agreed to write Hamilton, but Morse intended "to have him done before I get through." But Franklin and Adams would be difficult to do in new ways: "all Americans over 20 years of age imagine, at least, that they know all about [Franklin] . . . & certainly they are as sick of hearing his name as the Athenians were that of Aristides the Just," and Morse himself was sick of reading of Adams. All three, however, could be admitted if "good writers" could be secured. Aaron Burr was eliminated by agreement between editor and publisher. Pickering, whom Houghton, Mifflin did not want anyway, was dropped when Lodge, who had considered writing it, changed his mind and took up Hamilton. Houghton, Mifflin seems to have doubted the merit of including Andrew Jackson, perhaps on political grounds, but Morse defended the choice: "He was of limited intellect & did more mischief than all other presidents & statesmen put together, but his influence was immense & lasting; he is a most brilliant topic." Equally important, "his

life, if well done, would be the most popular & valuable of the series."
In this case, political importance and potential commercial success
justified inclusion.

When the publishers announced the series in the summer of 1881,
they described two purposes, which combined their original vision
with Morse's: "First, of avoiding the traversing of ground already sufficiently familiar. Second, of presenting in the complete series a thorough sketch of the whole history of the period covered by it." In order
to make the series "a valuable and permanent addition to historical
literature," all the authors would be "persons who have made the study
of our history a chief pursuit, who are familiar with all its facts, thoroughly instinct with its spirit, and able to trace hidden connections and
to draw from the great undigested mass of material its true significance
and philosophy." Here was the historical vision of the emerging profession of history, which eschewed mere antiquarianism (fascination with
the undigested mass of material) for a broader vision of historical progress. And Houghton, Mifflin promised to bring the fruits of such
"profound study" to "the general reader" who might not read Hermann
Von Holst's *Constitutional History of the United States* but could certainly appeciate his life of John C. Calhoun.[44]

The authors of the American Statesmen volumes included a larger
proportion of academic professionals than did the original Men of
Letters writers, perhaps because American history had by the 1880s
become more institutionalized than had American literature. Sumner,
Von Holst, Tyler, and James K. Hosmer (who wrote Samuel Adams)
all taught in universities; Daniel Coit Gilman (*James Monroe*) was the
first president of Johns Hopkins University, which had initiated American higher education along the German model. In all, nearly half of
the American Statesmen authors were professors; the other half included journalists, attorneys, and political figures. Several men were
engaged to write for both series: Sydney Howard Gay, who wrote
James Madison for Morse, was supposed to write a life of Edmund
Quincy for Warner (which never appeared), and Thomas Wentworth
Higginson, who wrote *Margaret Fuller Ossoli*, was originally slated to
produce the Benjamin Franklin volume in the Statesmen series. In the
end, the Statesmen series was dominated by Harvard men of affairs,
many from Boston and Cambridge. Morse played a far greater authorial role in the Statesmen than did Warner in the Men of Letters: he
wrote the lives of John Quincy Adams, Jefferson, John Adams, Franklin, and the two-volume Lincoln. Henry Cabot Lodge wrote four vol-

umes (Hamilton, Daniel Webster, and two on Washington), Theodore Roosevelt two (Thomas Hart Benton and Gouverneur Morris).[45]

When Houghton, Mifflin and Company announced the American Men of Letters and the American Statesmen in September 1881, the firm and the editors had high hopes for both and perceived connections between the two. The clearest links between the series were material. Morse asked the firm in 1881 whether "you mean to make the two series—Men of Letters & Statesmen—alike" in "shape, size, & style of volume"; six months later the publisher sent Warner a copy of Morse's life of John Quincy Adams as an example of "style."[46] Despite their differently colored bindings (the Statesmen in navy blue, with a half-inch band of gold stars across the top; the Men of Letters in burgundy and without the stars), the two sets of books resembled each other in numerous physical characteristics. The volumes were identical in size ($7^1/_8$ inches high, $4^3/_4$ inches deep). Both their spines featured the subject's name at the top, with the author's immediately below, the series title in the middle, and "Houghton Mifflin & Co." at the bottom; the front covers of each were stamped with the name of the series and editor. The half-title pages, which identified the series and author, and the title pages were typographically identical. With rare exceptions, the typography of the text was also similar: left-hand pages were headed with the subject's name, right-hand pages with the chapter title; the style and size of type were generally uniform. In both series, the leader on left-hand pages was the subject's name; on right-hand pages, the chapter title. Occasional exceptions to typographical uniformity resulted from the publishers' desire to maintain a consistent page length throughout the series: longer volumes were printed with more lines per page than the typical twenty-nine to thirty-two and occasionally in smaller typeface, in order to keep all the volumes around three hundred pages.[47] The Statesmen and Men of Letters volumes differed materially from each other in only one principal respect: the Men of Letters books contained frontispiece portraits of the subjects, while the Statesmen volumes did not.

The most striking material connection between the series lay in the advertisements at the back of the volumes. Most of the volumes examined for this study contained advertisements for other Houghton, Mifflin publications, as was the firm's custom. In these books, however, the advertisements were for the series themselves. And often the advertisements in the volumes of one series promoted those of the other series. An 1888 printing of William Graham Sumner's *Andrew Jackson* (originally published in 1882) contained ads for both the Statesmen and the Men of Letters volumes issued thus far, followed by the firm's list of "Standard and Popular Library Books." Conversely, many printings of American Men of Letters volumes advertised the American Statesmen series. (By the end of the century, some of these books also advertised the American Commonwealths series, a set of volumes on the states of the Union that began around the same time as the Statesmen and Men of Letters but never achieved their fame.)[48] The ads suggest that Houghton, Mifflin may well have envisioned a common market for these sets of biographies. Within a decade, however, connection would give way to comparison, and the Men of Letters series would suffer by the contrast.

∾ THE CULTURAL WORK OF THE ∾ HOUGHTON, MIFFLIN SERIES

The American Statesmen and American Men of Letters began with the mission of providing general readers with the outlines of American literary and political history, in volumes concise and inexpensive enough to gain a popular readership yet written by men with literary skill and historical knowledge. Given the variety of authors, it was not surprising that the volumes differed rather widely within each series: some (including Woodberry's *Edgar Allan Poe* and Gilman's *James Monroe*) were based on extensive research in primary documents, while others drew primarily on previously published biographies; a few (including Edward Cary's *George William Curtis*) resembled "lives and letters" in their copious extracts from the subjects' correspondence. Authors' relationships to their subjects also differed. Some authors emphasized the value of distance for critical biography. Warner wrote in his *Washington Irving* that, two decades since his subject's death, "It is time . . . to make an impartial study of the author's literary rank and achievement."[49] Similarly, Edward M. Shepard opened his *Martin Van Buren* by eschewing the partisanship that, he claimed, had previously dominated assessments of Van Buren's career, a partisanship "seriously inconsistent with the fairness and truth of history.[50] But others had been selected precisely because they had known their subjects or had lived in their subjects' milieu; in these cases the goal was to understand the "inner" life of the subject. Higginson, for example, placed himself in a middle distance from Fuller: although he had not known her intimately, he had known members of her immediate family and had spent his life in Cambridge, surrounded by her influence. This stance was not atypical: authors (especially in the Men of Letters) offered assessments based not on scientific objectivity but on familiar sympathy. These differences notwithstanding, it is possible to identify several philosophical strands that recur within each series, usually linked to the relationship between the Revolutionary or antebellum past and the Gilded Age present. In each case, the question involved the nature of progress: many of the writers in the American Men of Letters shared an ambivalence toward literary realism, which by the 1880s had superseded romanticism in critical and popular estimation; numerous American Statesmen volumes advanced a Whig philosophy of political reform and a critique of excessive democracy.

The American Men of Letters series offered both individual portraits in American literary history and a vision of that history itself.[51] Most of the individual portraits suggested the connection between the literary man and his origins. Cooper's upbringing along the Hudson, Noah Webster's childhood in vestigially Puritan Connecticut, and Fuller's sternly academic girlhood home all shaped the authors' conceptions of authorship. In some cases, family traits became central to the author's own character: Fuller possessed her ancestors' "New England vigor—which was a Roman vigor, touched by Christianity."[52] In others, the connection seemed born of revolt: for example, Nathaniel Parker Willis's emergence as something of a dandy and as a sentimental writer sprang in part from a reaction against his Calvinist parents' strictures. John L. Kijinski has suggested that writers in the English Men of Letters series generally presented their subjects as models of middle-class respectability.[53] No such overarching model can be applied to the biographies in the American Men of Letters; indeed, given the series' objective of showing the various literary cultures of the United States, such uniformity would be unlikely. Many of the writers proposed clearly individual theses about their subjects: Warner's Irving, though an American, was predominantly a cosmopolitan man of letters; Higginson's Fuller, in contrast to the prevailing view of her obsession with "self-culture," was a woman of public action and "executive force"; Scudder's Webster represented not just Federalism but also an individualism that had since been superseded by more corporate, national forms of endeavor.[54]

Several themes, however, emerged throughout many of the volumes—most of them connected to the relationship between past and present. For some writers in the series, the ostensible primitivism or

Volumes in the American Statesmen series

John T. Morse, Jr., *John Quincy Adams* (1882)

Henry Cabot Lodge, *Alexander Hamilton* (1882)

Hermann Von Holst, *John C. Calhoun* (1882)

William G. Sumner, *Andrew Jackson as a Public Man: What He Was, What Chances He Had, and What He Did with Them* (1882)

Henry Adams, *John Randolph* (1882)

Daniel C. Gilman, *James Monroe in his Relations to the Public Service during Half a Century 1776 to 1826* (1883)

John T. Morse, Jr., *Thomas Jefferson* (1883)

Henry Cabot Lodge, *Daniel Webster* (1883)

John Austin Stevens, *Albert Gallatin* (1883)

Sydney Howard Gay, *James Madison* (1884)

John T. Morse, Jr., *John Adams* (1884)

Allan B. Magruder, *John Marshall* (1885)

James K. Hosmer, *Samuel Adams* (1885)

Theodore Roosevelt, *Thomas Hart Benton* (1887)

Carl Schurz, *Henry Clay*, 2 vols. (1887)

Moses Coit Tyler, *Patrick Henry* (1887)

Theodore Roosevelt, *Gouverneur Morris* (1888)

Edward M. Shepard, *Martin Van Buren* (1888)

Henry Cabot Lodge, *George Washington*, 2 vols. (1889)

John T. Morse, Jr., *Benjamin Franklin* (1889)

George Pellew, *John Jay* (1890)

A. C. McLaughlin, *Lewis Cass* (1891)

John T. Morse, Jr., *Abraham Lincoln*, 2 vols. (1893)

Thornton K. Lothrop, *William H. Seward* (1896)

S. W. McCall, *Thaddeus Stevens* (1899)

Albert Bushnell Hart, *Salmon P. Chase* (1899)

Charles Francis Adams, Jr., *Charles Francis Adams* (1900)

Moorfield Storey, *Charles Sumner* (1900)

paucity of the past became a source of strength, in contrast to the more prosperous but less hardy present. If the ordinary colonist's access to books in Noah Webster's Connecticut "was poverty-stricken as compared with the abundant resources of our own day,—if the Hartford of 1765 is to be contrasted with that of 1881, to the manifest disadvantage of the former,—one would wish to remember that in the very sterility of that life there was a certain iron which entered into the constitution of the people who lived it. If there were not the leisure and culture of

Volumes in the American Men of Letters series
Charles Dudley Warner, *Washington Irving* (1881)
Horace E. Scudder, *Noah Webster* (1882)
F. B. Sanborn, *Henry D. Thoreau* (1882)
Octavius Brooks Frothingham, *George Ripley* (1882)
Thomas R. Lounsbury, *James Fenimore Cooper* (1883)
Thomas Wentworth Higginson, *Margaret Fuller Ossoli* (1884)
Oliver Wendell Holmes, *Ralph Waldo Emerson* (1885)
George E. Woodberry, *Edgar Allan Poe* (1885)
Henry A. Beers, *Nathaniel Parker Willis* (1885)
John Bach McMaster, *Benjamin Franklin as a Man of Letters* (1887)
John Bigelow, *William Cullen Bryant* (1890)
William P. Trent, *William Gilmore Simms* (1892)
Edward Cary, *George William Curtis* (1894)
Albert H. Smyth, *Bayard Taylor* (1896)
George E. Woodberry, *Nathaniel Hawthorne* (1902)*
Thomas Wentworth Higginson, *Henry Wadsworth Longfellow* (1902)*
George Rice Carpenter, *John Greenleaf Whittier* (1903)*
Rollo Ogden, *William Hickling Prescott* (1904)*
Henry Dwight Sedgwick, *Francis Parkman* (1904)*
Edwin Mims, *Sidney Lanier* (1905)**
Ferris Greenslet, *James Russell Lowell* (1905)**
Bliss Perry, *Walt Whitman* (1906)**

*works published as part of the "Second Series" of American Men of Letters, after Charles Dudley Warner's death in 1900.
**originally published outside the series, but added to it by Houghton, Mifflin in 1912. (See Michael Winship, ed., *Bibliography of American Literature. Volume Eight: Charles Warren Stoddard to Susan Bogert Warner* [New Haven and London: Yale University Press, 1990], p. 483).

the present day, neither were there the mental indolence and dissipation."[55] Though Fuller "lived at a time when life in America was hard for all literary people, from the absence of remuneration, the small supply of books, the habit of jealousy among authors, and the lingering prevalence of the colonial spirit," she also lived in a "fresh, glowing, youthful, hopeful, courageous period" that had since passed away.[56] Thanks to "the flood of new books, written with the single purpose of satisfying the wants of the day, produced and distributed with marvelous cheapness and facility," wrote Warner, "the standard works of approved literature," including the writings of Irving, now went unread.[57] Between past and present lay a chasm.

In political terms, this chasm was the Civil War; in literary terms, it was the movement to realism, repeatedly cited in the volumes as an antithesis to America's literary past. Numerous authors suggested that their subjects' fall from prominence resulted from the rise of realism. Warner argued that vogue for realism had led readers to discount Irving and Sir Walter Scott and replace them with the transitory and journalistic. Irving "belonged to the idealists," which for Warner was a positive trait: "he escaped the desperate realism of this generation, which has no outcome, and is likely to produce little that is noble.[58] William P. Trent attributed the decline of Simms's reputation to the same source—and similarly emphasized the "ennobling qualities of great romances," which must be the chief argument if "the friends of romance are to make any firm stand against the attacks of the realists."[59] Henry A. Beers, who stated the point most directly, began his *Nathaniel Parker Willis* in this vein: Willis "has sunk into comparative oblivion" because "Every generation begins by imitating the literary fashions of the last, and ends with a reaction against them. At present 'realism' has the floor, sentiment is at a discount, and Willis's glittering, high-colored pictures of society, with their easy optimism and their unlikeness to hard fact, have little to say to the readers of Zola and Henry James."[60] By the time Willis died in 1867, "a new literature had grown up in America. The bells of morning tinkled faintly and far off, lost in the noise of fife and drum, and the war opened its chasm between the present and the past."[61] If realism was thus the philosophical and literary force that had eclipsed much of America's literary past, the authors of the American Men of Letters volumes called for recognition of, if not return to, the earlier romanticism.

But they were quick to distinguish romanticism from sentimentalism—and to criticize the latter in terms that were often clearly gendered. Warner pointedly refuted the charge that the Knickerbocker school had given birth to sentimentalism, which he regarded as a "surface disease" with a "bathetic tone." Irving's "manly sentiment and true tenderness" had not brought about "the sentimental gush" of those who succeeded him but who had lost his "corrective humor [and] his literary art." On the other hand, despite Irving's charm his work still lacked "intellectual virility," in Warner's words.[62] Beers faced a greater challenge, since Willis clearly belonged to the sentimentalists. He offered his subject no quarter, criticizing most of Willis's productions as ephemeral effusions, even though Willis himself had criticized the kind of writing found in annual gift books as "yearly flotillas of trash."[63]

Higginson, of course, dealt with the question of gender most directly in his *Margaret Fuller Ossoli*.[64] Significantly, Higginson combined Fuller's public activity and assertion with the traits associated with Victorian womanhood, to create a portrait of a woman who pushed but ultimately did not exceed the limits of the gender. Higginson's Fuller was predominantly a woman of public action: initiating the Conversations (which fueled the reform activity of women listeners), founding and editing *The Dial*, writing for New York newspapers, all in an era when such attainments generally lay outside woman's province. But "with all her Roman ambition," she remained "'a very woman' at heart," who ultimately married for love and died in a shipwreck with her husband and child.[65] To reinforce this impression, Higginson included a full chapter of letters between Fuller and her husband. For a woman author, this domestic denouement made sense; for a man like Irving or Willis, sentimentalism was clearly a sign of weakness.

In the schema of the American Men of Letters, before the realistic present and the romantic past lay the deep past of the colonial period—against which the authors of the early republic reacted. In this sense these figures were most clearly "American" men of letters: they asserted America's literary independence from England. Webster, with his idiosyncratic but clearly patriotic grammar, speller, and dictionary, was the first, seeking to give the United States a national culture to match its national political institutions. (Once again, the relationship between past and present became important here. For Horace Scudder, the solitariness of Webster's pursuit was as significant as its Americanness; in the 1880s projects like dictionaries and Bible revisions were the work of groups of men, churches, and publishers, not individuals.) Fuller grew up "when our literature was still essentially colonial" and became "a literary pioneer," launching "the first thoroughly American literary enterprise," for "whatever else it was," Transcendentalism "was indigenous."[66] Lounsbury's Cooper and Trent's Simms also represented truly American writing; Warner's Irving, even if he spent seventeen years in Europe and considered himself predominantly a cosmopolitan man of letters, returned home because of his enthusiasm "for the land and the people he supremely loved."[67] Warner's title, then, had been right from the start: the series asserted an "American" literary history, offered a vision of literary manliness that denigrated the sentimental, and suggested a progression of American "letters" that moved from colonial antecedents to the idealistic past to the realistic world of the 1880s.

The American Statesmen series displayed both its authors' individual interpretations of their subjects and a more general Whiggish orientation that celebrated the orderly progress of America, and in particular of the American North. Distinct authorial visions clearly existed. For example, Hermann Von Holst's *John C. Calhoun* was not just a biography but equally an analysis and critique of Calhoun's pro-slavery political and constitutional philosophy. In shifting from nationalist support for the War of 1812 and internal improvements to championship of sectionalism, Calhoun declined from "the statesman" to "the attorney of a special cause," according to Holst.[68] In this interpretation, Holst repeated for the popular audience of the American Statesmen series the central argument of his *Constitutional History of the United States,* which Peter Novick has characterized as "one long legal barrage at the doctrine of states' rights."[69] As Lois Hughson has argued, Henry Adams's *John Randolph* reflected its author's lifelong "ambivalence about personal power and its relation to accomplishment," a theme dominant as well in Adams's contemporaneous biography of Albert Gallatin and his *History of the United States of America during the Administrations of Thomas Jefferson and James Madison.* Adams also described Randolph's political experience as an "education" (although one that the headstrong Virginian ultimately ignored), a model not unlike what would appear in *The Education of Henry Adams.*[70] And William Graham Sumner's *Andrew Jackson* lauded the Supreme Court's ascendancy under John Marshall as the bulwark against the abuses of "a surging democracy"—a view that reflected Sumner's own Gilded Age belief in the judiciary as the guardian of stability.[71]

Many of these individual authorial visions, however, cohere around a set of principles that might be described as "whig," with particular criticism for the philosophy and policies of Jefferson and Jackson. Morse, the most frequent author in the series, praised Benjamin Franklin's "genuine . . . faith in man" over the "exaggerated gospel of the people" preached by "Democrats of the revolutionary school in France and the Jeffersonian school in the United States."[72] In Lodge's *George Washington,* Jefferson appears as a plotter who sought to undermine his rival Hamilton and to discredit his enemies with charges of monarchism.[73] According to William Graham Sumner, Jefferson's Republican party "was filled with ill-informed and ill-regulated sympathy for the French Revolutionists" and, if successful in 1796, "would, by importing Jacobinism into this country, have overthrown constitutional liberty here"; as president, Jefferson overturned Washington's prudent diplomatic precedents and precipitated the "fruitless war" of 1812.[74] The Federalists were not without their faults in these biographies, but these tended to be personal flaws rather than philosophical dangers: the "vanity" of Morse's John Adams and the "uncharitable" nature of his John Quincy Adams help to account for their lack of popularity.[75] But this very unpopularity becomes a badge of honor: John Quincy Adams, "hardly abused and cruelly misappreciated in his own day," was ultimately honored by "subsequent generations . . . as one of the greatest of American statesmen" for his accomplishments and his character.

The antithesis of the Adamses was Andrew Jackson. Morse, who believed Jackson politically dangerous and "of limited intellect," must have been pleased by Sumner's volume, which criticized many of Jackson's policies and depicted Old Hickory as immensely popular but equally reckless. In foreign policy, for example, Jackson encouraged "The filibustering spirit, one law for ourselves and another for every one else."[76] As Henry Clay's antagonist, Jackson also made his way into Carl Schurz's volumes. Schurz portrayed the intense drama of Jackson's and Clay's rivalry: Jackson, though "very ignorant," possessed the genius of command and a bravery that inspired those around him; Clay, though occasionally inclined toward "peremptory command" and intolerant of "adverse opinion," possessed "the leadership of a statesman zealously striving to promote great principles."[77] Schurz quickly made clear which of these titans represented evil: immediately after taking office, Jackson swept out the appointees of his predecessor, cloaking the spoils system in the name of "reform." For Schurz, abolitionist and civil-service reformer, "Never was the word 'reform' uttered with a more sinister meaning."[78] On one side stood "statesmen" like John Quincy Adams and Clay—significantly, Morse and Schurz used the word "statesman" to describe Jackson's enemies—who supported a nationalist economic philosophy and a strong union. On the other stood the forces of disorder (like Jackson and, to a lesser extent, Jefferson) and slavery (Calhoun).

This vision connects the biographers with the political reformers of the 1880s, the northern, upper-middle-class "mugwumps" who stood for civil-service reform and against the rowdy partisanship that had built the nation's major parties. Indeed, many of the men who wrote for Morse were involved in political reform movements. The oldest of them, like Schurz and Sydney Howard Gay (who wrote his *James Madison* "from the Federalist point of view"), had been abolitionists; after the Civil War Schurz turned his attentions to civil-service reform.[79] The younger men like Theodore Roosevelt and Lodge were the successors to these earlier moral reformers: aristocratic in background, generally college educated, and often Republican. Not surprisingly, they criticized in the past what they perceived as the antecedents of contemporary ills: the spoils system of Jackson had presaged the Gilded Age urban political machines that mugwumps condemned. It is important to recognize that not all of the authors shared this outlook. Shepard, for example, defended Jefferson's "enormous formative influence" against the "so partial and sometimes so partisan . . . historians of our early national politics" who saw Jeffersonian democracy as the forerunner of Jacksonian corruption, and praised Van Buren—the premier spoilsman, in the Whig view—as a master of *both* the "exalted art of the politician" and the "consummate art of the statesman."[80] But more frequently, the tone and philosophy of late Victorian genteel reform permeated the American Statesmen volumes.

∾ RECEPTION AND REPACKAGING ∾

By 1890 the American Statesmen and American Men of Letters series had become American literary institutions, recognized by potential contributors as valuable sites of publication for their work. Hence Houghton, Mifflin and the editors Warner and Morse began to receive suggestions for possible subjects, usually from people who wanted to write the biographies themselves. Eugene L. Didier of Baltimore proposed to write the life of the southern novelist John Pendleton Kennedy for the American Men of Letters; the prominent biographer James Parton suggested Thomas Paine, "the first of his class in North America, the first to live by his pen"; J. Brander Matthews wondered whether John Howard Payne, the early American dramatist and author of "Home, Sweet Home," might "be made the vehicle of an interesting account of the stage in these United States in the first quarter of this century."[81] Warner seems to have rejected all of these ideas. Morse received two inquiries about Thomas Hart Benton (whom he eventually added to the series) and a proposal from J. Hampden Doughty to write William H. Seward's life (which was too recent for Morse's plan in 1887 but became part of the "second series" in 1898). He also rejected biographies of Richard Henry Lee and DeWitt Clinton ("outside of New York State he would now excite little interest"), and "sent a similar response to a young lady who thought that Millard Fillmore! was entitled to a place among 'American Statesmen.' "[82]

Becoming a literary institution could also have an underside, as William Everett—whom Warner had approached about writing the life of Prescott—revealed. Everett hesitated to undertake the book for a variety of reasons, including the compensation the publishers proposed (the standard ten percent royalty on copies sold). But his greatest complaint lay in the constraints he perceived in writing for a series. If Everett understood Warner's plan correctly, he wrote,

> it does not correspond to my way of looking at distinguished authors. The development of American Literature is to me an absolutely intangible thing. I can understand that there may be such a thing, but I do not see how you can write about an individual with reference to it. . . . I know what *men* are; I have not the least conception of *developments*. I could perhaps tell the story of Prescott's life and works; but himself as the centre of a group,—like the fancy pictures called Irving and his friends,—is not only beyond my execution, but even my understanding. He wrote with no such consciousness,—and hence to me the thing did not exist.

Moreover, Everett complained that the book's "design" could not possibly be his own, "when it is a publisher's scheme, under an editor's care . . . an assigned task, with countless limitations fencing it in." If the publishers were willing to pay him an agreeable fixed sum for this "task-work," he might consider accepting; but he was being asked to perform the equivalent of manual labor without any assured return. Everett perceived a contradiction: Houghton, Mifflin claimed to engage "men of letters" to write the volumes in the series, but treated them as laborers, much like pressmen but without the guarantee of compensation.[83]

Even as the two series gained a national reputation (while other publishers' series quietly emerged and expired during these years), by 1890 their fortunes were diverging. As early as 1885, Warner was having difficulty getting his contributors to complete (or, in some cases, even to begin) their work. Nine volumes had appeared by the end of 1885, but over the next eight years only three more came out. James Russell Lowell had agreed to write Hawthorne's life, but made no progress while minister to Great Britain and none afterward. George Washington Cable had agreed to do William Gilmore Simms but sent nothing to Warner. In all, about half of the originally announced authors failed to complete their books at all. Some were replaced, while other volumes—including those on Hawthorne and Longfellow—went

Table 1. Sales of American Men of Letters volumes (from date of publication to 1900)

	First two years	First five years	First ten years
Irving (1881)	2,840	5,087	7,706
Noah Webster (1882)	2,259	3,182	4,219
Thoreau (1882)	2,240	3,501	4,763
George Ripley (1882)	1,844	2,787	3,650
Cooper (1882)	2,059	3,324	4,617
Fuller Ossoli (1884)	2,710	3,644	4,813
Emerson (1884)	7,925	10,110	12,620
Poe (1885)	2,315	3,147	4,289
N. P. Willis (1885)	1,663	2,355	3,069
Franklin (1887)	3,299	4,427	5,786
Bryant (1890)	1,889	2,765	4,056
W. G. Simms (1892)	1,288	1,749	2,298
G. W. Curtis (1894)	3,020	3,661	4,369
Bayard Taylor (1896)	1,526	1,860	2,540
Averages	2,634	3,686	4,914
Averages without Emerson	2,227	3,191	4,321

Source: Houghton, Mifflin, and Company, Sales Books, vols. 31–32, Houghton Mifflin Papers, Houghton Library, Harvard University.

unwritten until after Warner's death in 1900. By June 1885 the publishers prodded Warner to move his authors along, a refrain that would become familiar; in March 1888, they wrote, "We are seriously concerned over the slow movement of the *Men of Letters* series. Promptness of action seems to us now of great importance," as they planned to begin new series and wanted to conclude the old ones. Houghton, Mifflin encouraged "discarding books which have no chance of life, or securing authors who can take hold of them with resolution."[84] Meanwhile the American Statesmen series proceeded rapidly. Morse often apologized to the publishers about authors' delays, but in fact his series grew constantly over the decade, with nine volumes in the first two years, eighteen by 1888, and twenty-three by 1893. Some of Morse's original contributors dropped out (Higginson, initially slated to write the life of Franklin, took this project to the American Men of Letters, then switched to Margaret Fuller; keeping an author for Martin Van Buren proved difficult), but most completed their agreed works within a few years. Schurz infuriated Morse, first by his delays and then by submitting two volumes on Clay and refusing to shorten them, but this was the exception.[85] Henry Oscar Houghton congratulated Morse for the fact that "your series has gone on more regularly than any other that we remember being connected with."[86]

Table 2. Sales of American Statesmen volumes (from date of publication to 1900)

	First two years	First five years	First ten years
J. Q. Adams (1882)	4,217	6,597	10,277
Hamilton (1882)	4,624	7,647	12,903
Calhoun (1882)	4,198	6,464	9,651
Jackson (1882)	3,868	6,115	9,581
Randolph (1882)	3,388	5,276	7,607
Monroe (1883)	3,287	4,997	7,109
Jefferson (1883)	3,812	6,628	12,116
D. Webster (1883)	4,102	7,354	12,104
Gallatin (1883)	2,569	4,307	6,310
Madison (1884)	2,794	4,585	6,769
John Adams (1884)	2,506	4,402	6,793
Marshall (1885)	2,956	4,668	6,744
S. Adams (1885)	2,727	4,589	6,846
Benton (1887)	2,984	4,260	5,963
Clay, 2 vols. (1887)	5,478	8,128	12,214
Henry (1887)	4,029	6,332	9,307
Morris (1888)	2,634	3,880	5,414
Van Buren (1888)	2,435	3,617	5,373
Washington, 2 vols. (1889)	4,476	6,757	10,510
Franklin (1889)	2,912	4,750	8,154
Jay (1890)	2,340	3,466	5,122
Cass (1891)	2,163	3,039	4,454
Lincoln, 2 vols. (1893)	5,650	8,729	—
Averages	3,485	5,504	8,242
Averages without Lincoln	3,386	5,357	—

Source: Houghton, Mifflin, and Company, Sales Books, vols. 31–32, Houghton Mifflin Papers, Houghton Library, Harvard University.

Note: Sales for works from 1898 forward are reduced because the appearance of the Standard Library Edition that year (not included in this table) diminished the sales for volumes of the regular edition. Thus works initially published after 1888 show a drop near the end of their first ten years. Volumes published between 1896 and 1899 are not included inasmuch as most of their sales were in the Standard Library Edition, nor are ten-year figures for Morse's *Abraham Lincoln*, whose second five years coincide with that edition.

The commercial fortunes of the series also diverged: the volumes in the American Statesmen far outsold those in the American Men of Letters (Tables 1–3). Predictably, every book sold best in its first two years of publication—but in those first years, volumes in the Statesmen series averaged 3,485 copies sold, while those in the Men of Letters averaged 2,634. The only exception to this pattern was Oliver Wendell Holmes's *Ralph Waldo Emerson* (1884), which sold three times the average in the Men of Letters, likely because of Emerson's recent death (in 1882), his continuing prominence, and Holmes's own fame. As the publishers had hoped from the start, this combination of subject and

Table 3. Average sales per book in each series, by year (with number of books in print)

	American Men of Letters		American Statesmen*	
	all vols.	old vols.	all vols.	old vols
1882	1,420 (5)	1,575 (1)	2,504 (5)	—
1883	743 (5)	743 (5)	1,972 (9)	1,555 (5)
1884	1,126 (7)	428 (5)	1,043 (11)	890 (9)
1885	1,214 (9)	1,076 (7)	1,098 (13)	896 (11)
1886	372 (9)	372 (9)	634 (13)	634 (13)
1887	575 (10)	359 (9)	1,162 (16)	740 (13)
1888	370 (10)	370 (10)	919 (18)	799 (16)
1889	308 (10)	308 (10)	879 (20)	677 (18)
1890	433 (11)	321 (10)	735 (21)	679 (20)
1891	224 (11)	224 (11)	624 (22)	572 (21)
1892	386 (12)	317 (11)	619 (22)	619 (22)
1893	198 (12)	198 (12)	691 (23)	511 (22)
1894	386 (13)	229 (12)	527 (23)	527 (23)
1895	296 (13)	296 (13)	515 (23)	515 (23)
1896	296 (14)	224 (13)	643 (24)	586 (23)
1897	206 (14)	206 (14)	600 (24)	600 (24)
1898	176 (14)	176 (14)	450 (24)	450 (24)

Source: Houghton, Mifflin, and Company, Sales Books, vols. 31–32, Houghton Mifflin Papers, Houghton Library, Harvard University.

Note: In both series, the appearance of new books invariably boosted the average for all volumes, since a new book sold especially well in its first year (or two, depending on the time of year it appeared). And the publication of new books also seems to have given a boost to the sales of old ones: witness the rise in sales for all but one old book in 1885, when Poe and Willis were issued on the heels of Holmes's Emerson, and the jump for everything in 1892, when Simms appeared (the first book in two years). The big drop in the Statesmen series in 1898 reflected the publication of the Standard Library and Large Paper (limited) editions, which at that point provided an additional form in which to buy these works. From 1887 on, the Statesmen series sold over twice as many copies per volume as the Men of Letters series in all but two years.

*Two-volume works are counted as one volume.

biographer proved hugely successful, selling 7,925 copies in its first two years. Removing *Emerson* from the averages, however, Men of Letters volumes sold a third fewer copies than Statesmen volumes in their first two years and only half as many copies over five years. Annual sales figures for the series indicate the magnitude of the gap: from 1887 on, the sales of previously published volumes in the Statesmen series more than doubled those of the Men of Letters volumes in all but two years. Ten Statesmen biographies sold better than the second-strongest Men of Letters life (Warner's *Irving*); indeed, some volumes in the Men of Letters series virtually disappeared from sales after their first few years.

Significantly, readers made choices not just *between* the series but also *within* them. The least popular volumes in the Men of Letters series were precisely those that reflected the publishers' and editor's desire for representativeness: Willis, the now-forgotten magazinist, and Simms, the southerner. The most popular were those still familiar to a late-century audience: Emerson, Irving, Franklin. Similarly, the bestsellers among the Statesmen were largely those Houghton, Mifflin had wanted included at the outset for their fame: Hamilton, Jefferson, Washington. Two New Englanders, John Quincy Adams and Daniel Webster, also sold exceedingly well, as did the two volumes on Henry Clay written by the prominent reformer Carl Schurz. The poorest sellers in this series may have been those whom readers did not remember or deemed ephemeral: Gouverneur Morris, Martin Van Buren, John Jay, Lewis Cass. Commercially, the firm had been right from the beginning—volumes on previously neglected subjects might possess historical novelty, but familiar favorites would sell better.

Despite these internal variations, the publishers emphasized the sales difference between the two series. H. O. Houghton at first attributed the poor sales of the Men of Letters to the delinquency of the volumes:

> I think the Series has suffered from the halting way in which we have brought out the new books, and I should like to have the remaining volumes of the Series brought out with greater promptness, and with as little intervening time between the issue of each, as is possible. This Series has not done nearly as well as the Statesmen Series. In fact, only one of the volumes, except Dr. Holmes's, for which the account is not yet made up, has paid for itself. That volume is the one written by you, which for several reasons was the least expensive of all. I do not despair of the Series, but I think we could do much better with it if the volumes should succeed each other faster, and with more regularity.[87]

In other words, the American Men of Letters series would sell better if readers perceived it *as* a series (as the bindings, title pages, and the rest indicated they should)—a perception that long delays made difficult. By 1898, the firm seems to have recognized another explanation for the difference: readers were more interested in the lives of political figures than in those of literary men. Men of letters, in fact, might be approached more readily through their works than through their lives. Thus in 1897 Houghton, Mifflin began planning a Standard Library Edition of the Statesmen series, which would parallel its Standard editions of its authors' works.

The new edition of the American Statesmen, which the firm advertised aggressively between 1898 and 1901, offered buyers both the material quality associated with Houghton, Mifflin's well-known Standard Library Editions of its authors' work and an explicit textual coherence previously lacking in the series. Formerly, coherence among the volumes had been primarily a matter of appearance: the material characteristics of the volumes were the same, but they appeared whenever authors completed them, in no particular order. Indeed, advertisements for the series before 1897 listed the volumes in the order in which they had originally been published. If many of the authors shared a political philosophy, there was still no overarching statement of such purpose.

Creating the new edition of the series involved both material and textual alteration. The volumes of the Standard Library Edition were to be prepared from "entirely new plates, made expressly for the edition," and to be printed on Croxley paper, "the paper that has been used with such uniform satisfaction in all Standard Library editions, having proved one of the most important factors in the great popularity of the series." The original Statesmen volumes contained no illustrations; each volume of the new edition contained four engraved portraits "from oil paintings, photographs, and other originals, not easily accessible, many of which have never before been reproduced." Facing the frontispiece portrait in each volume was an engraving of the subject's home, from Lincoln's boyhood log cabin to Monroe's Greek Revival plantation house. The binding, "a handsome shade of olive green cloth . . . imported expressly for this edition," was simpler and more elegant than the blue cloth with gold stars of the original edition; moreover, the volumes were larger than those of the earlier edition ($7^1/2$ inches high by 5 inches deep). Perhaps the most telling change in the bindings appeared on the spine. Where the spines of the original edition had announced the subject, author, and "American Statesmen," those in the Standard Library Edition added a Roman numeral: "James Monroe/Gilman/American Statesmen/XIV." This addition indicated placement in a sequence—and, indeed, the new edition possessed an order lacking among the original volumes.[88]

In preparing the new edition, Houghton, Mifflin engaged Morse once again, this time to make the series into a textual whole by writing a general introduction, placing the volumes into chronological sections, and preparing introductions to each section. Advertised from the start as a series of biographies that would illustrate the history of the nation, the American Statesmen series now became, in the words of

Houghton, Mifflin, "A political history of the United States, antedating the Revolution and extending through the Civil War and Reconstruction period." The five sections treated "The Revolutionary Period," "The Constructive Period," "The Jeffersonian Democracy," "Domestic Politics: The Tariff and Slavery" (significantly not "The Jacksonian Period"), and "The Civil War" (which included five new volumes written at the end of the century). Houghton, Mifflin also arranged for the preparation of a "topical index," which appeared as the thirty-second and final volume and likewise provided readers with connections between the volumes in the series.

As the publishers explained, the series provided American readers with not just a history of their past but also the information they needed in the present as citizens of a republic:

> In this country, where an intelligent understanding of all the great political questions of the day is expected of every citizen, there exists a necessity for some means of tracing the earlier history of the important problems that now confront us. . . . The "American Statesmen" Series supplies this need by presenting in biographical form the contribution of twenty-eight representative men to the political history of the country, selecting the subjects in such a way as to give a complete and perfect picture of the growth and development of the United States.[89]

In his general introduction, Morse explained publicly for the first time the "principle of selection" that, he now claimed, had shaped the series from the outset.

> The principle has been to make such a list of men in public life that the aggregation of all their biographies would give, in this personal shape, the history and the picture of the growth and development of the United States from the beginning of that agitation which led to the Revolution until the completion of that solidarity which we believe has resulted from the civil war and the subsequent reconstruction.

Several subjects, including Patrick Henry, Thomas Hart Benton, Lewis Cass, and John Randolph, had been chosen not primarily because they were great statesmen but because they represented elements of American political development essential for a complete history: Henry "the South in the period preceding the Revolution," Benton "the character of the Southwest," Cass "the Northwest—or what used to be called the Northwest not so very long ago," Randolph "the characteristics of Congress" in the early republic.[90] This vision, in fact, resembled Warner's original plan for the Men of Letters series, which included figures like Willis not because of their literary greatness but because of their representativeness of particular literary cultures. As the publishers wrote in the advertisement, these were "representative men."

The other part of Morse's "principle" codified the idea of "progress" that many of the volumes had suggested:

> It has been the editor's intention to deal with the advancement of the country. When the people have moved steadily along any road, the men who have led them on that road have been selected as subjects. When the people have refused to enter upon a road, or, having entered, have soon turned back from it, the leaders upon such inchoate or abandoned excursions have for the most part been rejected. Those who have been exponents of ideas and principles which have entered into the progress and have developed in a positive way the history of the nation have been chosen; those who have unfortunately linked themselves with rejected ideas and principles have themselves also been rejected.

Thus Governor Hutchinson of colonial Massachusetts (who opposed the Revolution), Stephen A. Douglas (whose policies "the people decisively condemned" in electing Lincoln), and Andrew Johnson (whose vision of Reconstruction lost to that of Thaddeus Stevens and Charles Sumner) did not merit places. Nor did Burr—whose "name would have been a degradation of the series" and whose "career was strictly selfish and personal," leaving "no permanent trace"—or James Buchanan, whose "wrong-headed blundering is sufficiently depicted for the purposes of this series by the lives of those who foiled him." The one exception, Calhoun, was included "for reasons so obvious that they need not be rehearsed."[91] (And Holst's volume on Calhoun demonstrated that its subject had led the deluded and inevitably doomed opposition to progress.) The series, thus organized, introduced, and indexed in the Standard Library Edition, presented a history of American democratic progress. Morse's references to "the people" suggested that the paths the nation followed were popularly sanctioned, and that the men worth including among "American Statesmen" earned inclusion by leading the way.

This narrative of orderly selection—which mirrors the series' own emphasis on social and political order—was clearly a construction that became possible only *after* the volumes had been originally published. As we have seen, the process by which subjects entered the American Statesmen series in the 1880s and early 1890s was far more haphazard. The series included Patrick Henry not because Morse or the publishers believed that a colonial Virginian was necessary but because they wanted Moses Coit Tyler to write a volume and Tyler chose Henry. Thomas Hart Benton was added to the list only after several correspondents suggested his name to Morse in the mid-1880s. And the re-creation of the series in a Standard Library Edition occurred only because the American Statesmen volumes had proven commercially successful in their first, less textually ordered, incarnation. Had the American Statesmen fared as poorly as the American Men of Letters, it would not have appeared in Houghton, Mifflin's "Offer Beginning the Twentieth Century" alongside Emerson, Hawthorne, and Dickens.

∾ CONCLUSION: ∾
CONSTRUCTING CULTURAL PANTHEONS

Between 1900 and 1927, Houghton, Mifflin and Company continued to sell the American Statesmen and American Men of Letters volumes and to pay royalties to their authors. New volumes appeared in both series: in the American Men of Letters, the biographies of Hawthorne, Longfellow, Parkman, and Prescott that Warner had never been able to bring to completion as well as lives of Whittier, Holmes, and Harte; in the American Statesmen, a "Second Series" of "men particularly influ-ential in the recent Political History of the Nation," including James G. Blaine, John Sherman, William McKinley, and Ulysses S. Grant.[92] As late as the 1920s, Houghton, Mifflin saw the possibilities of cultural work and commercial advantage in the American Statesmen. In 1920, the firm asked Henry Cabot Lodge—fresh from his Senate victory over Woodrow Wilson's League of Nations—to write a new introduction to his *George Washington,* which it intended to republish. Houghton, Mifflin suggested that Lodge "emphasize the importance of Wash-ington's message and . . . encourage the public to study his policies"— perhaps meaning Washington's Farewell Message, in which he (like Lodge in the League battle) warned Americans about entangling for-eign alliances. Upon receiving Lodge's new introduction, the firm wrote approvingly that it "connects up most admirably the past and present."[93] Two years later, the firm attempted unsuccessfully to "un-dertake a mail order campaign for the sale of the Series" in connection with the *Literary Digest.* "The *Literary Digest* will advertise the Series as an education in sound Americanism, and urge its wide reading as a background for forming judgments upon the political problems of today." Houghton, Mifflin next created an "inexpensive popular edition" of several volumes from the series, "under the title of Great Presidents," in order to stimulate "the demand for biographies among people who do not care to pay the higher price which it is now neces- sary to charge" for works like the Statesmen volumes.[94] These attempts to keep the series alive notwithstanding, the sales of the Statesmen series had been waning since as early as 1905. In 1927, Houghton, Mifflin bought out the authors' copyrights to both the Statesmen and the Men of Letters books (as well as the American Commonwealths), signifying the end of their commercial lives.

Ultimately the American Men of Letters series probably had more academic significance than did the American Statesmen series, for precisely the same reasons the Statesmen series sold better. The Ameri- can Men of Letters, as Kermit Vanderbilt explains, became an impor- tant source of information for the men who would write the pioneering Cambridge History of American Literature in the early twentieth cen- tury (and William Peterfield Trent, the senior editor of that project, had begun his academic career with William Gilmore Simms in the Men of Letters series).[95] The books in this series were, in many cases, the first treatments of their subjects (except for anthology squibs and in a few instances compendious lives and letters) and thus established the ground on which future scholars built. Their lack of popularity when published reflected the general lack of attention to American literature (and particularly to the writings of American romantics) at that point, but this same prior inattention made the studies all the more valuable to later scholars. The choice that Houghton, Mifflin and Morse made at the outset of the American Statesmen—to include a host of well- known figures like Washington, Franklin, and Hamilton—probably accounts for that series's better sales. Indeed, the volumes that sold best were precisely the ones that treated familiar subjects. But this same choice made the Statesmen series more derivative and more clearly the product of its authors' own political predilections. The Statesmen se- ries provided brief biographies of major American leaders for readers who might not have the opportunity to read these men's lives and letters or other, longer biographies that had come before. For middle- class readers and school libraries, the Statesmen series served precisely the function that Houghton, Mifflin advertised: it provided a bio- graphical history of the nation—and, after 1898, gave it a coherent order with a general index and introductions that tied the volumes together, creating a series in content where there had earlier been only a series in material form. But for scholars, most of these volumes, and certainly the most popular ones, traversed little new ground. And when the Progressive history writing of Charles Beard, Carl Becker, and others elevated the reputations of Jefferson and Jackson at the expense of the Federalists and Whigs, the interpretations of Morse, Lodge, and the other mugwump men of letters seemed dated at best, irrelevantly elitist at worst.[96]

The history of the American Statesmen and American Men of Letters series in their heyday—from their inception in 1880–81 to the repackaging of the Statesmen in 1898—provides a case study in late Victorian biographical publishing and in the actual practice of defining cultural canons. That the two series would become biographical institutions like Morley's English Men of Letters was by no means assured at the start. As the early history of both series reveals, publishers, editors, and authors all had their say in who "belonged": if the proposed author wanted to write about Edmund Quincy rather than Lydia Maria Child, Child would not end up in the series. As the various suggestions from readers indicated, the existence of the series did not simply create a commonly shared image of the nation's worthiest statesmen and men of letters but instead encouraged readers and authors to propose their own additions. Ultimately buyers' demands led the publishers to a conclusion about the relationship between statesmen, men of letters, and the genre of biography. Perhaps the problem with the Men of Letters series was not that the authors were slow to get their books finished; perhaps readers simply preferred reading authors' works to reading their lives. Biography provided the best way for readers to "know" political figures like Jefferson or Clay but not the straightest route to the heart of Emerson, Fuller, or Poe. When Houghton, Mifflin advertised the American Statesmen series with the works of Longfellow, Whittier, Dickens, and the rest in 1901, the firm was clearly making a commercial decision, but at the same time it implicitly acknowledged that its readers had made their choice.

∾ NOTES ∾

The research for this chapter was made possible by the Stanley J. Kahrl Fellowship, Houghton Library, and a Junior Faculty Research Award from the University of Nevada, Reno. I am grateful to Michael Winship, Jeffrey Groves, Kristin Robinson, Christopher Grasso, Elizabeth Raymond, and Dennis Dworkin, and to graduate seminars at Claremont Graduate School and the University of Nevada, Reno, for comments on earlier drafts. Quotations from manuscript correspondence are reprinted by permission of the Houghton Library, Harvard University; Houghton Mifflin Company; and the Watkinson Library, Trinity College.

1. Houghton, Mifflin and Company (hereafter HM&C), "Our Special Offer Beginning the Twentieth Century," advertisement, 21 Feb. 1901, Advertising Scrapbooks, Houghton, Mifflin Papers (bMS Am 1925), Houghton Library, Harvard University, Cambridge, Mass.

2. Several volumes were added to each of these series after the turn of the century: a "second series" of political figures from the Gilded Age was appended to the Statesmen, and long-delayed lives of Hawthorne and Longfellow, as well as biographies of Prescott and others, were added to the Men of Letters. This essay, however, considers each series to be the works published in it up to 1899, for several reasons. The Statesmen series was repackaged as a coherent "whole" in 1898, making the later volumes clearly an appendage that had nothing to do with the earlier publishing history. Charles Dudley Warner, the editor of the Men of Letters series, died in 1900; subsequent volumes in that series thus belong to a later chapter of the series history than this essay describes.

3. HM&C, announcement for American Statesmen series, c. 1881, Houghton, Mifflin Papers; HM&C, proof copy of announcement for "American Men of Letters," enclosed with HM&C to Charles Dudley Warner (hereafter CDW), 6 Aug. 1881. Charles Dudley Warner Collection, Watkinson Library, Trinity College, Hartford, Conn. (hereafter Warner Collection).

4. HM&C, preliminary advertisement for "American Statesmen" (c. 1881), Houghton, Mifflin Papers. On the claims to literary preeminence of Houghton, Mifflin and Ticknor and Fields, see Richard Brodhead, *Cultures of Letters: Scenes of Reading and Writing in Nineteenth-Century America* (Chicago: U of Chicago P, 1992).

5. Literary anthologies of the 1840s and 1850s, most famously Rufus Wilmot Griswold's *The Poets and Poetry of America* and *The Female Poets of America,* usually contained brief biographies of their subjects. However, those brief lives were often written by the poets themselves (and edited, sometimes unfavorably, by the compilers). On Griswold and the anthologists, see Richard D. Altick, *Lives and Letters: A History of Literary Biography in England and America* (New York: Knopf, 1965) 268–69; on the alteration of poets' autobiographical sketches, see Scott Evan Casper, "Constructing American Lives: The Cultural History of Biography in Nineteenth-Century America," diss., Yale U, 1992, 284n84. A related genre of the 1850s was the "homes of famous men" book, made famous by Putnam's *Homes of American Authors* (New York: Putnam, 1853) and *Homes of American Statesmen* (New York: Putnam, 1854).

6. Sparks's Library differed from many other American publishers' "library

series" in the Jacksonian era (such as the widely distributed Harper's Family Library), which consisted mainly of works previously published elsewhere and reproduced in the absence of international copyright laws. On the emergence of "library series" in the 1830s and 1840s, see Ezra Greenspan, "Evert Duyckinck and the History of Wiley and Putnam's Library of American Books, 1845–1847," *American Literature* 64 (1992): 681. Wiley and Putnam's Library of American Books was the exception to the general pattern: a series of new volumes, contracted and copyrighted specifically for this series in an attempt to promote the original work of American authors.

7. "Advertisement" (dated January 1834), for "The Library of American Biography, Conducted by Jared Sparks," in *Library of American Biography,* ed. Jared Sparks (1834; New York: Harper and Brothers, 1848), 1:iv. For further discussion of the Library of American Biography, see Herbert Baxter Adams, *The Life and Writings of Jared Sparks,* 2 vols. (Boston: Houghton, Mifflin, 1893) 2:187–207.

8. On these strains of biographical criticism in the mid-nineteenth century, see Casper ch. 7.

9. F. J. M. Korsten, "The 'English Men of Letters' Series: A Monument of Late-Victorian Literary Criticism," *English Studies* 6 (1992): 509.

10. Korsten 512.

11. John L. Kijinski, "John Morley's 'English Men of Letters' Series and the Politics of Reading," *Victorian Studies* 34 (1991): 216, 220–21.

12. "Books of the Month," *Atlantic Monthly* 50 (1882): 285–86.

13. John Torrey Morse, Jr., (hereafter JTM) to HM&C, 21 Mar. 1881, Houghton, Mifflin Papers. See also George Haven Putnam to CDW, 7 July 1880, 16 July 1880, Warner Collection.

14. William Dean Howells to Charles Dudley Warner, 27 Dec. 1879, Warner Collection.

15. George Haven Putnam to CDW, 5 Jan. 1880, Warner Collection.

16. John Morley to William Dean Howells (telegraph message), n.d. (but almost certainly 20 Jan. 1880), Warner Collection.

17. Howells to CDW, 12 Mar. 1880, Warner Collection.

18. CDW to Howells, 15 Mar. 1880, William Dean Howells Collection (bMS Am 1784), Houghton Library, Harvard University.

19. Putnam to CDW, 7 July 1880, Warner Collection.

20. On the reorganization of Houghton's publishing firm, see Ellen B. Ballou, *The Building of the House: Houghton Mifflin's Formative Years* (Boston: Houghton Mifflin, 1970) 276–79.

21. Henry Oscar Houghton to CDW, 22 Nov. 1880, Warner Collection. Houghton's letter responds to an earlier letter from Warner, not surviving.

22. Houghton to CDW, 24 Nov. 1880, Warner Collection.

23. On Warner, Fields, and the editorship of the series, see H. O. Houghton

to CDW, 17 Jan., 22 Jan., 5 Feb., 20 Apr., 17 May, 5 July 1881, all Warner Collection; HM&C to CDW, 18 Apr., 25 Apr., 30 Apr., 17 May, 2 June 1881, all Warner Collection; CDW to HM&C, 1 June 1881, Houghton, Mifflin Papers.

24. H. O. Houghton to CDW, 22 Jan. 1881, Warner Collection.

25. H. O. Houghton to CDW, 7 Jan. 1881, Warner Collection.

26. CDW to HM&C, 14 June 1881, Houghton, Mifflin Papers. Quotations in the subsequent paragraph appear in the same letter.

27. H. O. Houghton to CDW, 28 Jan. 1881, Warner Collection.

28. For references to the "American Men and Women of Letters," see H. O. Houghton to CDW, 5 Feb. 1881; HM&C to CDW, 11 Apr., 18 Apr., 25 Apr., 30 Apr., 17 May, 13 July, 19 July 1881, all Warner Collection. For the proof copy of the announcement with title changed to "American Men of Letters," see HM&C to CDW, 6 Aug. 1881, Warner Collection.

29. Proof copy of "American Men of Letters" announcement, in HM&C to CDW, 6 Aug. 1881, Warner Collection. On the bindings associated with subscription firms and with Ticknor and Fields, see the essays by Nancy Cook and Jeffrey D. Groves in this volume. Examples of the decorative bindings used by subscription firms on volumes of collected biography appear on Harriet Beecher Stowe, *Men of Our Times; or, Leading Patriots of the Day* (Hartford: Hartford Publishing Co., 1868), and James Parton, *People's Book of Biography; or, Short Lives of the Most Interesting Persons of All Ages and Countries* (Hartford: A. S. Hale and Company, 1868).

30. H. O. Houghton to CDW, 5 Feb. 1881, Warner Collection.

31. HM&C to CDW, 25 Apr. 1881, Warner Collection. On Warner's eventual selection of William Gilmore Simms as the southern subject and of William Peterfield Trent as Simms's biographer, see John McCardell, "Trent's *Simms:* The Making of a Biography," in *A Master's Due: Essays in Honor of David Herbert Donald,* ed. William J. Casper, Jr., Michael F. Holt, and John McCardell (Baton Rouge: Louisiana State UP, 1985) 179–203.

32. HM&C to CDW, 25 Apr. 1881, Warner Collection.

33. CDW to Horace E. Scudder, 15 Sept. 1881, Horace E. Scudder Papers (bMS Am 801.4), Houghton Library, Harvard University.

34. CDW to HM&C, 22 Jan. 1885; H. O. Houghton to CDW, 23 Jan. 1885, both Houghton, Mifflin Papers.

35. CDW to HM&C, 14 Jan. 1885, Houghton, Mifflin Papers.

36. CDW to HM&C, 22 Nov. 1895, Houghton, Mifflin Papers.

37. HM&C to CDW, 31 Jan. 1884, Warner Collection.

38. H. O. Houghton to CDW, 23 Jan. 1885, Houghton, Mifflin Papers.

39. HM&C to CDW, 26 Mar. 1898, Warner Collection; CDW to HM&C, 15 May 1898, Houghton, Mifflin Papers. See also George Monteiro, "Whitman, Warner, and the American Men of Letters Series," *Walt Whitman Quarterly Review* 1 (March 1984): 26–27. After Warner's death in 1900, Whitman finally was added, in a 1906 volume by Bliss Perry.

40. See, for instance, CDW to HM&C, 8 Nov. 1895, in which Warner describes why Howells would be the ideal author for Longfellow's biography. Houghton, Mifflin Papers.

41. Kermit L. Vanderbilt, *American Literature and the Academy: The Roots, Growth, and Maturity of a Profession* (Philadelphia: U of Pennsylvania P, 1986) chs. 6–7, esp. 108–9.

42. John T. Morse, Jr., "Incidents Connected with the American Statesmen Series," *Proceedings of the Massachusetts Historical Society* 64 (November 1931) 371. This article offers Morse's recollections of editing the series, including his difficulties with Carl Schurz (who wrote *Henry Clay*) and the plagiarism of Allan Magruder (who wrote *John Marshall*). Morse's memory of the series' origins is colored somewhat by the 1898 reordering of the series (and the fifty years that had passed between its inception and this article): from the extant correspondence, it is clear that his vision was less coherent in 1880–81 than it became over the course of the series' publication. See Oscar Handlin, "John Torrey Morse," *Dictionary of American Biography*, ed. Robert Livingston Schuyler and Edward T. James (New York: Charles Scribner's Sons, 1958) 22:475–76.

43. JTM to HM&C, 30 Apr. 1881, Houghton, Mifflin Papers. All quotations in this and the next paragraph are from this letter.

44. Advertisement for "American Statesmen" series, Advertising Scrapbooks, Houghton, Mifflin Papers.

45. As Morse recalled, Lodge had asked him to include Roosevelt because "Theodore has nothing to do—in a word, *he needs the money.*" Morse, "Incidents" 381.

46. JTM to HM&C, 1 Sept. 1881; H. O. Houghton to CDW, 8 Mar. 1882, both Houghton, Mifflin Papers. Another connection at this stage concerned one subject: Benjamin Franklin. Morse, at the outset disinclined to include Franklin, had added him to his list of Statesmen (with Higginson as author) at Houghton's urging. But Warner wanted Franklin for the Men of Letters and suggested to the publishers that the author of *Poor Richard's Almanac* and the *Autobiography* be transferred to his list. Morse apparently agreed, though over the next few years some question remained about where Franklin belonged. Eventually lives of Franklin appeared in both series.

47. On the publishers' desire to maintain "a harmony of design and substantial uniformity of size," see HM&C to CDW, 18 Apr. 1881, Warner Collection. Eventually, as the Statesmen series became commercially successful, the publishers allowed its volumes to approach four hundred pages.

48. On the American Commonwealths Series, see Ballou 339. Ballou suggests that the three series—Commonwealths, Statesmen, and Men of Letters—together formed part of Houghton, Mifflin's educational endeavors. But the Statesmen and Men of Letters series also stood apart for their larger trade appeal. The publishers and editors did not refer to the Commonwealths when

writing about the other two series, but they clearly did make connections between the Statesmen and the Men of Letters.

49. Charles Dudley Warner, *Washington Irving* (Boston: Houghton, Mifflin, 1881) 2.

50. Edward M. Shepard, *Martin Van Buren* (Boston: Houghton, Mifflin, 1888) 3.

51. The volumes of the American Men of Letters that appeared during Warner's editorship (1881–1900) fall roughly into two categories: books commissioned especially for the series and books prepared originally for other purposes that found a home in the American Men of Letters. For example, Octavius Brooks Frothingham wrote his biography of George Ripley soon after Ripley's death in 1880 as a memorial volume and agreed to adapt it for inclusion in the series. Similarly, Edward Cary's life of George William Curtis was not originally intended for the series but was a memorial work written less than two years after Curtis's death in 1892. Both Frothingham's *Ripley* and Cary's *Curtis* contained far more extracts from their subjects' letters than the typical volume in the series; they lay somewhere between the "life and letters" treatment and the more concise analytical biography envisioned by Warner and the publishers. The works commissioned for the series—which are the ones discussed here—included far less quotation and were more clearly works of composition and interpretation rather than compilation. See HM&C to CDW, 21 Dec. 1881; Frothingham to CDW, 21 Dec. 1881, both Warner Collection.

52. Thomas Wentworth Higginson, *Margaret Fuller Ossoli* (Boston: Houghton, Mifflin, 1884) 8.

53. Kijinski 213–15.

54. Warner, *Washington Irving* 297; Higginson 130; Horace E. Scudder, *Noah Webster* (Boston: Houghton, Mifflin, 1881) 293–94.

55. Scudder 26.

56. Higginson 312–13.

57. Warner, *Washington Irving* 8.

58. Warner, *Washington Irving* 293.

59. William P. Trent, *William Gilmore Simms* (Boston: Houghton, Mifflin, 1892) 328.

60. Henry A. Beers, *Nathaniel Parker Willis* (Boston: Houghton, Mifflin, 1885) 2–3.

61. Beers 351.

62. Warner, *Washington Irving* 19–20, 300.

63. Beers 82.

64. See also Julia Ward Howe, *Margaret Fuller* (Boston: Roberts Bros., 1883).

65. Higginson 233.

66. Higginson 130–32.

67. Warner, *Washington Irving* 161.

68. Hermann Von Holst, *John C. Calhoun* (1882; Boston: Houghton, Mifflin, 1899) 29. Though Holst's volume does narrate the history of Calhoun's political career, the critique of states' rights and slavery is paramount; Calhoun appears primarily as "the representative of an *idea*" (7) and, ultimately, as "the greatest and purest of proslavery fanatics" (351).

69. Peter Novick, *That Noble Dream: The "Objectivity Question" and the American Historical Profession* (Cambridge: Cambridge UP, 1988) 76.

70. Lois Hughson, *From Biography to History: The Historical Imagination and American Fiction, 1880–1940* (Charlottesville: UP of Virginia, 1988) 30. Hughson, ch. 2, discusses Adams's *John Randolph* (1882) and his *The Life of Albert Gallatin* persuasively in the context of Adams's philosophy of history.

71. William Graham Sumner, *Andrew Jackson* (Boston: Houghton, Mifflin, 1882) 362.

72. John T. Morse, Jr., *Benjamin Franklin* (Boston: Houghton, Mifflin, 1889) 415.

73. Henry Cabot Lodge, *George Washington*, 2 vols. (Boston: Houghton, Mifflin, 1889), 2:219–25.

74. Sumner 11–12.

75. John T. Morse, Jr., *John Adams* (Boston: Houghton, Mifflin, 1884) 264; Morse, *John Quincy Adams* (1882; Boston: Houghton, Mifflin, 1899) 12.

76. Sumner 359.

77. Carl Schurz, *Henry Clay*, 2 vols. (Boston: Houghton, Mifflin, 1889) 1:321, 324–25.

78. Schurz 1:333.

79. "Sydney Howard Gay," *Dictionary of American Biography* 7:195.

80. Shepard 5, 397.

81. Eugene L. Didier to HM&C, 27 Jan. 1885; HM&C to CDW, 30 Jan. 1885; James Parton to HM&C, 21 Apr. 1885; HM&C to CDW, 22 Apr. 1885; J. Brander Matthews to CDW, 23 Oct. 1882, all Warner Collection.

82. JTM to HM&C, 12 Aug. 1884, 12 Oct. 1887, 30 Nov. 1887, 22 Dec. 1887, all Houghton, Mifflin Papers.

83. William Everett to CDW, 14 May 1888, Warner Collection. Other authors in the series complained about aspects of the editing, particularly the general prescription that volumes should run approximately three hundred pages. In at least one case, Lounsbury's *James Fenimore Cooper*, the publishers used a smaller typeface and more lines to the page in order to keep the volume to 306 pages. Other authors' complaints involved particulars that were not specific to the series form, such as the permitted number of galley corrections and the terms of the royalty.

84. HM&C to CDW, 5 June 1885, 24 Oct. 1885, 19 Jan. 1886, 2 Mar. 1888, all Warner Collection.

85. See Morse, "Incidents" 378–80.

86. H. O. Houghton to JTM, 9 Apr. 1884, Houghton, Mifflin Papers.

87. H. O. Houghton to CDW, 17 Feb. 1885, Houghton, Mifflin Papers.

88. HM&C, "Standard Library Edition/American Statesmen" (advertisement), 6 Oct. 1898, Advertising Scrapbooks, Houghton, Mifflin Papers. Binding details taken from Daniel C. Gilman, *James Monroe* (1883; Boston: Houghton, Mifflin, 1899).

At the same time Houghton, Mifflin created the Standard Library Edition of the American Statesmen series, the firm also created a "Large Paper Edition," limited to five hundred copies. This edition, whose "very fine antique laid paper, deckle edges" was, at 8 inches high by $5^3/8$ inches deep, larger than the Standard Library Edition ($6^7/8$ inches by $4^5/8$ inches), could be purchased in "polished buckram" for $3.50 per volume or in "the finest French levant" for $7.50 per volume. The Standard Library Edition sold for $1.50 per volume in cloth or $3.50 per volume in half morocco. The numbered edition sold out within the first year. See "American Statesmen/Large-Paper Edition" (advertisement), 31 May 1898, Advertising Scrapbooks, Houghton, Mifflin Papers.

89. HM&C, "Standard Library Edition/American Statesmen" 2.

90. John T. Morse, Jr., "Editor's Introduction," in Morse, *Benjamin Franklin* (Boston: Houghton, Mifflin, 1898) v–vii.

91. Morse, "Editor's Introduction" vii–x.

92. "American Statesmen" (advertisement), in the back of a 1915 printing of John T. Morse, Jr., *Benjamin Franklin* (Boston: Houghton, Mifflin, 1889).

93. HM&C to Henry Cabot Lodge, 5 Apr., 21 Apr. 1920, both Houghton, Mifflin Papers.

94. HM&C to Albert Bushnell Hart, 16 Feb. 1922: HM&C to Henry Cabot Lodge, 12 Sept. 1924, both Houghton, Mifflin Papers.

95. Vanderbilt 105–6, 155.

96. On Progressive historiography, see Novick 92–97.

Materiality as Performance:
The Forming of Helen Hunt Jackson's
Ramona

MICHELE MOYLAN

ᖇ A THEORY OF ᖇ
MATERIALITY AS PERFORMANCE

Oɴᴇ ᴡᴀʏ ᴏꜰ ᴜɴᴅᴇʀsᴛᴀɴᴅɪɴɢ ᴛʜᴇ relationship between a text's materiality (including illustrations, bindings, typography, advertising sheets) and literary meaning is to assume that materiality functions like other conventions of literature: it constitutes one aspect of the semiotic system that readers have learned to understand as part of literary meaning. In this sense, materiality, like such other literary conventions as genre or narrative voice, contributes to what Peter Rabinowitz calls a "readerly standpoint," or Iser calls the "ideal reader."[1] Thus, for example, a particular set of illustrations for a novel might encourage the reader to interpret the text one way, while another illustrator's work could lead the reader to a far different understanding. In this sense, materiality functions as a causal agent in interpretation.

The material text might alternatively be understood from the other end of the interpretive experience, expressing part of what Hans Robert Jauss has called the text's horizon of expectation.[2] The material text, in other words, might represent the meaning or the range of possible meanings that a particular culture group has found in a work. Seen this way, illustrations are not interpretive cause but effect—a representation of meaning already found. To use the previous example, then, a text's illustrations would represent the meaning that a particular cultural group had found in the text; they would constitute response, not text—reading, not writing.

These two approaches to understanding the meaning of textual materiality seem contradictory, or at least paradoxical. A mediating ground is available, however, if we think of textual materiality as what the hermeneutician Hans-Georg Gadamer calls "presentation," or what I will call "performance."[3] Like a concerto played by orchestra or a play presented by a theatrical company, texts "mean" when they are performed. We can look at textual materiality as one expression of such an interpretive performance.

Joel Weinsheimer, translator of Gadamer's *Truth and Meaning,* explains Gadamer's theory of interpretive presentation, or performance. It is not: "something a critical subject does to a literary object; quite the contrary . . . [it] is the practice of the work—if you will, the work's working. The interpreter does not create the work (as subjectivists are always claiming) but only plays a part in it. Yet this participation nevertheless brings the work into being, for a work whose mode of being is presentation [i.e., performance] does not exist apart from the presentations of it (as objectivists are always claiming)."[4]

This model has several implications central to exploring the relationship between the material text and literary meaning. First, the text itself has no fully realized meaning and cannot therefore possess the secret of its interpretation. Performed meaning—in this case the material form of the book—is not "outside" the text; it is instead the fulfillment of textual meaning. Second, as Weinsheimer points out, Gadamer's performative hermeneutic implies a third presence besides text and reader in the interpretive act—an audience: interpretation "is essentially and not just accidentally communal. Interpretation is not only interpretation of something, by someone; it is also to someone."[5] Interpretive performance not only makes meaning from the text, it takes that meaning on the road and tries to sell it to others as well. It reenters, in other words, the world of culture as an agent of change. Thus, the material text as performance is *both* cause and effect—writing and reading.

Finally, Gadamer's model provides a space for such concepts as authorial intention and "implied readers." Like any other performer of a text's meaning, the author can leave a record of interpretation that attempts to persuade future readers. The author's interpretation can be written into the text itself (as many authors have attempted to do with characters who function as readers' guides, for example), but that interpretation can also become a part of the material text. As I will show, Helen Hunt Jackson insisted on constructing the physical form of her novel *Ramona* in such a way as to encourage readers toward her own interpretation. Literary performance, then, seeks to persuade others to read as the original interpreter has read, and thus it not only represents the cultural values of the original reader but also promotes an "ideal" reader for the text. When that interpretation is written into the literary or material text, or when that interpretation becomes otherwise dominant, future readers must contend with it—they may choose to read with or against it, but that meaning is difficult to ignore.

∾ THE CASE OF ∾
HELEN HUNT JACKSON'S *RAMONA*

Ramona, the novel Helen Hunt Jackson published in 1884, intending to sensitize eastern readers to the plight of western Indians, particularly the California Mission Indians, has appealed to generations of readers from a variety of regions and socioeconomic classes. The story traces the life of an orphan girl, Ramona, raised by wealthy Spanish relatives in what would soon become California. When Ramona reaches maturity, she falls in love with an Indian, Alessandro. After choosing to abandon her Spanish heritage to run off with Alessandro, Ramona learns that she is half Indian. The two finally marry and seem happy, but soon after they face a series of persecutions from whites that eventually drive them into hiding high in the California mountains. Alessandro goes crazy from the persecution, steals a horse, and is shot, leaving behind Ramona and their infant girl. The story ends with Ramona marrying the wealthy Spanish cousin with whom she had grown up and leaving America hoping for a better life in Mexico.

Published in the same year as *Huckleberry Finn*, *Ramona* first ran as a six-month serial in the *Christian Union* and subsequently amassed tremendous sales figures both in the United States and abroad. In 1885, for example, *Ramona* sold 21,000 copies as one of the year's best-sellers, and by 1900 readers had purchased more than 74,000 copies. Despite the lack of cheap reprint editions, the novel continued to sell roughly 10,000 copies per year for most years through 1935. Held by 68 percent of U.S. libraries in 1893, it was one of only three contemporary novels owned by 50 percent or more of the public libraries in the United States.[6] Indeed, at least one library had enormous trouble meeting public demand for the novel: in 1914 the Los Angeles Public Library was circulating 105 copies of *Ramona* but still had a waiting list; by 1946 the library had bought over 1,000 copies of the novel.[7]

Not only have library patrons read copies of the novel into tatters, but the variety of films, plays, and pageants the novel inspired further reflects the story's popularity. After D. W. Griffith's first film adaptation of the novel in 1910, *Ramona* was dramatized on film three more times. One film (1928, starring Dolores Del Rio and Warner Baxter) ushered in the age of talkies, and one (1936, starring Loretta Young and Don Ameche) the age of Technicolor. By 1914 Carlyle Channing Davis and William A. Alderson, authors of *The True Story of "Ramona,"* could account for fifty-three theater versions, and many others have since appeared.[8] And a springtime "Ramona pageant," described in a 1984 full-page *Newsweek* article as a "breathtaking piece of entertainment," has played to sell-out crowds in California almost every year since 1923.[9]

Never out of print, *Ramona* has been translated into "all known languages" and has been printed hundreds of times in dozens of editions.[10] The popularity of *Uncle Tom's Cabin* was phenomenal, but in *Ramona* Harriet Beecher Stowe's novel had a worthy rival. Clearly a powerful explanatory myth for generations of American readers, *Ramona* deserves serious attention from literary and cultural scholars alike.

Perhaps because of its popularity, this novel's reception history demonstrates clearly the enduring although complicated relationship between material form and interpretation that characterizes literary performance. Throughout its long history, the material forms of *Ramona* have reflected meaning already found in the text at the same time that they have attempted to sell that meaning to future readers. In the following sections of this essay, I will explain six possible interpretations of Jackson's novels and demonstrate the ways in which those interpretations have been manifested in both the material texts and readers' responses to those texts. In some cases, as when Jackson controlled the packaging of her novel to promote her own interpretation of it, cause and effect relationships between meaning and form are relatively clear. In other cases, cause and effect are impossible to assign— the form exists as both the result of previous readings and the cause of subsequent ones.

Authorial Intention

In 1884, when Helen Hunt Jackson published her most famous novel, she knew clearly the impact she intended her story to have. If *Ramona* "would do for the Indian a thousandth part what *Uncle Tom's Cabin* did for the Negro," she wrote, "I would be thankful for the rest of my life." Not only was Jackson clear about her intended effect, she also had a purposeful narrative strategy: "What I wanted to do was to draw a picture so winning and alluring in the beginning of the story that the reader would become thoroughly interested in the characters before he dreamed of what was before him;—and would have swallowed a big dose of information on the Indian question, without knowing it."[11] *Ramona* would seduce its readers, not lecture them; beckon them to succumb to the pleasure and romance of the story, not exhort them— until, without their awareness, the fiction would convince them of the nobility of the American Indians, a race naturally possessed of grace, courage, family and community loyalty, and strong religious values, whose nobility was undergoing systematic destruction by a powerful, corrupt, white male American culture.[12]

Given Jackson's clear and explicit purpose for *Ramona*, it should come as no surprise that some readers did respond primarily to the story's social criticism. *Ramona*'s message seems to have contributed to a national atmosphere making possible the passage of the Dawes Act of 1887 and other legislation sympathetic to Indian issues.[13] Charles Fletcher Lummis, who founded the Sequoya League in Los Angeles in 1892 for the purpose of helping Indians, was influenced by Jackson's writings, as were turn-of-the-century activists involved in the Women's National Indian Association.[14] D. W. Griffith's 1910 film adaptation (starring Mary Pickford and subtitled "A Story of the White Man's Injustice to the Indian") also emphasized Jackson's message. The "Bi-ograph Bulletin," a broadside used to advertise the film, featured a picture of Ramona weeping over the dead body of Alessandro, and the text stated that Griffith intended the film to be not only "recreative," but "instructive"; it "most graphically illustrates the white man's injustice to the Indian."[15] Significantly, the "Bulletin" also frequently mentioned Jackson, suggesting that in 1910 her name could still draw an audience and authenticate her story. The Griffith film's overt insistence on "the white man's injustice to the Indian" stood as a rare exception among the dramatic adaptations of *Ramona*, which generally downplayed the story's political message.

The material texts of the early editions of Jackson's novel reflected her intended message and reinforced the story's social criticism. Roberts Brothers, the novel's first publisher, printed early editions of *Ramona* with advertising sheets offering Jackson's *A Century of Dishonor* (1881), a mostly factual, prose attempt to focus the country's attention on the mistreatment of Indians. This edition also included a copy of a letter from Jackson thanking the firm for publishing both texts so that readers who finished *Ramona* wanting more information about Indians would have a ready source to turn to. By explicitly linking *Ramona* with *A Century of Dishonor,* Jackson and her publishers encouraged her readers to interpret the story as social criticism and a call to action.

Jackson further encouraged this reading by publishing the novel under her own name. Although Jackson was a prolific and reasonably good poet and fiction writer, during her career she published everything except *A Century of Dishonor* and *Ramona* under pseudonyms. By identifying herself directly with the text, Jackson lent important credence to the "truth value" of *Ramona,* for her experience in 1882 as an official "Indian agent" sent to study and report on the conditions of California Indians gave her criticism of government policies a force and credibility difficult to refute. Helen Hunt Jackson's name on the binding invited readers to see the novel as an exposé detailing despicable American treatment of blameless Indians. Even readers ignorant of Jackson's background and expert knowledge of Indian affairs soon learned of them, for a spate of books and articles, each claiming to expose the "real" characters and events behind the Ramona story, quickly appeared. By 1889, moreover, Roberts Brothers added to the original text of *Ramona* a seven-page supplement (written by Edward Roberts) entitled "Ramona's Home." It described a visit to the novel's locale taken by Roberts and Jackson. In 1899 Little, Brown brought out an edition of the novel that included an "explanatory" text by A. C. Vroman and T. F. Barnes. That same year Little, Brown also published editions containing illustrations based on photographs taken of the land and people of southern California. By 1908 Jackson's publisher was producing a companion text to *Ramona* entitled *Through Ramona's Country.* Although Jackson, like Stowe, claimed to have received divine aid in the writing of her story, she and her publishers quickly read the public's desire for the novel to become documentary, and they capitalized on this desire by supplementing the original story with all the sociological and geographical verification they could muster. As with *Uncle Tom's Cabin, Ramona's* value as social didacticism increased when readers could feel confident that they were reading a "true" portrayal of Indians and their living conditions.

Savage Indians

Over time, however, many readers have arrived at interpretations of *Ramona* that directly opposed what Jackson had intended (thereby demonstrating the limited power of authorial intention). Jackson's earliest readers often responded to the novel either by objecting to her portrayal of Indians, finding it romanticized and dangerous, or by reading *Ramona* as a call for continuing philanthropic efforts to "civilize" the Indians. Both responses dismissed any notion of Indians as "noble savages"—innately good when uncorrupted by the forces of civilization. In these readings Indians are inherently violent, subhuman, and evil, requiring either elimination or civilization.

In print, early response to the novel was dominated by readers eager to castigate Jackson for creating "fantasy" Indians too good to be true. Theodore Roosevelt called Jackson's work mere "feminine sentimentalism," while letter writers and editorialists filled the pages of western newspapers with debates about whether any Indians as "good" as those in *Ramona* had ever existed.[16] For example, one article from the *San Francisco Chronicle* tried to dispel the "entirely mistaken sentiments" that readers of *Ramona* would be likely to reach by presenting a counter-version: government agents are not insensitive, self-serving bureaucrats but concerned advocates for the Indians; government agents aside, moreover, Jackson's Indians are idealized and essentially false. Hadn't the San Jacinto *Register* revealed that the woman upon whom *Ramona* was based was "dissolute in the extreme. . . . short and shrewd, [a woman who] knows of her notoriety and makes merchandise of it?" The man who served as model for Alessandro, furthermore, was a "worthless horsethief and utterly unlike the noble Alessandro of the story." The author concluded, "The actors in 'Ramona' were the creations of her [Jackson's] brain and show us nearly perfect people who doubtless ought to have lived, but who doubtless never did."[17]

This journalist spoke for many of Jackson's contemporary western readers, who reportedly "inundated" her with letters "testifying, much to her disappointment, to the brutality of the Indians whom they claimed did indeed massacre whites."[18] Even modern critics have argued that "Mrs. Jackson never really knew the Indians for the pitifully squalid folks they were. Alessandro and Ramona are transplanted Castilians, not Indians."[19] Probably the most virulent proponent of the "savage Indian" position was Louis Reeves Harrison. In his review of the 1910 film adaptation of *Ramona,* Harrison interpreted Jackson's peaceful, nonthreatening Indians not as noble savages but as members of a defective species. He analyzed them through the lens of a loosely applied social Darwinism and concluded that they deserved to be eliminated: the "weak" Alessandro, wrote Harrison, "loses his head, winds up in miserable collapse, and is removed from the face of the earth in the cold-blooded way that nature eliminates the unfit."[20]

In their zeal to transform Indians, even many of the philanthropic responses to the Ramona story suggest the prevalence of the "savage Indian" ideology. For example, the Ramona Indian School, begun by Jackson's friends and supporters soon after her death, brought young Indian girls together for three to five years, removing them from their reservations and families and teaching them to create "decent" homes.[21] *Ramona* was a guidebook in this effort. Edmon Chase, the school's superintendent, wrote to Roberts Brothers: "This particular work ought to be in the hands of every teacher in this country and every woman who is a mother or may be one. The management of the children of the worst U.S. Apaches is entirely after the spirit of that little volume, and the effect is marvelous."[22] Clearly the Ramona School was intended to civilize the savageness out of a degraded race. As a representative response to *Ramona*, the existence of this school suggests that readers found it easy to ignore Jackson's attack on white American culture and to react to the racial plot with feelings of paternalism and pity rather than with guilt and desire for self-reform.

Testimony to the continuing power of this reading lives on in material representations of the text. Many of the best-selling editions of the novel contain illustrations by Herbert Morton Stoops (1888–1948), which first appeared in the 1932 Little, Brown edition. Stoops was most famous for his illustrations of Old West subjects for the adventure fiction ("Westerns") of *Blue Book* magazine, and his illustrations of *Ramona* reflect the Western genre's attitudes toward Indians. Although the Spanish and American characters are finely detailed and highly individualized, the Indian characters are virtually no more than black-haired circles, with slits for eyes, nose, and mouth, shrouded in Indian blankets (see Illustration 1). The depictions of Alessandro, the only Indian somewhat characterized, are best described in their contrast to the depictions of Felipe, the cousin whom Ramona eventually marries. Illustrations of Felipe emphasize his fine features, and he changes expression and appearance as the novel progresses. Alessandro, on the other hand, has broad, undefined features, his head often appears shadowed or covered, and he changes in neither expression nor appearance throughout the text, always looking sullen and vaguely threatening (see Illustration 2). In other words, the illustrations, simultaneously representing an interpretation of the story and promoting that interpreta-

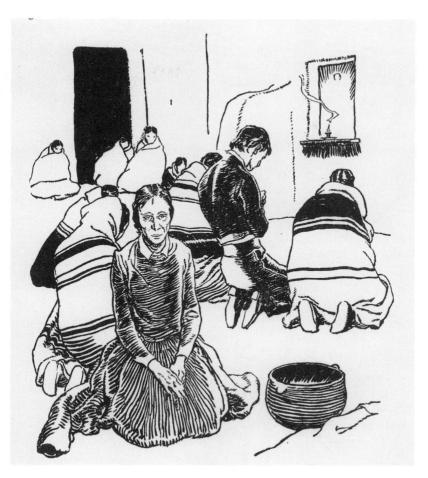

1. From *Ramona*, 1932. Published by arrangement with Little, Brown, and Company.

tion, portray the Indian as essentially inferior to European whites—underdeveloped, subhuman, threatening, and potentially savage.[23]

Erased Indians

Another meaning that readers have found in *Ramona* similarly works against Jackson's intention. In this interpretation, readers choose to respond to Ramona as Spanish rather than Indian. Fred Lewis Pattee lays out this reading of *Ramona* in *A History of American Literature since 1870:* "Ramona's Indian blood is not convincing to the reader. . . . There was small trace of the Indian about her: her beauty was by no means Indian—steel blue eyes and 'just enough olive tint in her complexion to underlie and enrich her skin without making it swarthy.' She

231

a

b

c

2. From *Ramona*, 1932. Published by arrangement with Little, Brown, and Company. (A) Felipe. (B) Alessandro and Ramona. (C) Felipe and Alessandro.

had been reared as a member of the patriarchal household of the More-nos, and in education and habit of life was as much Spanish as her foster brother Felipe."[24]

Writing in the section of Spiller's *Literary History of the United States* entitled "Western Record and Romance," Wallace Stegner provides a similar reading, arguing that Ramona does not seem at all Indian.[25] And William Scheick, in *The Half-Blood*, claims that when she leaves

America for Mexico, Ramona chooses her Spanish heritage and fails as a representative for the Indian race.[26]

This reading of *Ramona* has also been performed through material versions of the text. For example, the Avon edition of the novel, first published in 1970 and deliberately aimed at a popular readership, flagrantly encourages the reader to assume that Ramona is Spanish. The cover features a dark-skinned Ramona, but in Spanish rather than Indian dress (see Illustration 3). Furthermore, although the cover and flyleaf text refer to the "Indian Alessandro," they describe Ramona as a girl "of the Indian Country caught between two worlds." Her love is "star-crossed," it "def[ies] the custom of her people," and is "forbidden" because it is interracial.[27] This edition proceeds to emphasize the interracial relationship and to hint at its illicitness by quoting a passage in which Señora Gonzaga, Ramona's foster mother, having just found Ramona and Alessandro together, calls Ramona a "shameless creature." The editors then encourage the reader to discover how "Ramona would suffer again and again in her forbidden love." The obvious implication is that Ramona's "people" are Spanish and that she transgresses cultural boundaries when she chooses to love an Indian.

Other editions have also encouraged a reading of Ramona as Spanish rather than Indian. All the text's famous illustrators—Stoops, Henry Sandham (the artist who traveled with Jackson and illustrated what came to be known as the "Pasadena edition" of the novel), and N. C. Wyeth (who illustrated the 1939 Little, Brown edition)—delineated a clear color difference between Ramona and Alessandro and most often pictured Ramona in Spanish rather than Indian dress (see Illustration 4). And though the Grosset and Dunlap reprint edition, the first low-priced edition (copyrighted in 1912 but first released in 1934 at a price of seventy-five cents), contains almost no illustrations of characters, virtually all of its many illustrations depict Catholic icons or Gothic Spanish ruins and thereby emphasize the story's Spanish cultural background over the Indian.

By erasing Ramona's Indian heritage, readers have eliminated the possibility that the text could work toward social reform. If Ramona is not really Indian, then the story titillates readers with the possibility of miscegenation, which it later denies when Ramona marries Felipe. The story, as these readers understand it, does not criticize the encroaching American civilization.

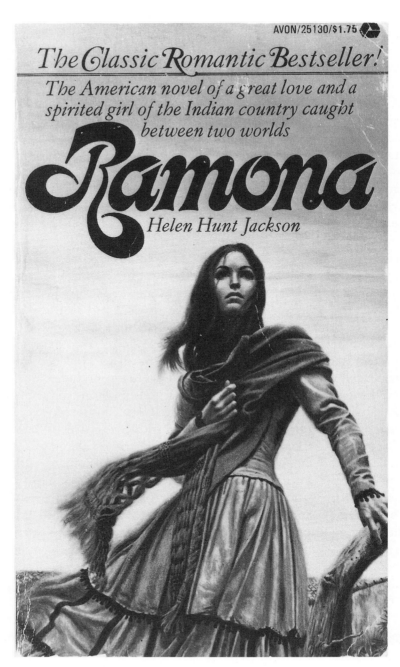

The Classic Romantic Bestseller!

The American novel of a great love and a
spirited girl of the Indian country caught
between two worlds

Ramona

Helen Hunt Jackson

AVON/25130/$1.75

3. Cover of the 1970 Avon paperback edition of *Ramona* by Helen Hunt Jackson.
Copyright © 1970 by Helen Hunt Jackson. Published by arrangement with Avon
Books, a division of the Hearst Corporation.

4. N. C. Wyeth illustration from *Ramona*, 1939. Published by arrangement with Little, Brown, and Company.

Love Story

One of the most common approaches to Jackson's story has been to see it in terms of its portrayal of Ramona and Alessandro's love affair. Unlike readings that construct Ramona as Spanish, and thus focus on her final return to the hacienda and her marriage to Felipe, this reading focuses primarily on the middle sections of the novel and the details of Ramona's relationship with Alessandro. Before she died, Jackson herself complained that readers misunderstood her book, focusing on its story (that is, on the romantic development) rather than its message.[28] Others of the story's historians have echoed this theme. For example, in promotional material distributed by the "Ramona Pageant Association," Stan Wyman writes that Jackson "failed to accomplish the goal she had set out for herself. The book was being read by the masses who focused on the love affair between Ramona and Alessandro."[29]

Perhaps the most telling evidence that readers have understood the story in terms of its tragic romance comes from their behavioral responses. One of the most popular stops on the "Ramona" tourist circuit (a major industry in some California towns throughout the 1950s) has been the place where local lore suggests that Ramona and Alessandro were married. At least through the 1940s, thousands made regular pilgrimages to this site.[30] Ramona's marriage site also plays host to the annual picnics of the "True Vow Keepers," a club whose membership includes only persons who have been married for fifty years or longer.[31]

The adaptations of the Ramona story that most emphatically stress the romance have generated strong sales. For example, in an advertisement published in 1928, Little, Brown encouraged booksellers to stock up on copies of the novel because, they said, book sales had increased a hundred percent in the wake of the romantic 1916 film adaptation. And the 1928 film version alone, in part aided by the popularity of its romantic theme song, "Ramona," grossed $1.5 million, or "four times the normal gross of a feature film."[32] Starring Dolores Del Rio and Warner Baxter and directed by Edwin Carewe, this film strongly emphasized the love affair between Ramona and Alessandro (see Illustration 5). One advertisement for it featured a mock cover of the novel with Del Rio and Baxter locked in a passionate embrace; the text read: "Millions have read the book! Millions will live the romance on the screen! . . . See 'Ramona!' Dream with her! Thrill with her! Love with her!" (See Illustration 6.)[33] Another advertisement showing a similar embrace read: "ROMANCE! Love that never dies . . . Love that bides, endures,

5. Dolores Del Rio and Warner Baxter as Ramona and Alessandro. Publicity still from the 1928 film of *Ramona*. Photo courtesy of Special Collections, Jones Library, Amherst, Mass.

and thrives on unwavering faith . . . Love Beautiful, sincere, sublime . . . Love that glorifies . . . Helen Hunt Jackson's American Love Classic."[34] From these advertisements a potential movie-goer would get no hint that the story had anything to do with Indians. The same could be said of the film's phenomenally popular theme song (written by Mabel Wayne with lyrics by L. Wolfe Gilbert). This song was actually released before the film as advertising, and its unprecedented success helped to create the film's audience. The song is ostensibly a love ballad from Alessandro to Ramona:

> Ramona, I hear the mission bells above.
> Ramona, they're ringing out our song of love,
> I press you, caress you, and bless the day you taught me to care, to always remember the rambling rose you wore in your hair,
> Ramona, when the day is done you'll hear my call,
> Ramona we'll meet beside the waterfall.
> I dread the dawn when I awake and find you gone,
> Ramona, I need you, my own.[35]

As with the film's advertisements, the song focuses exclusively on the love relationship, containing no suggestion of the original novel's so-

6. Advertisement for 1928 film of *Ramona*. Photo courtesy of Special Collections, Jones Library, Amherst, Mass.

cial or racial concerns and no indication of any tragedy beyond the romantic.

Probably none of the popular adaptations of the story stresses the romantic elements more than the Ramona Pageant does. As Daryl H. Miller writes, "each spring, love blooms anew between Ramona—a lovely half-Spanish, half-Indian woman—and Alessandro, the noble son of an Indian chief. And each spring their romance reaches the same tragic conclusion." Later, Miller quotes the director of the pageant: "Tear jerkers will always draw people."[36] Unlike most of the novel's illustrations, pictures of Ramona and Alessandro together dominate the pageant's promotional material.

This interpretation of *Ramona* is performed in the material text as well. The 1970 Avon edition of the novel (one of the more "popular" editions of the novel) also promotes the story in terms of the romance between Alessandro and Ramona. The front cover promises the prospective buyer a "Classic Romantic Bestseller," and the advertisements inside create a context disposing readers to focus on romance. One, promoting other books issued by the name publisher, encourages readers to buy "two best-selling approaches [*The Intimate Enemy* and *Pairing*] to better, more fulfilling relationships." This advertisement functions in much the same way as did the publisher's inclusion of Jackson's letter in early editions of the novel. It both encourages a particular reading of the novel, in this case as romance, and then it offers those readers someplace to go for expert advice on the subject.

California Tourism

The most powerful interpretive move that readers have made with this story is to understand it as a pastoral fable celebrating an ordered, idealized vision of the Spanish missions. (Ramona and Alessandro go to live at the missions for a short, relatively peaceful time after their marriage.) Readers thus interpreting Jackson's novel make *Ramona* into a mythic portrayal of an exotic, distant land, or, sometimes, little more than a California tourist tract. Tourists by the thousands, for example, have bought postcards ostensibly depicting the locales referred to in the story. During the late nineteenth century and early in the twentieth, hordes of tourists made pilgrimages to "Ramona sites," seeking to conjoin the powerful experience of mythic place gained through the Ramona story with actual locales around Hemet and San Jacinto. California newspapers have obliged visitors to the area by publishing full-page maps to the sites, such as the one entitled "Tour through Homeland of Ramona" appearing in a 1927 edition of the *Los Angeles Examiner*.[37]

Film adaptations of the Ramona story further emphasized the setting, often consuming enormous budgets to portray California accurately. For example, when D. W. Griffith and the Biograph Company filmed the first adaptation of the novel in 1910, "they sent a company of sixty-five actors out to California and kept them there for five months, so as to get the correct local color and scenery."[38] Both the 1916 Clune production (costing over a quarter of a million dollars) and the 1936 King production (costing over three-quarters of a million at a time when most films were in the range of two to four hundred thousand dollars) featured California scenery. Not surprisingly, most reviews of these film adaptations focused on their scenic beauty. For example, one reviewer wrote of the 1936 version that the film would "do much to make more widely known the glories of the 'golden state,'" while another wrote that "what is memorable and arresting about the film is its pictorial beauty."[39]

The story not only mythologized California for outsiders, it also defined the place and its history for the emigrants who poured into southern California in the last half of the nineteenth century. Kevin Starr, historian of southern California, suggests that Jackson's pastoral vision reflects the broader quest by migrating New England Protestants to define and order a relationship to western land and culture. The "New England mind," he argues, began at this time to "Mediterraneaniz[e]," or look to Catholicism and Latino cultures for usable traditions and history. *Ramona* partakes of this desire to delineate a usable past for rootless California immigrants by collapsing "American Southern California back onto the Spanish past," thereby providing a "healing past" that allows "Americans of Mrs. Jackson's time, fearful about themselves and what they had wrought in Southern California, . . . some warmth from the banked fires of the culture they had displaced."[40]

In 1884, when *Ramona* was first published, San Diego had a population estimated at five thousand; by 1888 the population had risen to thirty-two thousand, and a huge real estate boom was underway. Between 1880 and 1890 the population of Los Angeles quadrupled.[41] These newcomers, hungry for a usable past to help them forge a connection to the land, found in *Ramona* a myth that harmonized the native Catholic, Mexican, and Indian cultures as part of a utopian past while also narrating the transition from that past to the American present. By 1946 the Ramona story had been adopted by southern California to a staggering degree. Reviewing the Ramona phenomenon, Carey McWilliams found a town named "Ramona," fifty or more businesses with "Ramona" as part of their names, innumerable homes with illustrations from *Ramona* adorning the walls, and even a school system that for years required students to read several of Jackson's pieces on the history of southern California.[42] Furthermore, the Ramona Pageant, produced every year since 1923 in the mountains above Hemet and San Jacinto, uses hundreds of performers, virtually all from the local communities. As the promotional brochure for the 1991 production boasts, "local citizens have devoted 30, 40, even 50 or more years to the pageant."[43] Clearly, the Ramona story has created a focal point for southern California's definition of itself.

Although Jackson never intended her story to function as a pastoral fable, her story has been attacked by those who think its pastoralism falsely harmonizes and sweetens California's sordid history of racial tension. Richard Dillon best exemplifies this position, arguing that "what *Ramona* did to Southern California is saddening, for the author's intentions were so honorable. . . . All it did was to create a synthetic

California of the past peopled by Spanish Dons, gentle Franciscan padres, and noble redmen."[44] As Dillon suggests, this interpretation of the story requires nothing from its audience except nostalgic yearnings for a perfect world that never existed: readers, he writes, prefer to understand California "not in the clayey adobe of reality but in the shifting silver sands of more comfortable legend."[45]

Dillon states that readers' processes of making this story asocial (he refers specifically to reading *Ramona* as pastoral) suggest a frightening ability on the part of "the predominantly white Protestant population of Los Angeles . . . [to] master a (still) mind-boggling ambivalence and manage to keep their actual Indian and Mexican neighbors 'in their place' while adoring the cardboard 'Spaniards' and mission neophytes of Jackson's romance."[46] In other words, Dillon suggests that because readers detach this story from a social context, they can empathize with its characters without making the transition to social action in a world outside the text.

Equally striking is the predominantly white readership's ability to whitewash this story, to take out all trace of racial conflict with white-American culpability, and to adopt it as part of the constructed California history used primarily to "sell" things. When Jackson's novel first appeared, California newspapers ran many articles that conveyed Californians' defensive responses; and in their protestations that Jackson had gotten the story wrong, they betrayed their realization that they had been pilloried. Quickly, however, defensiveness gave way to a realization that this story would sell—not only itself but southern California as well. "Ramona tourism" became a major industry in southern California even before the turn of the century, and various towns and locales vied for the economic honor of being designated a "Ramona site." Throughout the 1880s, for instance, tourist trains stopped at Camulos so tourists from the East could see where Ramona lived.[47] Even by 1916, one chronicler of the Ramona phenomenon wrote that, "It is the most widely read book on California today, despite its age. One who is foremost in knowledge and experience as to the 'tourist crop' deems it a conservative estimate that this novel has been worth $50,000,000 to Southern California."[48] Similarly, the Ramona Pageant (staged almost exclusively by local white residents wearing black wigs) has "sold" California's mission history to thousands of tourists every year for almost seventy years (see Illustration 7).[49] Indeed, Richard Dillon has suggested that the Ramona industry rivals Disneyland and Knott's Berry Farm in its creation of a mythical land of illusion.[50] Mere actors in a grand western cabaret that has no relation to the present,

7. Brochure for Ramona Pageant. Photo courtesy of Special Collections, Jones Library, Amherst, Mass.

that assigns no responsibility and thus no guilt, Native Americans and Hispanics alike are nostalgically coopted and sold as part of the grand American story.

The novel's original publishers quickly recognized their audience's fascination with California and shaped their editions accordingly: Roberts Brothers even brought out an edition containing many sheets blank to be filled in by special photographs of California prepared by the publishers, or by readers' own sketches or paintings memorializing their visit to California.[51] Little, Brown's 1905 edition added the subtitle "Helen Jackson's Famous Romance of Southern California." Many editions of *Ramona* commanded unusually high prices in nineteenth- and early twentieth-century America. Frequently the books were beautifully illustrated and bound in a variety of leathers or even in silk. They became works of art, early versions of our "coffee-table" books, bought to evoke the distant land to which the book's owner had traveled or wished to travel.

Multiculturalism

In 1988, Signet Classics published a new edition of Jackson's novel that attempted to recover the story's intention of social criticism. Cover text advertised the story as chronicling "the fading Spanish order, the decline of Indian tribal communities . . . and, inevitably, the brutal intrusion of whites." The comparison with *Uncle Tom's Cabin* is once again evoked: "*Ramona* was linked with *Uncle Tom's Cabin* as one of the great ethical novels of the century." Its introduction, written by Michael Dorris, himself a Modoc Indian, informs modern readers of Jackson's expertise on Indian matters while arguing that her novel did, albeit indirectly, improve conditions for Indians.

Of course, the interpretation performed by the Signet text represents a set of cultural values, as do all the various readings of the Ramona story. The Signet text wants to reach an academic audience no longer accepting of white cooptation of Indian or Latino cultures. Thus, Dorris emphasizes that though *Ramona* may show vestiges of a nineteenth-century white paternalism toward Indians and Mexicans alike, the story's essential meaning is captured by the struggle of those native cultures to avoid domination and erasure. Dorris writes, "the defiant spirit that produced *Ramona* is the answer to complacency, to defeat, to injustice."[52] Already the attempt to incorporate Jackson's work into contemporary critical paradigms has borne some fruit. Valerie Sherer Mathes's 1990 study, *Helen Hunt Jackson and Her Reform Legacy*, attempts to recover Jackson's work as an important part of nineteenth-century Indian activism, and the 1992 American Studies Association conference featured a panel on *Ramona*. Nevertheless, although its introduction by a Native American seems intended to lend the Signet edition an authority that a story about Indians written by a white woman might otherwise lack for contemporary cultural scholars, Jackson's own race as well as her somewhat problematic politics may hamper the full acceptance of *Ramona* into the current literary canon. As James R. Kincaid suggested in a 1992 *New York Times* review of writing by American Indians, white liberals practice one of the most pervasive forms of racism: in trying so hard to understand and sympathize, these liberals can see only the Indians of their own imaginations.[53] No doubt this charge could be leveled at the paternalism implicit in Jackson's nostalgic celebration of mission culture (though given the wholesale genocide being practiced by the American government, paternalism might well have been the lesser of two evils). But even if scholars never adopt the text, the history of the Ramona story remains an important record of American popular thought, and the novel will probably continue to be read and "rewritten" by generations to come as Americans continue to struggle with their cultural heritage.

Clearly, *Ramona*'s history demonstrates that textual meaning, even within the seemingly simple realm of "popular" literature, is neither unitary nor fixed, and it is certainly not fully determined by authorial intent. Rather, readers' continual recreations of the Ramona story suggest that literary meaning can best be understood using the metaphor of performance. Texts "mean" only when they are "performed"—that is, when they are read and interpreted, a process that conjoins text, history, and culture. The interpretations of *Ramona* developed by readers from various regions, different genders, and successive generations stand as a record of the cultural values and assumptions of those readers—especially white Americans' strong and abiding belief throughout the late nineteenth and early twentieth century that they could rationalize away the nation's continuing racial problems and its legacy of racial guilt.

∾ NOTES ∾

Some of this material appears in an earlier essay entitled "Reading the Indians: The Ramona Myth in American Culture," *Prospects: An Annual of American Culture Studies* 18 (1993): 153–86. Thanks to the University of Minnesota for providing me with a research grant enabling me to study the Jackson material at the Jones Library in Amherst, Massachusetts. Thanks also to the American Antiquarian Society for financial support enabling me to attend their Seminar in the History of the Book. I gratefully acknowledge the helpful comments of Edward M. Griffin, who graciously read early versions of this essay.

1. Peter Rabinowitz, *Before Reading: Narrative Conventions and the Politics of Interpretation* (Ithaca: Cornell UP, 1987); Wolfgang Iser, *The Act of Reading: A Theory of Aesthetic Response* (Baltimore: Johns Hopkins UP, 1978).

2. Hans Robert Jauss, "Literary History as a Challenge to Literary Theory," in *Toward an Aesthetic of Reception*, trans. Timothy Bahti (Minneapolis: U of Minnesota P, 1982).

3. Other theorists and scholars also employ the term "performance": speech act theorists refer to the "performative" as a part of speech that calls for a particular response from auditor or reader, scholars write "performance" histories of plays and films, and in *Authorship and Audience: Literary Performance in the American Renaissance,* Stephen Railton refers to the act of writing literature as a "performance" (Princeton, N.J.: Princeton UP, 1991). These uses share with mine a sense that meaning happens communally—through something shared by speaker and auditor, through the production of a play, or through the *public* act of writing, which foregrounds the audience's role in shaping written texts.

4. Joel Weinsheimer, "Suppose Theory Is Dead," *Philosophy and Literature* 16 (1992): 251–65.

5. Weinsheimer 259.

6. James D. Hart, *The Popular Book: A History of America's Literary Taste* (Berkeley: U of California P, 1950) 183.

7. Carey McWilliams, "Southern California: Ersatz Mythology," *Common Ground* 6 (Winter 1946): 31.

8. Carlyle Channing Davis and William A. Alderson, *The True Story of "Ramona"* (New York: Dodge, 1914) 256.

9. Because of the popularity of the novel and these dramatic versions, the "Ramona story" has become known to a great many people who have never read the novel. Nevertheless, I consider their responses to be a part of the reading history of *Ramona.* Therefore, when I specifically refer to readings of the actual novel, I shall make that clear by using the title, *Ramona,* or by specifying "the novel." Otherwise, I shall use the term "story" to refer to the many versions of the basic plot that people may have picked up through dramatic versions, newspaper articles, or the popular culture.

10. McWilliams 32.

11. Quoted in Ruth Friend, "Helen Hunt Jackson: A Critical Study" (Ph.D. diss., Kent State University, 1985) 264, 294.

12. Jackson's approach very much echoes Washington Irving's as he describes it in "To the Reader," from *Tales of a Traveler* (1824): "I am not, therefore, for those barefaced tales which carry their moral on the surface, staring one in the face; they are enough to deter the squeamish reader. On the contrary, I have often hid my moral from sight, and disguised it as much as possible by sweets and spices, so that while the simple reader is listening with open mouth to a ghost or a love story, he may have a bolus of sound morality popped down his throat, and be never the wiser for the fraud" (*Tales of a Traveler,* ed. Judith Gilbin Haig [Boston: Twayne, 1987] 4).

13. See Albert Keiser, *The Indian in American Literature* (New York: Oxford UP, 1933) 284; Allan Nevins, "Helen Hunt Jackson, Sentimentalist vs. Realist," *American Scholar* 10 (1941): 284; and Michael Dorris, Introduction to Helen Hunt Jackson, *Ramona* (New York: Signet-NAL, 1988) xvii.

14. McWilliams 33; Valerie Sherer Mathes, *Helen Hunt Jackson and Her Reform Legacy* (Austin: U of Texas P, 1990) 92.

15. *Biograph Bulletins: 1908–1912* (New York: Octagon Books, 1973) 197.

16. Theodore Roosevelt, *The Winning of the West* (New York: Putnam's, 1920) 41–42. Roosevelt refers specifically to *A Century of Dishonor,* but his comments seem equally applicable to *Ramona.*

17. "An Ideal Destroyed," *San Francisco Chronicle* (Jackson Manuscript Folder 13, Jones Library, Amherst, Mass.).

18. Michael Marsden, "Helen Hunt Jackson: Docudramatist of the American Indian," *Markham Review* 10 (Fall/Winter 1980–81): 17.

19. Lawrence Clark Powell, *Land of Fiction: Thirty-two Novels and Stories about California, from "Ramona" to "The Loved One"* (Los Angeles: Glen Dawson, 1952) i.

20. Louis Reeves Harrison, *The Moving Picture World* 6, no. 22 (June 4, 1910): 933.

21. Emily Pierce, "Helen Hunt Jackson: What She Wrote, How She Lived, and Where She Is Buried," *Leslies* (Jackson Manuscript Folder 1, Jones Library, Amherst, Mass.): 316.

22. Edmon Chase, letter to Roberts Brothers, Boston, n.d., 1890 (Jackson Manuscript Folder 12, Jones Library, Amherst, Mass.).

23. In many ways the illustrations of *Ramona* perform the same function as does Aunt Ri (a white woman who befriends Ramona and Alessandro)—that of a "ficelle" or reader's friend. They interpret the action and help to promote a particular reading of the text.

24. Fred Lewis Pattee, *A History of American Literature since 1870* (New York: Century Company, 1915) 256.

25. Robert Spiller, et al., *Literary History of the United States*, 4th ed. (New York: Macmillan, 1974) 869.

26. William Scheick, *Half-Blood: A Cultural Symbol in 19th-Century American Fiction* (Lexington: UP of Kentucky, 1979) 45.

27. Helen Hunt Jackson, *Ramona* (New York: Avon Books, 1970).

28. Certainly, Jackson's own choice of narrative strategy (to hide her moral within a more readily acceptable story) has contributed to the penchant of readers to focus on the story rather than the message. Nevertheless, Jackson seemed to have felt that she had been explicit enough about the message that her readers *should* have understood it.

29. Stan Wyman, "Righting a Wrong: Author of Novel Wanted to Help Indian People." Distributed by "Ramona Pageant Association Inc.," n.a.

30. McWilliams 32.

31. McWilliams 32.

32. "Those Theme Songs," *New York Times Encyclopedia of Film: 1937–40*, ed. Gene Brown (New York: Times Books, 1984): Aug. 4, 1929A.

33. Jackson Manuscript Folder 15, Jones Library, Amherst, Mass.

34. Jackson Manuscript Folder 15, Jones Library, Amherst, Mass.

35. Readers familiar with Jackson's novel will realize that Ramona is not famous for wearing roses in her hair. The reference in the song was probably meant to echo the film's second promotional device, the development of a new strain of roses called the "Ramona" rose.

36. Daryl H. Miller, "Love Conquers All at Ramona Pageant: San Jacinto Again Glows with Spirit of the Old West in Long-Running Tear-Jerker." Distributed by the "Ramona Pageant Association, Inc.," n.a.

37. *Los Angeles Examiner*, Sunday, January 9, 1927 (Jackson Manuscript Folder 13, Jones Library, Amherst, Mass.).

38. "Is the Moving Picture to Be the Play of the Future?" in Brown, *New York Times Encyclopedia of Film: 1896–1928*, August 1911. The author goes on to add that since during the story an Indian village is destroyed: "to get a

faithful likeness of the devastation, the Biograph Company purchased a village and burnt it down."

39. *Motion Picture Review Digest* (1, no. 54 Dec. 28, 1936 [New York: H. H. Wilson Company]): 111–12.

40. Kevin Starr, *Inventing the Dream: California through the Progressive Era* (New York: Oxford UP, 1985) 61.

41. David Lavender, *California: Land of New Beginnings* (New York: Harper and Row, 1972) 313, 317.

42. McWilliams 32.

43. "The Ramona Pageant: 1991 Season" (San Jacinto, Calif.: Ramona Pageant Association, 1991) 3.

44. Richard Dillon, *Humbugs and Heroes: A Gallery of California Pioneers* (Garden City, N.Y.: Doubleday, 1970) 172.

45. Dillon 173.

46. Dillon 172.

47. McWilliams 31

48. "Southern California: The Home of Ramona" (Jackson Manuscript Folder 14, Jones Library, Amherst, Mass.).

49. The Ramona Pageant was not the only outdoor drama to sell the mission myth to residents and visitors alike in the early twentieth century. Starr notes that though the Ramona Pageant has outlasted all others, *The Mission Play*, which had its own playhouse in San Gabriel seating 1,450, was seen by "an estimated 2.5 million people between 1912 and 1929," and its author/founder, John Steven McGroarty, "was named poet laureate of California, knighted by the pope and the king of Spain, and twice elected to Congress" (88).

50. Dillon 173.

51. "Ramona Interleaved: Suggested Photographs, Covers, Pen, Ink Sketches, Medieval Book Marks, Etc." (Jackson Manuscript Folder 14, Jones Library, Amherst, Mass.).

52. Dorris xviii.

53. James R. Kincaid, "Who Gets to Tell Their Stories?" *The New York Times Book Review* 3 May 1992: 1+.

Packaging Literature for the High Schools: From the Riverside Literature Series to Literature and Life

LANE STILES

Soon after America's entry into the First World War, Scott, Foresman and Company of Chicago commissioned Edwin Greenlaw of the University of North Carolina to produce two schoolbook collections of patriotic literature, one for the high school market and one for the college market. Greenlaw was, in the words of Gerald Graff, "one of the imposing figures of early twentieth-century scholarship": Kenan Professor of English and dean of the graduate school at the University of North Carolina, a noted scholar of Spenser, and editor of *Studies in Philology*.[1] Notwithstanding whatever commercial motives may have inspired Scott, Foresman to initiate the projects, Greenlaw had something more in mind than just capitalizing on war hysteria. *Builders of Democracy* (1918), the first of the two collections and the one directed toward the high school market, was an assemblage of "poems, stories, extracts from histories of high literary value, and even state papers" primarily selected, Greenlaw acknowledged, "as a propaganda for good citizenship";[2] but the book was also designed to illustrate "certain conceptions about the teaching of English"—namely, that literature should be regarded "as the bible of the human spirit, its records as authentic as battle records or dynasties or constitutions, its interpretations as divine as the spirit of man."[3]

This larger, ostensibly humanistic purpose also informed the second collection that Greenlaw produced for Scott, Foresman: *The Great Tradition* (1919), which was subtitled "A Book of Selections from English and American Prose and Poetry, Illustrating the National Ideals of Freedom, Faith, and Conduct." In the introduction, Greenlaw—and his coeditor, James Holly Hanford—went so far as to deny that the book was "an anthology of patriotic literature" at all, or that it contained any of "the poetry and prose of national aggrandizement."[4] Given that three of the sixteen contemporary selections were by Woodrow Wilson and that the rest consisted of pieces like John Dewey's "The Mind of Germany" and Viscount Grey's "The Significance of America's Entry into the War," Greenlaw's denials may seem disingenuous, but his point was really that the book represented something more than a mere patriotic anthology, something more than even the standard college literature anthology. Where typical anthologies, according to Greenlaw, presented literature in a highly specialized and often irrelevant fashion to "elementary" college students ("listing chronologically a large number of authors, with specimens of their work"), Greenlaw's anthology promised to bring order, unity, and pertinence to literary study by eliminating those authors who were of advanced academic interest only (the English poet Abraham Cowley, for example) and by organizing those authors of more general interest according to their "ideas."[5] By "ideas" Greenlaw meant "the dominant ideas of successive epochs in the national life of the two great English speaking peoples, as these ideas have received large and permanent expression in literature."[6] Like *Builders of Democracy*, *The Great Tradition* was to be read as "a bible of the English speaking peoples on both sides of the Atlantic, made up of scriptures that we value not for flawless art but for their interpretation of the spirit of the race."[7] Greenlaw did not specify who "we" was in this case—who was doing the valuing and how—but in the next sentence he did assert his own priestly authority, if indirectly through the passive voice, as a privileged interpreter of this "great tradition": "Whatever has been admitted has been chosen because it seemed to have some bearing on the right interpretation of this spirit and to have the quality of permanence."[8]

Despite Greenlaw's claims for the permanence of the books, Scott, Foresman's hopes for their success ended with the war;[9] but Greenlaw's plan for making literature more relevant to the lives of nonspecialists by selecting, combining, and arranging texts according to their "values" proved to have a much longer life. In 1922 Scott Foresman released the first of four volumes of a new English and American literature anthology for the high schools edited by Greenlaw.[10] *Literature and Life,* as the series was called, was one of the first modern high school literature anthologies. It was also one of the most successful, dominating the literature textbook market for over two decades and influencing English instruction for long after that.[11] The four graded books, one for each year of high school, contained more than a chronological listing of literary texts; they constituted an entire English and American literature curriculum, with a carefully planned and detailed scope and sequence. The format of the *Literature and Life* series—hundreds of disparate literary texts bundled by "theme or content" and wrapped in layer after layer of biography, history, criticism, explication, formal analysis, appreciation, citizenship training, and composition and literacy instruction—may seem unremarkable to us now, but perhaps no other single form of packaging has more influenced how Americans in this century have come to identify, interpret, and value "classic" literature. The very familiarity of the format is tacit evidence of this influence.

∾ THE MATERIALITY OF THE ∾ *LITERATURE AND LIFE* SERIES

Terms like "format" and "packaging" point to the significance of the materiality of the *Literature and Life* series, a significance that is part and parcel of whatever meaning these books may have had: literary, cultural, or historical. When I speak of the materiality of a text, I am referring to all aspects of its physical presentation. In general, the materiality of a book would include obvious physical features such as bindings, paper, design, illustration, and typography; "textual" appendages such as advertisements, editorial addenda, and front and back matter; and other, less localized aspects such as the manner of production and dissemination of the book. In the specific case of *Literature and Life,* which presented a great number of literary texts, materiality would also include the selection and arrangement of those texts.

The significance of the materiality of *Literature and Life* as I will discuss it rests on two rather broad but closely related claims. The first derives from Jane Tompkins's assertion that "readers are always situated, or circumstanced, in relation to a work" and "there is never a case in which circumstances do not affect the way people read and hence *what* they read—the text itself."[12] One way that readers are situated in relation to a text—indeed, *always* situated in relation to *any* text—is through the materiality of that text.

In this regard, it would be difficult to think of a form of literary packaging in this century that has worked more diligently to situate readers of canonical texts than that represented by this series. With its multiple layers of editorial wrapping, *Literature and Life* mediated deliberately, thoroughly, and continuously between text and reader, at times "situating" the pupil as emphatically as a teacher's seating chart. Yet it also worked to condition readings less intentionally. Among the things I want to consider in this essay, then, is not only how the materiality of the *Literature and Life* series explicitly situated readers (or, at least, how it declared its intentions to situate them—a consequential distinction) but also how it implicitly situated readers, particularly in relation to classic literature.

My second claim concerning the materiality of the series depends upon an expanded notion of textuality. In addition to being a (quite literal) context that conditions readings, materiality is itself a text—one that can be read as, among other things, a record of its own production, or more precisely, of the traditions, institutions, and formations that produced it.[13] In other words, the material text situates readings of itself. What this means concretely in respect to *Literature and Life* is that the packaging can be interpreted as a record of the practices of American public education and textbook publishing in the early part of this century, a time when the practices of both institutions were being consolidated and professionalized on a national scale. What I want to offer in the rest of this essay is a very brief reading of this material text, a reading that considers the materiality of the *Literature and Life* series both as a context for the literary texts it re-presented and as a text that represented its own institutional origins and history. As it turns out, these two stories are so interrelated, there is no practical way to separate them.

∾ LITERATURE ANTHOLOGIES VERSUS ∾ "SEPARATE CLASSICS"

In the foreword to the teacher's handbook for the series, Greenlaw described *Literature and Life* as "an entirely new presentation of literature in the high school," offering a "wealth of material" that "would enable teachers to substitute a more extensive type of study for the over-intensive analysis of a few selections which so often prejudiced students against literature."[14] The form of presentation that Greenlaw was reacting against was the "course based on a series of separate classics." "Until recently," he noted in the introduction, "it was the usual method" but a method that tended to be "ineffective" because it was "based on some mechanical plan or no plan at all."[15] In its place, Greenlaw proposed a course based on an anthology—one that was integrated, progressive, and cumulative, however, and not a "mere" anthology: "If we make a mere anthology, a collection of all sorts of things, we have only a glorified magazine in which story, essay, and poem are pleasantly mingled for an evening's entertainment, or a quite arbitrary selection to illustrate literary history, or a collection of types."[16]

While not "an entirely new presentation of literature," Greenlaw's proposal was novel in many respects. Although popular literature anthologies had been produced for general consumption in the United States for many years, literature anthologies intended solely for high school students were a rarity before the arrival of *Literature and Life*. In fact, the formal study of English and American literature in the schools was itself a rarity until the end of the nineteenth century. Throughout much of the nineteenth century, if American schoolchildren experienced classic literature in the schools at all, they usually did so secondarily, through primers, grammars, readers, spellers, rhetorics, elocution manuals, and literary histories. In the second half of the nineteenth century, however, the study of English and American literature began to take a more prominent place in the school curriculum. One reason for this was the extension of the theory of "mental discipline," which had long been used to justify the study of classical languages, to include the study of modern languages. Under the influence of German philology, American educators came to believe that if the grammars of modern languages like English were as complex, formal, and rigorous as Greek or Latin, then there was no reason not to include English-language literature in the curriculum. Indeed, there were good reasons—practicality, relevance, economy, patriotism—to *prefer* English language to classical language instruction. In essence, English-language literary texts entered the schools at the end of the nineteenth century as already "classic," that is, with the same pedagogical status as traditional Greek and Latin texts.[17] The prevailing method for teaching these modern classics was also the same: formal rhetorical and philological analysis.[18]

Among the first persons to define and exploit the potential market for English and American classics in American high schools was Horace E. Scudder of the Boston firm of Houghton Mifflin.[19] As a prominent educational theorist, Scudder argued persuasively, in Arnoldian fashion, for the acculturating benefits of classic literature. As a prominent publishing figure, Scudder helped to make such literature widely available and reasonably affordable to the public schools. Starting in 1882 with Longfellow's *Evangeline,* Scudder began to reissue Houghton Mifflin's literary backlist—a pedigree of English and American titles with roots reaching back to the firm's notable ancestor, Ticknor and Fields—in inexpensive school editions.[20] The Riverside Literature Series promised "the best scholarship in the country," and most volumes were annotated ("over-annotated," Greenlaw and others would complain), illustrated, and supplemented with biographical and critical information. The series, and others like it, quickly came to dominate the emerging high school market and continued to dominate until they were gradually displaced by anthologies like Greenlaw's.[21]

Greenlaw objected to the high school English course based on separate classics series like the Riverside Literature Series on four grounds. First, "no matter how well-made such a course may be, *the student is not aware of its plan.*" Second, such a course tends to be "heterogenous, successive rather than organic," and therefore it cannot produce "permanent" knowledge. Third, "the unskilled teacher is doomed to ineffectiveness if not downright failure" if he or she is not provided with a method of organization. And fourth, "there are mechanical objections to the separate classic plan": books must be ordered well in advance; it is difficult to obtain an economy of scale; abler students are not provided with enough reading; and "since the texts for the entire year are not at hand, and since individual classics are commonly over-edited, there is danger of dwelling too long on a single classic, or of studying the life out of it."[22]

Each of these objections was, to one degree or another, both a criticism of individually packaged classics and an advocacy for a new type of packaging. For example, the first objection—that even if a course were organized around separate classics, students would have no way of understanding the organization—implied two things: that literary texts for students should be organized collectively and that this organization should be made explicit to the student. *Literature and Life* claimed to do both these things. Each volume of the series began with an introduction containing guidelines for using the book as well as a rationale of the anthology's overall organization. This rationale was reinforced by additional types of "editorial apparatus": tables of contents; section introductions; tables and charts; illustrations; footnotes; endnotes; questions and topics for class discussions, compositions, reports, and other assignments; bibliographies; suggestions for further reading; independent reading lists; and assorted appendices and indexes.[23] "The result," argued Greenlaw, "is a growing consciousness of power and in-

terest impossible when one small separately edited classic succeeds another, in an endless succession. The masterpieces of literature, old and
new, short and long, are here used as chapters or paragraphs or songs in
the great Book of Literature, which is the true subject of study."[24]

Students probably did engage the editorial apparatus on some level,
if only because Greenlaw advised teachers to quiz students on "historical or expository matter" using examinations like the following:

> Franklin's worthiest contribution to American literature is his ——
> because it is one of the truest expressions of an early ——. The only real
> poet of Revolutionary times is ——, who was the first to treat of the
> —— in beautiful verse. The first writers to give us a truly national
> literature wrote from —— to ——, because they exhibited intellectual
> ——. One of the masterpieces of American humor is Irving's *Knicker-
> bocker History;* but his —— contains two compositions, *Rip van Winkle*
> and ——, that have never been surpassed for —— of conception. He
> revealed to his countrymen the —— of our native legends. Cooper's
> most famous contribution to literature is the ——, which record the
> romance of the westward march of the ——. They should be read in the
> order: ——. Cooper interests us by his —— narrative, but his charac-
> ters are ——.[25]

But we might wonder whether such editorial "devices," as Greenlaw
labeled them, really contributed much to a student's "growing consciousness of power and interest" in literature.

We might wonder as well how effectively the packaging remedied
Greenlaw's second objection to the course based on separate classics:
that it tended to be heterogenous rather than organic, successive rather
than progressive and cumulative. For practical reasons, literary anthologies are typically made up of compact selections—poems, short
stories, essays, speeches, and excerpts from longer works—and *Literature and Life* was no exception. Its four volumes contained only two
complete novels (and short novels at that) out of over six hundred
selections: *Silas Marner* and *Treasure Island.* As for the six novels anthologized in part, Greenlaw admitted that "the editors do not believe
that reading these selected chapters is a substitute for the complete
reading," but he rationalized their inclusion by arguing that the selections were "complete in themselves," "of pivotal importance in the
structure of the book," "provided with such a setting as to make intelligent use of them possible," and, most importantly, "the very best
means of arousing a student's interest in a book."[26]

Even if we allow Greenlaw the possibility of constructing a coherent canon from short works and fragments (or from any body of literature, for that matter), the packaging that he designed to convey this coherence may have actually worked against it. *Literature and Life* offered a comprehensive selection of literary texts for "extensive" rather than "intensive" reading—a selection so comprehensive that each volume contained "far more than a year's work," regardless of how much time was dedicated to literature instruction in the classroom.[27] Commonly, teachers have taken one of two pedagogical approaches to comprehensive textbooks. They have either started at the beginning and progressed as far as possible in the allotted time; or else they have recapitulated their own educational experiences by choosing familiar texts and then teaching those texts as they were taught them. The continuity of Greenlaw's plan would have been disrupted in either case. To be fair to Greenlaw, a good portion of the teacher's handbook was dedicated to helping teachers select and organize the material for classroom purposes; but whether teachers, who, for the most part, were overworked and undertrained, would have followed Greenlaw's advice is doubtful. A national study of English instruction conducted by Dora V. Smith ten years after the release of *Literature and Life* found that teachers were using anthologies primarily as supplements for separately bound classics (the same way that they had once used literary histories) and that "[b]etween 40 and 50 per cent of the courses offer[ed] no type of organization whatever, presenting mere lists of classics for study."[28] Nine years later, in 1941, another survey by Smith yielded similar results: Although progressive anthologies like Greenlaw's were in common use, the traditional method of "intensive reading of a single selection by all members of the class in common [was] still the major procedure used in the teaching of literature."[29]

Greenlaw's third objection to individually packaged classics—that the unskilled teacher needed a formal method of organization—touched on an issue that went beyond the immediate materiality of such books. From the beginning, schools in the United States suffered from a chronic lack of sufficiently trained teachers. Toward the end of the nineteenth century and into the twentieth century, this situation began to improve: normal schools and teachers colleges proliferated; the first graduate programs in education, most notably at Teachers College, Columbia University, were instituted; certification programs became more commonplace; and professional organizations like the American Federation of Teachers (AFT) and the National Council of Teachers of English (NCTE) were founded. Still, even in the third decade of the twentieth century, there were many relatively unskilled teachers in schools across America.

Historically, American educators relied on textbooks to compensate for the lack of expertise in the classroom. Textbooks, in effect, drove curricula in America, and that remained the case for literature courses even as English instruction became more professionalized. After World War I, progressivist reform movements led to a spate of handbooks and articles on textbook selection that continued to blame the necessity for textbooks on the lack of adequately trained teachers.[30] Paradoxically, however, these handbooks also appealed to the professionalism of teachers as the presenters of textbooks.[31] This conflicted sense of the status of teachers was reflected in Greenlaw's teacher's handbook. One problem with separate classics, he wrote, was that unskilled teachers had no plan to follow. On the other hand, "it is not true that a course based on a complete text instead of on separate classics necessarily hampers a teacher's freedom": *Literature and Life* "allows the teacher as little or as much freedom as he desires."[32]

Greenlaw had to be somewhat politic in this regard because in a pragmatic way the principal user of the text was not the high school student but the high school teacher, who functioned as a proxy for Greenlaw's cultural authority in the classroom—as a privileged interpreter, like Greenlaw, of Anglo-Saxon tradition.[33] This authoritative role was materially embodied in the teacher's handbook, which possessed a status that more closely approximated the authority of the series' message than did that of the common student textbook.[34] A unique text positing a unique reader, the handbook mediated hierarchically (if invisibly) between the students and the main volumes of the series through the agency of the teacher (just as the teacher mediated hierarchically between Greenlaw and the students). As a material text, the handbook reflected both the residual and emerging aspects of the teaching profession: delimiting the autonomy of the (by implication) unskilled teacher even as it reinforced the teacher's authoritative status in the classroom.

∾ AMERICAN EDUCATION, TEXTBOOK PUBLISHING, ∾ AND THE HIGH SCHOOL LITERARY CANON

To understand Greenlaw's fourth objection to classics series—what he broadly labels "mechanical objections"—it may be helpful to consider in more detail the institutionalization of English and American literature studies in American high schools, a process that was itself, to a significant extent, a response to the institutionalization of vernacular studies in American colleges and universities. When Harvard announced in 1873 that six English literary texts would form the basis of a composition examination for college admission the following year, secondary schools had for the first time a compelling institutional reason for teaching English literature: to prepare students for college entrance.[35] Other colleges soon followed Harvard's example, instituting their own English literature–based entrance examinations; however, each formulated its own list of required texts, and this lack of uniformity resulted in a great deal of confusion and inefficiency for those schools involved in preparing students for college. Similar confusion and inefficiency reigned in other subject areas for the same reason.

In 1892, after years of mounting dissatisfaction among secondary school educators, leaders of the National Education Association (NEA) called for the appointment of a Committee of Ten on Secondary School Studies to study the problem of standardizing college entrance requirements. An early indication of the emerging status of English instruction was the Committee of Ten's designation of English as one of only nine fields for which conferences would be called.[36] The 1894 report of the committee officially confirmed this status by placing English studies on a par with classical studies and by legitimizing literary study per se—that is, as a valid subject in and of itself and not merely an adjunct to composition, rhetoric, or literacy instruction (although the Committee of Ten did suggest that rhetoric and philology should provide the methodological tools for literary analysis). English was also the only subject that the Committee of Ten recommended for four full years of study in the high school—yet another sign of its rising institutional importance.[37] The Committee of Ten urged teachers to give students as much direct contact with literature as possible. Literary history was to be subordinated to the study of literary works and their authors, with the possible exception being the fourth year of high school when students might be proffered a chronological history of "our literature as a whole."[38] The writers of the report could refer comfortably to a cultural heritage of "our literature as a whole" because the committee was made up almost entirely of representatives of elite institutions: colleges, universities, and private preparatory schools. They could also, therefore, and with no apparent sense of contradiction, present secondary school educators with a plan of coursework that was almost completely oriented toward college preparation while, at the same time, declaring that the purpose of high school was preparation for practical life.[39]

That same year, 1894, the National Conference on Uniform Entrance Requirements in English was organized and began to hold its first meetings. The National Conference, which was originally composed of delegates from the Association of Colleges and Preparatory Schools of the Middle States and Maryland, the Commission of Colleges in New England on Admission Examinations, and the New England Association of Colleges and Preparatory Schools, endorsed the recommendations of the Committee of Ten and established the first uniform reading lists for college entrance. The lists were divided into two categories: a short list, for "deep study," of a half-dozen or so titles that formed the basis of the examination that year; and a longer list for "wide" study, aimed at building general knowledge. According to Arthur N. Applebee, this division reflected "a practice that had already developed informally in high schools faced with a proliferation of titles and with requirements for close, analytic study which often seemed antithetical to more humanistic goals. The use of two lists offered a compromise between the two conflicting points of view, the shorter list belonging firmly to the advocates of disciplined study, the longer list to the proponents of appreciation."[40]

It was not surprising that the National Conference, composed as it was of organizations of colleges and preparatory schools, considered the main goal of high school English instruction to be to prepare students for college, or that it believed that the uniform reading lists should constitute the foundation for a national curriculum. Like the Committee of Ten, the National Conference could endorse a rigorous curriculum of classic literature for all high school students because it assumed that all students would benefit both culturally and intellectually from such a curriculum—culturally, by being exposed to the best of a shared tradition (and to the meliorating ethos inherent in such a tradition); intellectually, because of the mental discipline demanded by the formal study of such difficult texts.

The effects of the emphasis on uniform lists were predictable. Although the National Conference articulated lists for general reading as well as careful study, teachers tended to focus their instruction on the short lists—on those few texts, in other words, that were specifically tested on the college entrance exams. The uniform lists very quickly came to dictate high school curricula.[41]

The institutionalization of college entrance examinations in English literature in the 1870s precipitated a demand for complete literary texts that could be studied closely, and by the end of the 1880s, annotated school editions of standard works like those that came to make up the Riverside Literature Series were in fairly widespread use.[42] One reason that the Riverside Literature Series fared so well among its competitors was its ability to draw from Houghton Mifflin's large and well-established literary backlist, which included a number of standard British authors as well as what might be called the first strong canon in American literature: Emerson, Hawthorne, Holmes, Longfellow, Lowell, Thoreau, and Whittier. The prominence of this list was reflected in the strong correlation between the titles in the Riverside Literature Series and those on the uniform lists. The correlation was a strong selling point for the series and was prominently detailed in advertisements printed in many of the books themselves. Sometimes the very subtitles of the books signaled how they were to be used: "for careful study." Ballou notes that in 1900, when Houghton Mifflin published *College Entrance Requirements in English for Careful Study,* forty-six of the forty-nine titles listed were in the Riverside series. She adds: "Clearly Houghton Mifflin need not depart far from its own backlog to supply the reading needs of high school students."[43] By 1922, when *Literature and Life* was published, the Riverside Literature Series included over three hundred titles and accounted for more than a million dollars in annual sales. Most of the titles in the series were either English classics in the public domain or New England writers whose copyrights Houghton Mifflin had owned or controlled.[44]

Houghton Mifflin's niche in the high school literature textbook market was solidified in the 1880s and 1890s by the early variability and instability of college entrance requirements. Schools saved money by ordering only those few individual texts that were required for close study by a particular college or list for that year, and the stabilization of the lists at the turn of the century did nothing to alter this practice. What did begin to subvert it, however, was a growing reaction among many educators in the first decade of the twentieth century against what they perceived to be the overdomination of the high school curriculum by colleges and universities. Influenced by a number of factors—the child study movement of G. Stanley Hall, the democratic theories of John Dewey, various progressivist, functionalist, and scientific movements in education (including psychological research refuting the theory of mental discipline), and a general professionalization of secondary school instruction—these educators, in Applebee's words, wanted "to transform the high school, and with it the high school curriculum in English, from a 'fitting school' oriented toward college entrance, into a 'common school,' a school for the people, whose chief function would be preparation for life."[45]

The reaction against college domination of the secondary school curriculum ultimately led to the founding of the National Council of Teachers of English in 1911. Among the first actions of the NCTE was to promote two programs aimed at weakening the colleges' hold over the reading curriculum: the distribution of home reading lists and the funding of school libraries. Both programs attempted to subvert the dominant way that literature was being materially presented to students—in officially sanctioned classroom editions of a few classic texts edited for intensive rhetorical and philological study. In 1916, the College Entrance Examination Board, which had been formed in 1900 to govern the uniform lists, responded to the NCTE's criticisms by offering an alternative to the standard examination (or what was by then referred to as the "Restricted Plan"). This alternative, the "Comprehensive Plan," tested a student's general knowledge of English literature and could be taken in place of the standard examination. While this new option theoretically freed the high schools from the dominance of the uniform lists, many if not most schools continued to be guided by the short lists, and the canon of classics institutionalized by the lists persisted largely intact even after the Restricted Plan was terminated in 1931.[46]

The defining document of the high school revolt against the colleges was *Reorganization of English in Secondary Schools* (1917), also known as the Hosic Report, compiled by James Fleming Hosic following several years of discussion between members of the NEA Round Table Committee on College Entrance Requirements and the NCTE Committee on the High School Course in English. The Hosic Report reiterated the NCTE's belief that preparation for college should be secondary to preparation for life: "Most of the graduates of the high school go, not into a higher institution, but into 'life.' Hence the course in English should be organized with reference to basic personal and social needs rather than with reference to college-entrance requirements."[47] Noting that American high school populations were growing larger and more diversified, the report concluded that "a varying social background must be assumed and a considerable range of subject matter provided" for students. At the same time, the report contended that democratizing the high schools is "not incompatible with the desire to preserve a reasonable uniformity of aims and a body of common culture."[48]

The means for maintaining a common culture in this diverse environment, as it turned out, was a familiar one—"classics," or "great books"—but with a difference: they must be *properly* presented. The main trouble lay rather in the use of "over-edited" classics that promulgated outmoded and inappropriately formal methodologies of literary study for high school students than "in our choice of books," the report declared. "Classic literature still has an appeal for healthy-minded young people, if it is sympathetically and wisely presented." The report did acknowledge a place for "the modern and the easy" in the high school curriculum. And "with the admission of a large foreign element into our schools, and the steadily increasing number of boys and girls seeking a directly utilitarian education," there was also some justification for "the reading in class of books not truly deserving the name of literature"; but such books were acceptable only "where there is little previous cultivation to build on," and only temporarily so, their use being "but a means to an end, and the end the introduction to a literature broad in its humanity, and rich and full in its spiritual appeal."[49]

The Hosic Report continued the National Conference practice of dividing reading into two lists: one list of classics, like the old National Conference lists for deep study, intended "for class work"; the other, like the wide study lists, "for individual reading." The report also outlined a sequential and progressive reading curriculum based on the authors' sense of what was psychologically and developmentally appropriate for each age level. Because "the 14 or 15 year old boy loves action and adventure," "stirring narrative, full of movement and manly virtues" should be the focus of the curriculum in the eighth and ninth grades. Because boys and girls in the tenth grade "are just entering into manhood and womanhood," the school should attempt to divert them from reading about "the love of men and women for each other," which, no doubt, "will fill much of their leisure time," and direct them toward "broader and more comprehensive ideals of human duty and service."[50] If the proper groundwork was laid in the tenth grade, students could then discuss frankly "the relations of men and women to each other" in the eleventh grade. For the final year of instruction, a "literary" course organized chronologically and including both American and English literature was recommended—a recommendation that recalled the Committee of Ten's endorsement of a chronological history of "our literature as a whole." In fact, there were many aspects of the Hosic Report that recalled the Report of the Committee of Ten and even the reports of the National Conference, for despite their reformist intentions, the contributors to the Hosic Report held fundamentally the same attitudes about the values of classic literature as had their predecessors. What needed to be reformed, they believed, was methodology, not content, and so instead of reinventing the canon of the uniform lists, the Hosic Report merely reinstitutionalized it—in reading lists "for class work."[51]

If the Hosic Report did not transform the standard list of classics, it did help to provoke a transformation in the way classic literature was materially presented to students, which is to say, comprehensively rather than exclusively, extensively rather intensively. In the barest practical terms, this meant anthologizing texts instead of packaging them individually.[52] War delayed the response from textbook publishers, but with peace came an abundance of high school literature anthologies, many edited by educators associated with the NCTE.[53] Anthologies were an attractive alternative to separate classics for both publishers and educators. For textbook publishers, the uniform adoption of a single four-year anthology series, as opposed to the random purchase of multiple titles from separate classics series, promised fewer problems with sales and distribution and increased market share and profits. For educators, the uniform adoption of a single title promised economy of scale and less inconvenience and cost when changing texts; it was also an effective tool for consolidating administrative power and furthering the process of standardization and centralization that had come to define the culture of American public education.[54] Unlike separate classics, an anthology series could be formatted to reflect a wide range—even a conflicting range—of pedagogical theories and practices so as to appeal to a very broad audience; an anthology series could also be more quickly and cheaply revised to reflect current and evolving trends in education and literary study. With the public schools increasingly providing free textbooks for schoolchildren (a practice that textbook publishers looked very favorably upon), educators needed books that were not only more economical but more durable, and hardbound anthologies were clearly superior to paperbound separate classics in this respect.[55] Similarly, educators were coming to expect the physical make-up of a textbook (or what was often referred to in handbooks for textbook selection as "mechanical" make-up) to embody the most current educational research on legibility, design, visual interest, and organization, and the packaging of anthologies was better suited to such ends than was that of separate classics.[56]

Like many of the new anthology series, Greenlaw's *Literature and*

Life resounded with echoes of the Hosic Report.[57] There was, for example, a close correspondence between the organization of *Literature and Life* and the curriculum outlined in the Hosic Report. The first two *Literature and Life* volumes emphasized adventure and narrative; the third, social relations; the fourth was a historical survey of English and American literature. Like the Hosic Report, *Literature and Life* classified texts into two categories: those intended for class study and those for study at home. The most "difficult" pieces Greenlaw recommended for class study, and, more often than not, these pieces were the standard classics found on the short lists.

Greenlaw's canon of American writers in *Literature and Life* was the old one of Emerson, Hawthorne, Holmes, Longfellow, Lowell, Thoreau, and Whittier. There was little evidence of the emerging canon of the modern American academy: Herman Melville was still the Melville of *Typee* and *Omoo*, Mark Twain was a regionalist, and Emily Dickinson was nowhere to be seen. A substantial amount of contemporary American poetry, including works by Robert Frost, Amy Lowell, Edgar Lee Masters, Edwin Arlington Robinson, and Carl Sandburg, was included in the series, even though poetry was, in Greenlaw's estimation, "the most difficult form of literature to teach." But there was much less contemporary American prose, fiction or nonfiction, apparently because it was harder to locate that "manifestation of the same impulse that produced Shakespeare's dramas and Milton's epic" in such prose. "The Story of American Literature," a historical survey at the end of book two, contained only four samples of "prevailing types of prose": the essays "Snaring a Bushmaster" by William Beebe, "Some African Gun-Bearers" by Theodore Roosevelt, and "Our Mothers" by Christopher Morley; and the short story "Romance" by Simeon Strunsky.

Although Greenlaw, like the authors of the Hosic Report, was occasionally critical of some types of contemporary literature, his assurances that the modern texts in the series were, like the standard classics, "an expression of the changeless soul of man" and "material of undoubted beauty and excellence" were probably superfluous.[58] The very selection of the texts, their proximity to traditional classics, and their placement at the end of a chronological series of standard works materially announced their status more loudly than anything Greenlaw could say. Every anthology is, after all, a de facto canon. Selecting texts is inevitably a process of attaching values to them, values that pass reciprocally from one text to another. In separate classics series, the material mechanism for this exchange of values is uniform bindings. In anthologies, physical proximity conditions relationships between texts. Whether thematically, chronologically, or typologically arranged, texts in anthologies are wrenched out of their original material contexts, and out of their original historical and cultural contexts, and set into new contexts.

Greenlaw mainly arranged texts in *Literature and Life* by theme— "The World of Adventure," "Ideals of Democracy," "The Service of Nature to Man," "The Chivalric Ideal," "Finding New Worlds," "Men and Manners." Each thematic grouping was both explicitly and implicitly an argument for the classic status of every text that it contained (if not necessarily in terms of literary quality, then in terms of ideas) and for Greenlaw's nationalistic version of a continuous and dominant Anglo-Saxon tradition. Theodore Roosevelt's "The Development of the American Nation," for example, served as the concluding statement on the theme "The National Ideal" in a section initiated by Shakespeare's *King Henry the Fifth;* and under the capacious theme of "Man and His Fellows," Roosevelt and Woodrow Wilson advanced the democratic and humanitarian ideas of Robert Burns and Charles Dickens.

As these thematic groupings suggest, one of the principal aims of *Literature and Life* was to instill patriotism and good citizenship: "The course is designed for the training of the future rulers of our country, which Plato held to be the chief end of education."[59] But other aspects of the series' organization suggested uses that were not so congruent with Greenlaw's professed ends.[60] Despite numerous protestations that his was *not* "an anthology arranged according to types or literary history," Greenlaw did arrange texts typologically and historically as well as thematically. Thematic sections were subdivided into types like "Folk Ballads," "Historical Drama," "The Personal Essay and Letter," and "The One-Act Play"; and the final third of volume 2 and all of volume 4 were given over to formal literary histories. Indeed, the structure of volume 4 suspiciously resembled the old-fashioned "plan of listing chronologically a large number of authors, with specimens of their work" that Greenlaw had railed against in the introduction to the college text *The Great Tradition.* In that introduction, Greenlaw had used Abraham Cowley as his particular whipping boy: "Many authors, significant for historical reasons, are appropriately studied in advanced courses where the chief emphasis is on the history and development of English literature as an art, but have no value to the elementary student except for their contribution to his lumber-room of facts."[61] In the first chapter of the *Literature and Life* teacher's handbook, Greenlaw again singled out Cowley as an author "of no slightest interest" to the student, and asked: "Why should students who are not to be professors of English or literary critics but who are heading for all sorts of careers—farming, shop-keeping, bond selling, real estate, insurance, law, medicine—why should all these students be put through a systematic course in English authors chronologically—and professionally—arranged?"[62]

Yet, who should be cited, however briefly, in a chronological study of English authors in the fourth volume of the *Literature and Life* series but Abraham Cowley. And even Greenlaw's bourgeoisie of farmers, shopkeepers, bond salesmen, real estate brokers, insurance agents, lawyers, and doctors would have been hard-pressed to find much practical value in some of the specialized information contained in book four's expansive history of English literature (except, perhaps, for what it contributed to each one's "lumber-room of facts"). That a formal survey of the sort traditionally associated with college prep courses concluded a series that proclaimed itself to be sequential and cumulative materially signaled a purpose for *Literature and Life* that seemed to belie Greenlaw's declared purpose of preparing students for practical life.

Greenlaw admitted that book four did *appear* "to be a history of English literature with copious selections," including those "masterpieces usually recommended in courses of study," adding: "Thus the book, commercially speaking, offers a history plus a half dozen of the classics commonly most elaborately annotated, at a price well below that of separate volumes."[63] But although such an assessment might be "essentially correct," he went on, it was "extremely superficial" because it did not take into account how the overall structure of the series systematically and organically prepared the student for such a history. What Greenlaw seemed to be arguing here was that *Literature and Life* did a better job of preparing students for college preparation than did other courses, and at a cheaper price. This was at least the way that some educators assessed the series. The practical fact was that only a minority of the population was actually graduating from high school in the 1920s; the ninth and tenth grades were terminal grades for many more people than were the eleventh and twelfth grades. The overall structure of *Literature and Life* reflected this fact. The first two volumes were organized toward more functionalist and practical ends than were the last two, which emphasized more traditional and elitist approaches to literary study. James W. Olson contends that this mixed structure "probably contributed to the commercial success of the series" because "teachers of juniors and seniors were undoubtedly under greater pressure to prepare students for college, while teachers of the first two grades probably felt more ideological pressure from the functionalists."[64] By including the standard works from the uniform lists, annotating those works as profusely as individually bound classics, and providing the tools for traditional literary analysis in the editorial apparatus, Greenlaw made it easy for teachers to use his progressive anthology in decidedly nonprogressive ways.

The physical presentation of the literary texts in the *Literature and Life* series not only supported specialized uses for classic literature but also encouraged a kind of social stratification of instruction impractical in courses built around separate classics. With its abundance of selections, some meant for "close and detailed study" and some to "be read rapidly," some intended for class study and some for home reading, *Literature and Life* was designed to be adapted to students of varying abilities and needs; but grouping students by ability or channeling them into vocational, college preparatory, or other special programs was also an effective way of reinforcing racial, ethnic, gender, and class distinctions within a supposedly uniform system of public education. Using mass education simultaneously to empower the individual and to enforce social conformity was a contradiction as old as the common school movement itself, and the use of classic literature to acculturate the masses was informed by a similar sort of republican impulse, as well as by century-old romantic convictions of the ethical power of literature. From Scudder to Greenlaw, this belief in the social efficacy of classic literature in the high schools was remarkably consistent.

Greenlaw's "humanism," as embodied in the materiality of the series, also contributed to its hegemonic work. Good citizenship, according to Greenlaw, depended upon a "sense of racial solidarity." Nominally, Greenlaw was referring to the human race, but throughout the series the terms "human race" and "Anglo-Saxon race" were used interchangeably. This identification essentialized and universalized certain dominant cultural values while effectively silencing nonhegemonic voices. A particularly egregious case in point is provided by Theodore Roosevelt's "Some African Gun-Bearers," which was placed near the end of "The Story of American Literature" in book two. In his essay, Roosevelt lampooned Africans as "children, with a grasshopper inability for continuity of thought and realization of the future" and as "file-toothed cannibals," some of whom "were still in the kirtle-of-banana-leaves cultural stage."[65] Greenlaw's selection of this text as one of only four examples of contemporary American prose, his placement of it at the end of a long history of canonical American literature, and his contextualizing of it in the editorial apparatus as a modern classic in the humanist tradition of the ancient classics effectively depoliticized its racist and imperialistic ideology even as it validated it.

It is difficult to ascertain objectively how successful *Literature and Life* was at inculcating its "humanist" values, but there is some evidence from this period to suggest that instruction in classic literature generally was not as effective as—or effective in the ways that—its supporters hoped. Greenlaw himself spoke pessimistically of the average high school student's reading ability: "[H]alf of the ninth-year boys and girls understand less than half of the literature they are asked to study in class. Some understand it extremely well. Others understand almost none of it. But the duller half of the class gains only vague or misleading notions from the printed page."[66]

Greenlaw's conception of reading ability went "beyond mere recognition of words, size of vocabulary, expertness in pronunciation," beyond even literal comprehension, to embrace disciplinary and cultural literacies. For Greenlaw, students read well when they reproduced his particular interpretive strategies and cultural assumptions. Like the contributors to the Hosic Report, Greenlaw concerned himself with the actual reading practices of high school students primarily to the extent of offering a corrective or prophylactic for them; but there were significant differences between what and how students read for themselves and what and how they read for their teachers. These differences were illustrated in a study done by Charles Sumner Crow and published by the Teachers College, Columbia University, in 1924.[67] Crow gave over two thousand seniors from twenty-seven high schools a list of seventy-four standard English and American classics and asked the students to rank them according to four separate criteria. In the category of "aesthetic" value ("artistic, impressed me with its beauty of thought and expression"), the students listed Van Dyke's "The Story of the Other Wise Man" first, Longfellow's *Evangeline* (the all-time best-selling Riverside classic) second, Shelley's "To a Skylark" third, Bryant's "Thanatopsis" fourth, and Milton's "L'Allegro" sixth. However, when the same seventy-four classics were ranked according to their "leisure time" value ("interesting, entertaining, excellent book for my leisure time" versus "tiresome, irksome for me"), "The Story of the

Other Wise Man" fell to eighth, *Evangeline* to twenty-first, "Thana-topsis" to fifty-ninth, "To a Skylark" to sixty-fourth, and "L'Allegro" to sixty-sixth place. The results of the study suggest that instruction in classic literature may have been more effective at teaching high school students to valorize texts than to value them in any real or personal way.

∾ NOTES ∾

1. Gerald Graff, *Professing Literature: An Institutional History* (Chicago: U of Chicago P, 1987) 140.

2. Edwin Greenlaw, ed., *Builders of Democracy* (Chicago: Scott, Foresman, 1918) iii.

3. Greenlaw, *Builders* vi.

4. Edwin Greenlaw and James Holly Hanford, eds., *The Great Tradition* (Chicago: Scott, Foresman, 1919) xiv.

5. Greenlaw and Hanford xvii.

6. Greenlaw and Hanford xiii.

7. Greenlaw and Hanford xv.

8. Greenlaw and Hanford xv.

9. John Tebbel, *A History of Book Publishing in the United States,* 4 vols. (New York: R. R. Bowker, 1972–81) 2:441.

10. Volume 2 was also released in 1922, volume 3 in 1923, and volume 4 in 1924. *Literature and Life* was coedited by William H. Elson (who developed the Elson Readers series for Scott, Foresman), Christine M. Keck, Clarence Stratton, and Dudley Miles. For purposes of simplification, however, and because Greenlaw was the general editor of the series, I will refer to Greenlaw singly as editor. The consistency of voice and point of view in these books, as well as in the two wartime collections, would seem to justify this simplification.

11. Arthur N. Applebee, *Tradition and Reform in the Teaching of English: A History* (Urbana, Ill.: National Council of Teachers of English, 1972) 129; John Muth Bernd, "Approaches to the Teaching of Literature in the Secondary School, 1900–1956," diss., U of Wisconsin, 1957, 132; James Warren Olson, "The Nature of Literature Anthologies Used in the Teaching of High School English, 1917–1957," diss., U of Wisconsin, 1969, 100; Kay Hutchins Salter, "Reflections of English Curriculum Reform (1893–1924) in the 'Literature and Life' Texts," diss., U of Georgia, 1985, 175; Tebbel 2:441; Tebbel 3:223.

12. Jane Tompkins, "Masterpiece Theater: The Politics of Hawthorne's Literary Reputation," *American Quarterly* 36 (1984): 622.

13. The textbook represents a particularly rich record in this sense.

14. Edwin Greenlaw and Dudley Miles, *Teaching Literature: A Handbook for Use with the* Literature and Life *Series* (Chicago: Scott, Foresman, 1926) i.

15. Greenlaw and Miles, *Teaching Literature* 3.

16. Greenlaw and Miles, *Teaching Literature* 5. Apparently, the war was well behind Greenlaw, for he continues: "We may make an anthology of patriotic or political verse and prose, or another one dealing with industry, social relations, and geography, but these are source-books for other studies, not for literature."

17. More than a quarter of a century later, Greenlaw could still write: "Literature is conceived [in *Literature and Life*] as a form of knowledge, capable of supplying a discipline akin to that formerly supplied by the ancient classics" (*Teaching Literature* 7).

18. On the early history of literature textbooks in American schools, see Applebee 1–19; Charles Carpenter, *History of American Schoolbooks* (Philadelphia: U of Pennsylvania P, 1963) 160–67; John A. Nietz, *The Evolution of American Secondary School Textbooks* (Rutland, Vt.: Charles E. Tuttle, 1966) 28–43.

19. On Scudder's long relationship with Houghton Mifflin, see Ellen B. Ballou, *The Building of the House: Houghton Mifflin's Formative Years* (Boston: Houghton Mifflin, 1970). Richard Brodhead discusses Scudder's role in helping to institutionalize the American literary canon in *The School of Hawthorne* (New York: Oxford UP, 1986) 59–61.

20. The titles in the Riverside Literature Series were bound either in pale green paper for fifteen cents or brown linen for between twenty-five and sixty cents.

21. Other classic series included the Academy Classics (Allyn and Bacon, Boston), Annotated English Classics (Ginn, Boston), the Cambridge Literature Series (B. H. Sanborn, Boston), Eclectic English Classics (American Book, New York), English Classic Series (Maynard, Merrill; New York), English Readings for the Schools (Henry Holt, New York), English Star Series (Globe, New York), the Gateway Series of English Texts (American Book), Graded Classic Series (B. F. Johnson; Richmond, Virginia), Heath's English Classics (D. C. Heath, Boston), the Lake English Classics (Scott, Foresman; Chicago), the Lakeside Series of English Readings (Ainsworth, Chicago), Longmans' English Classics (Longmans, Green; New York), Macmillan's Pocket American and English Classics (Macmillan, New York), Merrill English Texts (Charles E. Merrill, New York), the Scribner English Classics (Charles Scribner's Sons, New York), the Silver Series of English Classics (Silver Burdett, New York), Standard Literature Series (University Publishing, New York), the Students' Series of English Classics (Leach, Sherrill and Sanborn; Boston), Ten Cent Classics (Educational Publishing, New York), and Twentieth Century Text-Books (D. Appleton, New York).

The following, from the preface to a Macmillan's Pocket American and English Classics edition of three Thomas De Quincey essays, typifies the editorial decision making that guided the formatting of these various series:

"In preparing this book, the editor has endeavored to keep constantly in mind its practical purpose—use in elementary and secondary schools. He has attempted, therefore, to supply such things as the students of these schools may reasonably demand: an accurate text,—that of Masson's edition; a brief sketch of De Quincey's life, with some comments on his personality and his place in our literature; a practical discussion of De Quincey's rhetorical merits and faults, to be used in connection with the text-book study of rhetoric; such information about Joan of Arc and Catalina de Erauso as is requisite to a proper understanding of the essays concerning them; a brief working bibliography; and numerous textual notes, including De Quincey's own, on the essays themselves" (Carol M. Newman, preface, *Joan of Arc, The English Mail-Coach, and The Spanish Military Nun*, by Thomas De Quincey [New York: Macmillan, 1905] v).

22. Greenlaw and Miles, *Teaching Literature* 3–4.

23. In the introduction to *The Great Tradition*, Greenlaw had made a similar argument for the importance of the "editorial apparatus": "The Table of Contents is therefore an integral part of the method of the book; it is to be carefully studied in order that the relationship of the particular selection to that section in which it is placed may be fully understood. Further helps will be found in the Index, which again is not a mere catalogue of facts, or a body of notes, but a commentary" (xvii).

24. Edwin Greenlaw and Clarence Stratton, eds., *Literature and Life* (Chicago: Scott, Foresman, 1922) 2:iii.

25. "The blanks are here filled in as they might be by a brilliant student": "Franklin's worthiest contribution to American literature is his *Autobiography* because it is one of the truest expressions of an early Americanism. The only real poet of Revolutionary times is Freneau, who was the first to treat of the Indian in beautiful verse. The first writers to give us a truly national literature wrote from 1787 to 1837, because they exhibited intellectual independence. One of the masterpieces of American humor is Irving's *Knickerbocker History;* but his *Sketch Book* contains two compositions, *Rip van Winkle* and *The Legend of Sleepy Hollow*, that have never been surpassed for originality of conception. He revealed to his countrymen the charm of our native legends. Cooper's most famous contribution to literature is the *Leather Stocking Tales*, which record the romance of the westward march of the pioneers. They should be read in the order: *Deerslayer, Last of the Mohicans, Pathfinder, Pioneers, Prairie.* Cooper interests us by his swift narrative, but his characters are simple" (*Teaching Literature* 77–78).

26. Greenlaw and Miles, *Teaching Literature* 72. The excerpted novels were Cooper's *The Spy*, Scott's *Ivanhoe* and *Quentin Durward*, Melville's *Typee*, Dickens's *A Tale of Two Cities*, and Thackeray's *Henry Esmond.*

27. Greenlaw and Miles, *Teaching Literature* 19. The terms "extensive" and "intensive" are used here as they were by educators in the early part of this cen-

tury to differentiate comprehensive reading from more limited and careful study, and should not be confused with their use by contemporary historians of the book to describe the revolution in reading styles associated with the expansion of print culture in the late eighteenth and early nineteenth centuries.

28. Dora V. Smith, *Instruction in English,* Office of Education Bulletin 1932, no. 17, National Survey of Secondary Education Monograph no. 20 (Washington, D.C.: Government Printing Office, 1933) 47–48. A brief comment published in Scott, Foresman's in-house newsletter to its sales force, *The Tin Horn,* supports one of Smith's observations: "While we are worrying about a few teachers who may not be pleased with the course laid down in LIT & LIFE, an Indiana principal tells Mr. Parsons he is using the Elson-Keck *course,* but buying the material in paper classics!" (*The Tin Horn* 4 Jan. 1923).

29. Dora V. Smith, *Evaluating Instruction in Secondary School English: A Report of a Division of the New York Regents' Inquiry into the Character and Cost of Public Education in New York State,* English Monograph no. 11 (Chicago: National Council of Teachers of English, 1941) 146–47. One of the reasons that Smith gives for the persistence of this practice is "that the teachers were taught these selections themselves and in their own training have not been given a sense of security in handling classroom discussion on materials of a different sort" (147).

30. For example, C. R. Maxwell wrote in 1921 that "America has not provided an adequate corps of highly trained teachers for the education of its children" and that "textbooks are indispensable tools in school" (*The Selection of Textbooks* [Boston: Houghton Mifflin, 1921] v, ix). A decade later Frank A. Jensen could still claim: "The percentage of trained teachers in most of our states is small, and the number of beginners each year is very large. As nearly all beginning teachers are textbook teachers during all their teaching days, the textbook is destined to continue to play an important part in American education for a long time to come" (*Current Procedure in Selecting Textbooks for the Elementary Schools in Cities of over 25,000 Population* [Philadelphia: J. B. Lippincott, 1931] 8). For a selected bibliography of early-twentieth-century titles on textbook selection, see Jensen 149–54.

31. Alfred L. Hall-Quest proclaimed the teacher and the textbook to be "the two pillars of instruction" (*The Textbook: How to Use and Judge It* [New York: Macmillan, 1918] 1).

32. Greenlaw and Miles, *Teaching Literature* 19.

33. The notion of a "consumer" of a text, with its multiple connotations of use and ownership, is nowhere more problematic than in reference to textbooks. Christopher Stray reminds us that textbooks "are typically books whose users are not their buyers. In many cases, books are not just imposed on pupils by teachers, but imposed first on teachers by their employers or by the state" ("Paradigms Regained: Towards a Historical Sociology of the Textbook," *Journal of Curriculum Studies* 26 [1994]: 4).

Although Greenlaw expressed the hope "that the boys and girls will wish to retain the four volumes as prized possessions" (*Teaching Literature* 43), the materiality of the books—their appearance, format, and cost—suggested a utility and status more appropriate to the schoolroom than the home. The materiality of the Riverside Literature Series, on the other hand, reached out to a larger audience. The Riverside books were, to borrow Stray's distinction, more "schoolbooks" than "textbooks"—closer in form and status to their earlier, nonpedagogical incarnations than were the texts anthologized in *Literature and Life*. The series, like other classics series, retained the trade practice of including advertisements and book lists in the front and end matter. Not only educators but students and their families were the implied consumers of these texts. (On the practice of including advertisements in textbooks, see John A. Nietz, *Old Textbooks* [Pittsburgh: U of Pittsburgh P, 1961] 7–8.)

34. Stray argues that the "disjunction between the authority of the message and the status of its medium is something that the textbook shares with the teacher. . . . Textbooks . . . transmit powerful messages but at a low level. Their audience consists of children and is thus itself low in status. Textbooks are the menial tools of powerful processes of transmission, the mundane channels through which they take place" (6).

35. The six titles were Shakespeare's *The Tempest, Julius Caesar,* and *The Merchant of Venice;* Goldsmith's *The Vicar of Wakefield;* and Scott's *Ivanhoe* and *Lay of the Last Minstrel*. In essence, literary studies were back-doored into the college curriculum as a subject for composition.

36. The other eight were Latin, Greek, other modern languages, mathematics, physical sciences, natural sciences, history and politics, and geography.

37. That *Literature and Life* was made up of four graded volumes, one for each year of high school, is a banal example of how the materiality of the series can be said to have reflected its institutional origins. Greenlaw's reconstruction of literary tradition to fit within this sequential and progressive framework offers a more complex example. For instance, Greenlaw's claim that the "succession of topics" in book one "corresponds closely (a) to the historical development of racial ideals and emotions shown in primitive literature; [and] (b) to the character and interests of the average pupil in the first year of high school" posits a theory of literary evolution akin to G. Stanley Hall's notion that the mind of the developing child recapitulates the history of its race (*Teaching Literature* 8).

38. *Report of the Committee of Ten on Secondary School Studies, with the Reports of the Conferences Arranged by the Committee* (New York: American Book, 1894) 91.

39. The Committee of Ten was not simply blinded by class ideology. The members sincerely believed in the theories of mental discipline and transfer of learning, arguing that the rigorous study of a few standard subjects was the most practical education a student could receive.

40. Applebee 31.

41. A useful summary of the rise of the uniform lists and their influence on the high school curriculum is Edna Hays's *College Entrance Requirements in English: Their Effects on the High School, An Historical Survey* (New York: Teachers College, Columbia University, 1936).

42. Applebee 34.

43. Ballou 511.

44. Ballou 513. By 1922, forty years after the inauguration of the Riverside Literature Series, a great number of Houghton Mifflin's copyrights on its early classics had expired, and Victorian-era "courtesy of trade" agreements among publishers were a thing of the past. As title after title entered the public domain, Houghton Mifflin's position in the high school literature market was increasingly vulnerable.

45. Applebee 46. The standard history of American education during the Progressive Era is Lawrence A. Cremin's *The Transformation of the School: Progressivism in American Education, 1876–1957* (New York: Knopf, 1961). See also Cremin, *American Education: The Metropolitan Experience, 1876–1980* (New York: Harper and Row, 1988). David B. Tyack considers roughly the same time period in his critique of the urbanization of American schools, *The One Best System: A History of American Urban Education* (Cambridge: Harvard UP, 1974).

46. Applebee 54. One piece of compelling evidence for the continued influence of the college entrance lists was *Literature and Life* itself, which scrupulously correlated every piece of literature it anthologized with both the Restrictive and Comprehensive Plans through 1931. In a 1932 national study of English instruction in the high schools, Dora V. Smith determined that "[t]he list of selections most frequently required for use with all pupils in common [was] roughly identical with that set for college entrance in 1890" (*Instruction in English* 87).

47. James Fleming Hosic, comp., *Reorganization of English in Secondary Schools*, Bureau of Education Bulletin 1917, no. 2 (Washington, D.C.: Government Printing Office, 1917) 26. "The crux of the whole difficulty of college entrance in English," Hosic declared in the preface, "is the formal examination" and the "flood of over-edited classics" it caused (6). Despite Hosic's repudiation of such packaging, a section outlining a suggested course in Ameian literature concluded: "Sufficient material for such a course may be found in the leaflets of the Riverside Literature Series" (84).

48. Hosic 26.

49. Hosic 65.

50. Hosic, 69, 70.

51. Applebee 67.

52. Olson distinguishes a true anthology, which thoroughly repackages and reformats a group of texts, from a mere volume of rebound individual classics,

in which the editorial and typographical identity of each classic, including its title page and numbering system, is preserved (xxiv). It was not uncommon for publishers of individual classics to bind as a set those classics appearing on the uniform lists for that year.

53. Applebee 128.

54. In 1923, a Scott, Foresman sales representative offered the following field report from Ohio: "Prin. and Supt. are interested most when you describe the endless TROUBLE in the H.S. because the classic did not come on time, because part of the class was supplied and part was not, because some teacher interfered with his plans and ordered an entirely different classic than he planned to use, etc., etc.

"Assurance that in each year the students would be reading *what* he wanted them to *when* he wanted them to . . . was the big feature to the *Supt.* in the drive which they now have organized all over the state" (*The Tin Horn* 16 Aug. 1923).

55. The debate over free textbooks involved many aspects of materiality, one of the more intriguing of which was the issue of hygiene. Observed Alfred L. Hall-Quest: "Unquestionably the strongest argument against free textbooks is [that] . . . [t]hey do carry germs of infectious diseases. A careful record of pupil and home health, however, and scrupulous disinfection of all books between terms would relieve this condition to no small extent" (54). We might speculate on what it meant for books to be perceived simultaneously as carriers of culture and carriers of disease.

56. Hall-Quest set out the following criteria for "mechanical make-up": "A good textbook should include a mechanical make-up based upon accepted standards of hygiene, art, design, adaptability to purpose, and upon sound principles of economic production, provided the last named should never be interpreted to mean that an inferior textbook be selected" (86). The notion of "hygiene" here refers to standards of typography, not standards of health. The guidelines Hall-Quest details are very specific. For example, the height of a character should be 1.5 mm minimum; the thickness of vertical stroke, .25 mm—or at most .3 mm.

57. The title of the series consciously echoed the Hosic Report's insistence that high school coursework should prepare students for life (as did the titles of such competing anthology series as Scribner's *Literature and Living* and Lippincott's *Reading for Life*).

58. Greenlaw's discomfort with popular fiction was apparent in his introduction to "Prevailing Types of Prose" in book two. Greenlaw cautioned the student that while Sinclair Lewis's novel *Main Street* might be "realistic," it was not "real": "For the author has drawn but half the picture. To the better sides of life, the finer aspirations and acts to be found in some proportion almost everywhere, the novelist has refused representation" (602).

59. Greenlaw and Miles, *Teaching Literature* 9.

60. Gerald Graff points out that "even though a certain ideology of citizenship obviously determined the canon, the existence of a canon does not guarantee that it will be taught in an ideologically consistent way. It seems significant, for example, that though Greenlaw's college text, *Literature and Life,* included a selection from the by now canonical *Silas Marner,* it justified doing so not on the grounds of that citizenship and idealism that were the ostensible theme of the anthology, but because it was a realistic work and thus 'especially desirable on account of the vogue of realism represented in the enormous popularity of *Main Street* and other books of its type,' the kind of reading the student 'will do when he leaves school'" (*Professing Literature* 131).

Graff consistently refers to *Literature and Life* as a "college text," but one of the innovations of the series was its direct address of the problem of articulation between high school and college. Although many anthologies were used in both high school and college classrooms, *Literature and Life* was intended exclusively for the high schools, and I have found no evidence that it was used otherwise.

61. Greenlaw and Hanford xv.

62. Greenlaw and Miles, *Teaching Literature* 16.

63. Greenlaw and Miles, *Teaching Literature* 15.

64. Olson 104–5. If *Literature and Life* was conflicted in its structure, it was only mirroring the conflicted rhetoric of the Hosic Report, which neatly finessed the ideological opposition between the traditionalists and the functionalists by arguing at once for the academic and the practical, the classical and the modern. Graff has recounted a similar conflict that was occurring about the same time in the academy between "scholars"—proponents of metods of literary history and analysis based on the older Germanic model of academic specialization—and "critics," who advocated more humanistic approaches to literary study. Greenlaw sided with the scholars in this debate. In *The Province of Literary History* (1931), Greenlaw distinguished the course of study suited to the undergraduate student (or generalist) from that appropriate for the graduate (or specialist), in effect, reproducing the functionalist/traditionalist split of *Literature and Life* (Graff 140–42).

65. Greenlaw and Stratton 605.

66. Greenlaw and Miles, *Teaching Literature* 26–27.

67. Charles Sumner Crow, *Evaluation of English Literature in the High School* (New York: Teachers College, Columbia University, 1924). Clearly, the *Literature and Life* series, whose volumes were released from 1922 to 1924, could not have been widely enough adopted by the time of Crow's study to register in his findings; but the results are worth considering anyway since many teachers continued to teach the standard works anthologized in the series as they had the separate classics.

Contributors

Scott E. Casper is assistant professor of history at the University of Nevada, Reno. His recent work includes "The Two Lives of Franklin Pierce: Hawthorne, Political Culture, and the Literary Market" (*American Literary History* 5 [Summer 1993]: 203–30), as well as articles in the *Journal of Women's History* and *American Art*. He is currently completing a book, *Constructing American Lives: Biography and Culture in Nineteenth-Century America*.

Nancy Cook is assistant professor of English at the University of Rhode Island. Recent publications include "Investment in Place: Thomas McGuane in Montana" in *Old West, New West*, edited by Barbara Meldrum (Moscow: U of Idaho P, 1993), and "More Names on Inscription Rock: Travel Writers on the Great Plains in the 1980s" in *Temperamental Journeys*, edited by Michael Kowalewski (Athens: U of Georgia P, 1992), as well as seven entries in *The Mark Twain Encyclopedia*, edited by J. R. LeMaster and James D. Wilson (New York: Garland, 1992).

Jeffrey D. Groves, associate professor of English at Harvey Mudd College in Claremont, California, has published articles on American literature in such journals as *NEQ* and *Legacy* and is a contributor to the forthcoming *American National Biography* (New York: Oxford UP). He is currently working on a book that will examine the relationship of literary promotion to canon formation in mid-nineteenth-century American literature.

Michael Kearns is associate professor of English at the University of Texas of the Permian Basin. He is the author of *Metaphors of Mind in Fiction and Psychology* (Lexington: UP of Kentucky, 1987), as well as numerous articles on literature and pedagogy.

Michele Moylan is an independent scholar who has taught at the University of Minnesota, Colorado College, and Hamline University. Her recent work includes "Reading the Indians: The Ramona Myth in American Culture" (*Prospects: An Annual Journal of American Cultural Studies* 18 [1993]) and a collection of essays entitled *Performing the American Nineteenth-Century Novel: Readers and the Cultural Construction of Meaning.*

Lane Stiles is senior editor of Mid-List Press in Minneapolis. He recently contributed to a forthcoming volume on American travel writers for the *Dictionary of Literary Biography* (Columbia, South Carolina: Bruccoli Clark Layman) and is currently working on a book-length study of American high school literature textbooks.

Amy M. Thomas is assistant professor of English at Montana State University. Her recent work includes "U.S. Literacy/Reading" in *The Encyclopedia of Social History,* edited by Peter Stearns (New York: Garland, 1994), and "Women's Reading," "Women's Literacy," and "Abigail Adams"—three essays in *The Oxford Companion to Women's Writing about the United States,* edited by Cathy Davidson and Linda Wagner-Martin (New York: Oxford UP, 1995). She is currently working on a book manuscript about nineteenth-century American readers and reading.

Kathleen Verduin is professor of English at Hope College and associate editor of *Studies in Medievalism.* She is organizer, with Leslie J. Workman, of the annual International Conference on Medievalism. She has published articles on Dante, on American literature, and on modern fiction. Her current work includes a book to be titled *Reading Dante in New England* and, with Leslie J. Workman, a comprehensive anthology, *Medievalism in America: A Documentary Anthology.*

Susan S. Williams is assistant professor of English at Ohio State University. Her essays on nineteenth-century American writers have appeared in *American Quarterly,* the *Henry James Review, Nineteenth-Century Literature,* the *New England Quarterly,* and *Narrative.* She has recently completed a book-length study of the interrelation between painted and photographic portraits and antebellum American fiction entitled *Confounding Images: Photography and Portraiture in Antebellum American Fiction* (U of Pennsylvania P, 1997) and is at work on a project on women writers and publishing culture in nineteenth-century America.

Index